The Human Side of American History

Edited by RICHARD C. BROWN, *Professor of History*
State University of New York College at Buffalo

Sixth printing, 1968

GINN AND COMPANY

Preface

Mr. Dooley Wants to
"Know What the Counthry Lived Iv"

"Mr. Dooley" was a fictional character who appeared in a weekly column created (in the 1890's) by Finley Peter Dunne, a Chicago newspaperman. In the column, Mr. Dooley carried on philosophical conversations in a broad Irish dialect with his friend, Mr. Hennessy. Source: By Finley Peter Dunne, in *American Heritage*, August, 1959, p. 84.

I know histhry isn't thrue, Hinnissy, because it aint like what I see ivry day. . . . If any wan comes along with a histhry . . . that'll show me the people fightin' . . . makin' love, gettin' married, owin' the groceryman and bein' without hard coal, I'll believe it, but not befure.

Historyans is like doctors. They are always lookin' fr symptoms. Those av thim that writes about their own times examines th' tongue an' feels th' pulse an' makes a wrong diagnosis. Th' other kind iv histhry is a post-mortem examination. It tells ye what a counthry died iv. But I'd like to know what it lived iv.

🌱 🌱 🌱 🌱 🌱 🌱 🌱

The *Human Side of American History* answers Mr. Dooley's pertinent question. From authentic first-hand accounts such as letters, diaries, journals, speeches, and news stories we learn what our country lived of. What is more we catch the spirit of what people lived, suffered, and died *for*. In these pages history comes alive. We are privileged to enjoy, to experience, to share. We feel we are there.

Excerpts are presented in order of time, and succinct titles contain clues to the content. Brief and informative introductions set the stage without stealing the scene from the interesting eyewitness accounts which follow.

This is a book which deserves to be read for its own sake.

Richard C. Brown

Library of Congress Catalogue Card Number: 62-3208

Home Office: BOSTON, MASSACHUSETTS 02117

Table of Contents

First Century A.D.

Strabo Writes of Lands and India West of Spain

The idea that new lands might be found to the west of the Pillars of Hercules (Strait of Gibraltar) was expressed as early as the first century A.D. by a Greek geographer named Strabo (ca. 63 B.C.–23 A.D.) in his *Geography*, Book I, Chap. IV, par. 6.

"The temperate zone makes a continuous circle by uniting with itself, so that, if the great size of the western sea did not prevent, we might sail from Spain to India on the same parallel [of latitude] . . . and it is possible that within the same temperate zone there may be two or even three inhabited lands. . . ."

First Century A.D.

Seneca Predicts Discovery of New Worlds

Soon after Strabo, the Roman philosopher and poet Seneca (3 B.C.–63 A.D.) wrote these prophetic lines in his play "Medea" (Act II, ll. 371ff.):

"In late years the time will come when Ocean will loose the bands of nature, and the earth will stretch out huge, and the sea will disclose new worlds, nor will Thule [the northern British islands] be the last [remotest] of lands."

Eighth Century A.D.

Bede Declares Earth a Sphere

Throughout the Middle Ages educated men continued to believe, as did the ancient Greeks, that the earth was a sphere. For example, "The Venerable Bede" of Northumbria, the first of the English historians, declared in his book *On the Nature of Things*, Ch. XLVI:

"The earth . . . is not perfectly round, owing to the inequalities of mountains and plains, [but] if all its lines be considered, it has the perfect form of a sphere."

ca. 1490

A Poet's Prophecy Precedes Columbus

Only a few years before Columbus sailed, a poet named Pulci, of Florence, Italy, wrote the following striking prophecy of a western voyage (*Morgante Maggiore*, Canto xxv, strophes 229, 230):

". . . his bark
The daring mariner shall urge far o'er
The western wave, a smooth and level plain.
. . . .
And Hercules might blush to learn how far
Beyond the limits [the Strait of Gibraltar] he had vainly set
The dullest sea-craft soon shall wing her way.
We shall descry another hemisphere.
. . . .
At our antipodes [opposite sides of the globe] are cities, states,
And thronged empires ne'er divined of yore."

2

1492

Columbus Contracts for Ten Percent

The terms of the agreement (Capitulation) between Columbus and King Ferdinand and Queen Isabella, six months before his historic voyage, are very interesting.

Source: Filson Young, *Christopher Columbus*, Vol. II, Appendix C, pp. 336–337.

"The things supplicated which your Highnesses give and declare to Christopher Columbus in some satisfaction for what he is to discover in the oceans, and for the voyage . . . he is about to make therein in the service of your Highnesses, are as follows:

"First: that [you make] . . . Don Christopher Columbus your Admiral in all those islands and mainlands which by his hand and industry shall be discovered or acquired . . . during his life. . . .

"Item, that all . . . merchandise, whether it be pearls, precious stones, gold, silver, spices, and all other things whatsoever . . . which may be bought, bartered, discovered, acquired or obtained . . . your Highnesses . . . will that he may have . . . the tenth part of all of them . . . the other nine parts remaining for your Highnesses. . . .

"These are executed and dispatched with the responses of your Highnesses . . . in the town of Santa Fe de la Vega de Granada, on the 17th day of April, in the year of the nativity of our Savior, Jesus Christ, 1492. I, the King. I, the queen. By order of the King and Queen.

John de Coloma   Registered, Calçena

The Admiral Describes the First "Indians"

> The original journal kept by Columbus on his first voyage
> of discovery has been lost. Bartolome de las Casas wrote an
> account of the historic voyage in 1500 from which these ex-
> cerpts are taken. He apparently had access to Columbus's jour-
> nal and claimed to use some of the Admiral's own words.
>
> Source: HART, ALBERT BUSHNELL (editor). *American His-
> tory Told by Contemporaries*, pp. 35–37. The Macmillan Com-
> pany, New York, 1906.

Wednesday, October 10. He sailed west-southwest, at the rate
of ten miles an hour and occasionally twelve, and at other times
seven, running between day and night fifty-nine leagues . . .
Here the crew could stand it no longer, they complained of
the long voyage, but the Admiral encouraged them as best he
could. . . .

Thursday, October 11th. He sailed to the west-southwest. . . .
They saw floating by the vessel a green rush. The men of the
Pinta saw a reed and a stick. In view of such signs they breathed
more freely and grew cheerful. Two hours after midnight they
had run about ninety miles. . . . As the Caravel *Pinta* was a
better sailer and had the lead, she made land and showed the
signals ordered by the Admiral. [Columbus was on board the
Santa Maria.] The land was first seen by a sailor called Rodrigo
de Triana. . . . They lowered all the sails . . . and lay to until
Friday when they reached a small island . . . called *Guanahani*
by the natives. [This is believed to be Watling Island, in the
Bahamas.]

Friday, October 12th. They soon saw people . . . and the
Admiral went on shore . . . Soon after a large crowd of natives
congregated there. What follows are the Admiral's own words:
"In order to win the friendship and affection of that people . . . I presented some of them with red caps and some strings
of glass beads which they placed around their necks, and with
other trifles of insignificant worth that delighted them. . . .
They afterwards came to the boats . . . swimming, bringing us
parrots, cotton thread in balls, and spears, and many other things,
which they bartered for others we gave them. . . . They re-

4

ceived everything and gave whatever they had with good will. But I thought them to be a very poor people. . . ."

"I saw but one very young girl, all the rest being young men, none of them being over thirty years of age; their forms being very well proportioned; their bodies graceful and their features handsome: their hair is as coarse as the hair of a horse's tail and cut short: they wear their hair over their eye brows except a little behind which they wear long, and which they never cut: some of them paint themselves black . . . and some paint themselves white, and some red . . . and some paint their faces, and some the whole body, and some their eyes only, and some their noses only."

"They do not carry arms and have no knowledge of them, for when I showed them the swords they took them by the edge, and through ignorance, cut themselves. They have no iron; their spears consist of staffs without iron, some of them having a fish's tooth at the end. . . . I saw some with scars on their bodies, and to my signs asking them what these meant, they answered (with signs) that people from neighboring islands wanted to capture them, and they had defended themselves. . . ."

"They must be good servants and very intelligent, because I see that they repeat very quickly what I told them, and it is my conviction that they would easily become Christians, for they seem not to have any sect. If it please our Lord, I will take six of them from here . . . that they may learn to speak [European languages]. I have seen here no beasts whatever, but parrot's only." All these are the words of the Admiral.

Dec. 1, 1504

Columbus Writes to His Son

> Columbus' last years were clouded with disappointment, poverty, and ill health. His promised revenues of ten per cent have not been given him and rivals have seized the trade with the Indies. He writes to his son Diego about his hopes that the Queen may remedy his wrongs—not knowing that she died four days before his letter was penned.
>
> Source: JOHN BOYD THATCHER, *Christopher Columbus*, Vol. III, pp. 318–325.

"My very dear son,

". . . I wish that you would write me more frequently. . . . Many couriers come daily and the news is of such a nature that in hearing it all my hair stands on end, it is so contrary to what my soul desires. . . .

". . . a good copy should be made of the chapter of the letter which their Highnesses wrote me, where they say they will fulfill their promises to me and will place you in possession of everything . . .

"[Tell them] of my sickness and that it is now impossible for me to go and kiss their Royal feet and hands, and that the Indies are being lost . . . that I have received nothing . . . and that I am living upon borrowed funds. . . .

"I will endeavor to have your uncle and brother start [for the court] tomorrow. Remember to write me very often. . . . May our Lord have you in His holy keeping.

"Your father who loves you as himself."

6

A Survivor Tells of Magellan's Expedition

Anthoyne Pigapheta, a Knight of Rhodes, was visiting Spain in 1519. He joined Magellan's expedition out of sheer curiosity "to experiment and go and see with mine own eyes a part of the awful things of ocean." On his return to Lisbon in 1522 he wrote the following letter.

Source: Pigapheta's *Narrative*, in *Hakluyt Society Publications*, Vol. LII, pp. 35–163.

"Monday, . . . the 10th of August [1519] . . . the fleet, . . . carrying crews of different nations to the number of 237 men in all the five ships, was ready to set sail from the mole of Seville. . . . We navigated between south and west; and we crossed [the Atlantic] as far as a country named Verzin [Brazil]. . . . At this place we had refreshments of victuals like fowls and meat of cows, also a variety of fruits of singular goodness. . . . The people of the said place gave, in order to have a knife or a fish-hook, five or six fowls, and for a comb they gave two geese, and for a small mirror or a pair of scissors. . . . For a king of cards, . . . they gave five fowls and thought they had cheated me. . . . They have boats which are made of a tree, all in one piece, which they call canoo. . . . Into these thirty or forty men enter, and their oars are made like iron shovels; and those who row these oars . . . look like enemies of hell. . . .

"Departing thence as far as 49½ degrees in the Antarctic heavens we entered a port to pass the winter, and remained there two whole months without ever seeing anybody. However one day we saw a giant on the shore dancing and leaping and singing, and whilst singing he put the sand and dust on his head . . . and he raised one finger on high, thinking that we came from heaven. He was so tall that the tallest of us came only to his waist. He had a large face painted red all around, and his eyes were painted yellow all around them, and he had two hearts painted on his cheeks; he had but little hair on his head, and it was painted white. . . .

"The captain caused food and drink to be given to this giant, and they showed him some things among them a steel mirror.

And when the giant saw his likeness in it, he was greatly terrified, leaping backwards so that he made three or four of our men fall down. . . . He was a long time with us, and at the end we baptized him and gave him the name of John. This giant pronounced the name of Jesus, the Pater Noster [Lord's prayer], and the Ave Maria [Hail, Mary!] as clearly as we did: but he had a terribly strong and loud voice. . . .

"After taking the course to the 52d degree of the said Antarctic sky . . . we found by miracle a strait . . . 110 leagues long. . . . It is surrounded by very high mountains covered with snow, and it was not possible to anchor with the anchors, because no bottom was found. . . .

"Wednesday, the 28th of November 1520, we . . . entered into the Pacific sea, where we remained three months and twenty days without taking in provisions, and we ate only old biscuits reduced to powder and full of grubs . . . and we drank water that was yellow and stinking. We also ate the oxhides which were under the main yard, . . . also the sawdust of wood, and rats which cost half a crown each: moreover enough of them were not to be got. . . .

"Besides those that died, twenty five or thirty fell ill of divers sicknesses . . . in such manner that very few remained healthy. However, thanks be to the Lord, I had no sickness. . . . And if our Lord and His Mother had not aided us . . . we should all have died of hunger in this vast sea, and I think that man will never again undertake to perform such a voyage. . . .

"Saturday, the 16th of March 1521, we arrived at daybreak in sight of a high island . . . named Zamal [Samar, in the Philippines]. . . . The people became very friendly and familiar with us, and the captain . . . conducted them to the ship and showed them all his goods, cloves, cinnamon, pepper, nutmeg, ginger, mace, gold, and all that was in the ship. He also had some shots fired with his artillery, at which they were so much afraid that they wished to jump from the ship into the sea. . . . These people are tawny, fat, and painted, and they anoint themselves with the oil of coconuts and sesame to preserve them from the sun and wind. Their hair is very black and long, reaching to the waist, and they carry small daggers and knives ornamented with gold. . . . They only half cook their victuals, and salt them very much, which makes them drink a great deal: and they drink much with

8

reeds, sucking the wine from vessels. Their repasts always last from five to six hours. . . .

> [After recounting the death of Magellan ("our mirror, light, comfort, and true guide") in a battle against the natives of the island of Matan, Pigapheta gives a long description of the journey through the East Indies, bringing up at the island of Timor, where the crew was regaled with the fabulous stories of Java, Siam, and China beyond.]

"Tuesday night on the 11th of February 1522, we left the Island of Timor and entered upon the great sea named Laut Chidol [Indian Ocean]. . . . In order to double the Cape of Good Hope we went as far as 42° South latitude. . . . Some of our men, and among them the sick, would have liked to land at a place belonging to the Portuguese called Mozambique, both because the ship [leaked] and because of the great cold which we suffered. . . . But the greater number of us, prizing honor more than life itself, decided on attempting at any risk to return to Spain. . . .

"We then sailed to the northwest for two whole months without ever taking rest; and in this short time we lost twenty-one men. . . . And if God had not granted us favorable weather, we should have all perished of hunger. . . . We touched at the Cape Verde Islands . . . and the inhabitants told us that it was Thursday, which was a great cause of wondering to us, since with us it was only Wednesday. . . . But we were afterwards advised that there was no error on our part, since as we had always sailed towards the west, following the course of the sun, and had returned to the same place, we must have gained twenty-four hours, as is clear to anyone who reflects upon it. . . .

"At last when it pleased Heaven, on Saturday the 6th of September 1522, we entered the bay of San Lucar; and of sixty men who composed our crew when we left Maluco, we were reduced to only eighteen, and these for the most part sick. Of the others, some died of hunger, some had run away at Timor, and some had been condemned to death for their crimes. From the day when we left this bay of San Lucar until our return thither, we reckoned that we had run more than [34,704 miles] and we had completed going round the earth from east to west.

"Monday the 8th of September we cast anchor near the mole of Seville, and discharged all the artillery.

"Tuesday we all went in shirts and barefoot, with a taper in our hands, to visit the shrine of Santa Maria of Victory. . . ."

The Chevalier Anthoyne Pigapheta

1540-1542

Coronado Explores the Great Plains

In 1540, Francisco Vásquez de Coronado led an expedition north from Mexico to find the "Seven Cities of Cibola," and "Quivira," a mythical golden kingdom. He found no gold, but he tells what he did find in this report to Charles I of Spain.
Source: WINSHIP, GEORGE PARKER (editor). *The Journey of Coronado, 1540-1542.* Allerton Book Co., New York, 1922.

After nine days' march I reached some plains, so vast that I did not find their limit anywhere . . . although I traveled over them for more than 300 leagues. And I found such a quantity of cows [buffaloes] in these . . . that it is impossible to number them. . . . And after seventeen days march I came to a settlement of Indians . . . who travel around with these cows, who do not plant, and who eat the raw flesh and drink the blood of the cows they kill, and they tan the skins of the cows, with which all the people of this country dress themselves here. They have little field tents made of the hides . . . very well made, in which they live while they travel around. . . . They have dogs which they load, which carry their tents and poles and belongings.

These people . . . could not give me any account of the country where the guides were taking me. I traveled five days more . . . until I reached some plains, with no more landmarks than as if we had been swallowed up in the sea. . . . And while we were lost in these plains, some horsemen who went off to hunt cows fell in with some Indians. . . . I obtained from these an account of the country where the guides were taking me, which was not like . . . my guides had described it. . . .

10

This news troubled me greatly, to find myself on these limitless plains, where I was in great need of water. . . . [Coronado therefore went ahead with only thirty horsemen and sent the rest of his force back to his base camp.]

It was the Lord's pleasure that, after having journeyed across these deserts seventy-seven days, I arrived at the province they call Quivira [Kansas]. The Indians are as barbarous as all those whom I have seen and passed before this; they do not have cloaks, nor cotton of which to make these, but use the skins of the cattle they kill. . . .

The province of Quivira is 950 leagues from Mexico. . . . The country itself is . . . very fat and black and . . . very well watered. . . . I found prunes like those of Spain and nuts and very good sweet grapes and mulberries. I have treated the natives . . . whom I found wherever I went, as well as was possible . . . and they have received no harm in any way from me or from those who went in my company.

I remained twenty-five days in this province of Quivira, so as to see and explore the country and also to find out whether there was anything beyond which could be of service to Your Majesty. . . . And what I am sure of is that there is not any gold nor any other metal in all that country. . . .

The account the guides gave me was false, because they wanted to persuade me to go on with the whole force, believing that as the way was through such uninhabited deserts, they would get us where we and our horses would die. . . . After having heard what was beyond [Quivira] I returned to provide for the force I had sent back . . . and to give Your Majesty an account. . . .

De Soto Dies and Is Buried in Secret

> In 1539 a large Spanish expedition, commanded by Hernando de Soto, landed in Florida. For four years De Soto's group explored what is now the southeastern part of the United States. They crossed the Mississippi and it became a watery grave for De Soto, as this account written by a member of the expedition discloses.
>
> Source: LEWIS, THEODORE H. (editor). "The Narrative of the Expedition of Hernando de Soto, by the Gentleman of Elvas," pp. 232–235 in *Spanish Explorers in the Southern United States, 1528–1543*. Barnes and Noble, Inc., New York, 1959.

May 20, 1542. The Governor [De Soto], conscious that the hour approached in which he should depart this life, commanded that all the King's officers should be called before him. . . . He confessed his deep obligations to them all. . . . [De Soto asked them to elect a new commander. The officers refused, saying they wished De Soto to name the man who would succeed him. De Soto chose a man known as Luys de Moscoso.]

May 21, 1542. The next day . . . departed this life the magnanimous, the virtuous, the intrepid captain, Don Hernando de Soto . . . Luys de Moscoso determined to conceal what had happened from the Indians; for De Soto had given them to understand that the Christians were immortal. [Also, the Indians both trusted and feared De Soto and the Spaniards thought the Indians would attack if they knew he was dead.] So soon as the death had taken place, Luys de Moscoso directed the body to be put secretly into a house, where it remained three days; and thence it was taken at night, by his order, to a gate of the town, and buried within.

May 25, 1542. The Indians, who had seen De Soto ill, finding him no longer, suspected the reason; and passing by where he lay buried they observed the ground loose, and, looking about, talked among themselves. This coming to the knowledge of Luys de Moscoso, he ordered the corpse to be taken up at night, and . . . it was taken out in a canoe and committed to the middle of the stream.

May 26, 1542. The Indian chief asked for De Soto saying:

"What has been done with my brother and lord, the Governor?" Luys de Moscoso told him that he had ascended into the skies, as he had done on many other occasions; but as he would have to be detained there for some time, he had left him in his stead. The chief sure that De Soto was dead ordered two well-proportioned young Indians to be brought, saying, that it was the usage of the country, when any lord died, to kill some persons who accompany and serve him on the way. . . .

And he told Luys de Moscoso to command their heads to be struck off, that they might go accordingly to attend his friend and master. Luys de Moscoso replied to him, that the Governor was not dead, but only gone into the heavens, having taken with him of his soldiers sufficient number for his need, and he besought him to let those Indians go, and from that time forward not to follow so evil a practice. They were presently ordered to be let loose, that they might return to their houses; but one of them refused to leave, alleging that he did not wish to remain in the power of one who, without cause, condemned him to die, and that he who had saved his life he desired to serve as long as he should live.

1609

Captain Smith Says "Work or Starve!"

The English colonists who landed at Jamestown in 1607 had great difficulty maintaining themselves during their first years in the new land. Some of the colonists were unwilling to work and here John Smith tells of the stern measures taken.

Source: HANDLIN, OSCAR (editor). *Readings in American History*, pp. 19–20. Alfred A. Knopf, New York, 1957.

. . . The laziness of the greatest number caused the President to advise as follows:

"Countrymen, the long experience of our late miseries, I hope is sufficient to persuade everyone to [correct] himself. . . . The greater part must be more industrious or starve . . . for the labors of thirty or forty honest and industrious men shall not be consumed to maintain an hundred and fifty idle [loafers]."

He also made a bulletin board, as a public memorial of every man's work, to encourage the good, and with shame to spur on the rest. . . . By this, many became very industrious. . . .

Now, we so quietly followed our business, that in three months . . . we made . . . tar, pitch, and soap ashes; produced . . . glass; made a well in the fort of excellent sweet water, which till then was lacking; built some twenty houses; recovered our church; provided nets and fish traps; and to stop . . . our disorderly thieves and the savages, built a blockhouse in the neck of our island . . . and none were allowed to pass . . . without the President's order.

Thirty or forty acres of ground we dug and planted. Of three sows in eighteen months, increased more than sixty pigs. And nearly five hundred chickens brought up themselves without care. . . . We also built a fort for a retreat near a convenient river upon a high commanding hill, very hard to be assaulted and easy to be defended. . . .

[Then the Jamestown colonists found that their corn supply, which they had put in casks to save for the winter, had rotted or been eaten by rats. They had to stop all their other work in order to provide food for the approaching winter.]

Sixty or eighty . . . were sent down the river to live upon oysters, and twenty . . . to try for fishing at Point Comfort. . . . Others went up the James River but nothing could be found but a few acorns.

[In this emergency, some colonists wanted to trade their tools and other possessions to the Indians for food. Others wanted to try to get back to England. But Smith insisted that they could gather food as well as the Indians could, and they should not give up their possessions to the Indians. He announced another "work or starve" order.]

"I will take a course so that you shall provide what is to be had. The sick shall not starve, but equally share of all our labors; and he that gathereth not every day as much as

14

I do, the next day shall be set beyond the river, and be banished from the fort as a drone, till he amend his conditions or starve." . . .

This order many murmured was very cruel, but it caused the most part to so well bestir themselves, that of two hundred . . . there died not more than seven. . . .

1620

Bradford Describes the Mayflower's *Voyage*

William Bradford, the second governor of Plymouth colony, was one of the Pilgrims on board the *Mayflower*. His account of the historic voyage appears below in the language and spelling of the early seventeenth century.

Source: DAVIS, WILLIAM T. (editor). *Bradford's History of Plymouth Plantation*, pp. 91–95. Barnes & Noble, Inc., New York, 1959.

Sept. 6, 1620. . . . They put to sea . . . with a prosperus winde, which continued for days . . . and which was some incouragmente unto them; yet according to the usuall maner many were afflicted with sea-sicknes. . . . [Bradford then tells of a young sailor who made fun of the Pilgrims because they were sea-sick. The sailor said he hoped they all would die, so he could help throw them overboard.] But it plased God before they came halfe seas over, to smite this yong man with a greeveous disease, of which he dyed in a desperate maner, and so was him selfe the first that was throwne overbord. . . .

After they had injoyed faire winds and weather . . . they were incountred many times with crosse winds and mette with many feirce stormes, with which the shipe was severely shaken, and her upper works made very leakie; and one of the maine beames in the midd ships was bowed and craked, which put them in some fear that the shipe could not be able to performe the vioage. [The Pilgrim leaders consulted with the captain of the *Mayflower*. After making some repairs, it was decided to sail on to America,

15

rather than to turn back.] So they committed themselves to the will of God, and resolved to proscede. . . .

And in one storm . . . a lusty yonge man named John Howland . . . was, with a toss of the shipe throwne into the sea; but it plased God that he caught hould of a long rope which hunge overbord, and rane out at length; yet he held his hould though he was many feet under water till he was hald up by the same rope to the top of the water, and then with a boat hooke and other means got into the shipe againe, and his life saved; and though he was somewhat ill with it, yet he lived many years after, and became a profitable member both in church and commone wealth. . . .

But to omite other things (that I may be brief) after longe beating at sea they fell with that land which is called Cape Cod. . . . After some deliberation . . . amongst them selves and with the master of the ship, they tacked aboute and resolved to stande for the southward . . . to find some place about Hudsons river for their habitation. [But after sailing south for about half a day, they ran into some shoals and rough breakers. So they returned to the north.] And the next day they gott into the Cape-harbor wher they ridd in saftie. . . .

Nov. 11, 1620. Being thus arived in a good harbor and brought safe to land, they fell upon their knees and blessed the God of heaven, who had brought them over the vast and furious ocean, and delivered them from all the periles and miseries therof, againe to set their feete on the firme and stable earth. . . .

1673

Colonial Postmasters Swear an Oath

By 1700 most of the English colonies had established postal systems and it was possible to send mail from one colony to another. New York's colonial government required postmasters to take this oath.

Source: BARCK, OSCAR T., and LEFLER, HUGH T. *Colonial America*, pp. 360–361. Used with permission of The Macmillan Company, New York, 1958.

You doe Sweare by the Everlasting God, that you will truly & faithfully discharge the trust reposed in you as a Post Master, and that you will neither directly nor indirectly detayne, conceale, or open any Letters, Packetts, or other Goods committed to your Charge, but carefully, honestly deliver or cause to be delivered all such Letters, Packetts, or other Goods to the Persons they properly belong unto, & that you will make all the Expedition in passing and repassing the several Stages with all speed, & to make noe more stay than necessarily belongs to the refreshing your selfe and Horse & in all things truly & soberly to comport yor selfe, so as belongs to the trust reposed in you as Post Master ought to doe.

1673

Marquette and Joliet Meet the Ilinois

> Frenchmen used the St. Lawrence, the Great Lakes, and other waterways to penetrate the interior of North America. Marquette, a missionary, and Joliet, a trader, journeyed from Lake Michigan across Wisconsin to the upper Mississippi which Marquette describes.
> Source: KELLOGG, LOUISE PHELPS (editor). *Early Narratives of the Northwest, 1634–1699*, pp. 236–239. Barnes & Noble, Inc., New York, 1953.

June 17, 1673. Here we are . . . on this . . . renowned river . . . whose peculiar features I have endeavored to note carefully. The Mississippi takes its rise in various lakes in the country to the north. It is narrow at the place where the Wisconsin River empties into it; its current, which flows southward, is slow and gentle. To the right is a large chain of very high mountains, and to the left are beautiful lands; . . . Its width is very unequal; sometimes it is three-fourths of a league, and sometimes it narrows to about six hundred feet.

We gently followed its course . . . as far as the 42nd. degree of latitude. Here we plainly saw that its aspect was completely changed. There are hardly any woods or mountains. . . . We saw only deer and cattle [buffaloes], . . . and swans without wings, because they drop their plumage in this country. From time to time, we came upon monstrous fish, one of which struck our canoe with such violence that I thought it would break the canoe to pieces. . . .

We continued to advance . . . without discovering anything except animals and birds but we kept well on our guard. . . . We make only a small fire on land, toward evening, to cook our meals; and, after supper, we . . . pass the night in our canoes, which we anchor in the river at some distance from the shore. This does not prevent us from always posting one of the party as a sentinel, for fear of a surprise. . . .

June 25, 1673. Finally . . . we perceived on the water's edge some tracks of men, and a narrow path. . . .

> [Marquette and Joliet left the rest of the party to guard their two canoes and followed the path. They found it led to an Indian village. Not wanting to startle the Indians by their sudden appearance, the two men stopped a short distance from the village and shouted.]

On hearing the shout, the savages quickly issued from their cabins. . . . Having no cause for distrust, as we were only two men and had given them notice of our arrival, they sent four old men to come and speak to us. Two of these bore tobacco pipes. . . . They walked slowly, and raised their pipes toward the sun, seemingly offering them to it to smoke, without, however, saying a word. . . . When they had drawn near, they stopped to consider us attentively. . . . I spoke to them first, and asked them who they were. They replied that they were Ilinois; and, as a token of peace, they offered us their pipes to smoke. They afterward invited us to enter their village, where all the people impatiently awaited us. . . .

> [Marquette, Joliet, and their party were treated well at the Illinois village, which is thought to have been in present-day Iowa. They stayed until the end of June, then continued down the Mississippi. They passed the mouth of the Ohio and got almost as far south as the Arkansas River, near the spot where De Soto died in 1541. On July 17, 1673, the Frenchmen started back up the Mississippi. By then they were sure the river flowed into the Gulf of Mexico and they did not want to be captured by the Spanish.]

░░

Jasper Danckaerts Views New York

Jasper Danckaerts was sent from Holland to the eastern seaboard in 1679 to look for a place of possible settlement for a little Dutch religious group. He was a keen observer and his diary gives us an excellent word-picture of New York when it had only 3500 people.

Source: BERGER, JOSEPH, and BERGER, DOROTHY. *Diary of America*, pp. 28ff. Simon and Schuster, Inc., New York, 1957.

Sept. 24th Sunday, 1679. In order to avoid scandal and for other reasons we went to church and found there truly a wild worldly world. I say wild, not only because the people are wild but because all the people . . . partake somewhat of the nature of the country.

The church being in the fort, we had an opportunity to look through the latter. It . . . is enclosed with a double row of palisades. . . . There were some brass pieces still bearing the marks of arms of the Netherlanders. . . .

The fort is built upon the point formed by the . . . East River, which is the water running between the Manhatans and Long Island, and the North River, which runs straight up to Fort Orange [Albany].

It has only one gate . . . opening upon a broad plain or street called the Broadway or Beaverway. Over this gate are the arms of the Duke of York.

29th Friday, 1679. We started . . . for Long Island. The outer shore . . . has before it several small islands . . . such as Coninen [Coney] Island. . . . Nobody lives upon it, but it is used in winter for keeping cattle, horses, oxen, hogs and others.

A considerable number of Indians live upon [Long Island]. We went . . . through the first village called Brenkelen . . . the people . . . made us very welcome, sharing with us . . . milk, cider, fruit or tobacco and especially . . . miserable rum . . . which is called by the Dutch *kill-devil*.

6th Friday [October, 1679]. We went from the city, following the Broadway. Upon both sides of this way were many habitations of Negroes, mulattoes, and whites. These Negroes were formerly . . . slaves of the West India Company, but, in consequence of the frequent changes and conquests of the country, they have obtained their freedom.

We left the village called the Bowery [from the *bouwery* (farm) of Peter Stuyvesant] . . . and went through the woods to New Harlem. . . .

11th Wednesday (Oct. 1679). We embarked early this morning [in friend Symon's skiff] and rode over to Staten Island . . . where ships, ready for sea, stop to take in water. . . . The woods are used for pasturing horses and cattle, for being an island, none of them can get off. Each person has marks [brands] upon his own, by which he can find them when he wants them. When the population of the country shall increase, these places will be taken up.

ca. 1688

A Colonial Cure for the Plague

> The medicines and medical treatment of colonial times make astounding reading today. Here is a recipe for making a powder that was supposed to cure the "plague" (probably smallpox or yellow fever).
>
> Source: BARCK, OSCAR T., and LEFLER, HUGH T. *Colonial America*, p. 427. The Macmillan Company, 1958.

In the month of March take toads as many as you will alive, putt them in an earthen pott, so that it will be half full, cover it with a broad tyle or iron plate; then (turn over) the pott so the bottom may be uppermost; put charcoales around it. Sett it on fire and lett it burn out and extinguish itself; when cold take out the toades, and in an iron mortar pound them very well.

Mary Lacey Has a Date with the Devil

In the summer of 1692, a witchcraft mania swept over several villages in Massachusetts. Hysterical young women confessed bewitchment and accused others as Mary Lacey did in this testimony.

Source: ANGLE, PAUL M. (editor and compiler). *The American Reader*, pp. 35–37. Rand McNally & Company, Chicago, 1958.

Question: "You are here accused for practicing witchcraft . . (How) do you do it?"
Answer: "I cannot tell. . . ."

. . . .

Q. "Do you acknowledge now you are a witch?"
A. "Yes."
Q. "How long have you been a witch?"
A. "Not (more than) a week."
Q. "Did the Devil appear to you?"
A. "Yes."
Q. "In what shape?"
A. "In the shape of a horse."
Q. "What did he say to you?"
A. "He bid me not to be afraid of any thing . . . but he has proved to be a liar from the beginning."

. . . .

Q. "Did he bid you worship him?"
A. "Yes; he bid me also to afflict persons."

. . . .

The judges: ". . . You must confess freely what you know in this matter."
Mary Lacey: ". . . the Devil came to me, and bid me obey him. . . ."
Q. "But how long ago?"
A. "A little more than a year."
Q. "Was that the first time?"
A. "Yes."

21

Q. "How long were you gone from your father, when you ran away?"

A. "Two days."

. . . .

Q. "Did the Devil appear to you then . . . ?"

A. "No, but he put such thoughts in my mind as not to obey my parents."

Q. "Who did the Devil bid you afflict?"

A. "Timothy Swan. Richard Carrier comes often a-nights and has me to afflict persons."

. . . .

Q. "How many witches are there in Andover?"

A. "I know no more, (except) Richard Carrier."

Q. "Tell all the truth."

A. "I cannot yet."

Q. "Did you . . . at any time . . . ride upon a stick or pole?"

A. "Yes."

Q. ". . . What sort of worship did you do the Devil?"

A. "He bid me pray to him and serve him and said he was a god and lord to me."

Q. "What meetings have you been at, at the village?"

A. "I was once there and Richard Carrier rode with me on a pole, and the Devil carried us."

. . . .

Q. "Was there not a man also among you there?"

A. "None but the Devil."

Q. "What shape was the Devil in then?"

A. "He was a black man, and had a high crowned hat."

Q. "Your mother and grandmother say there was a minister there. How many men did you see there?"

A. "I saw none but Richard Carrier."

Q. "Did you see none else?"

A. "There was a minister there, and I think he is now in prison."

Q. "Were there not two ministers there?"

A. "I cannot tell."

Q. "Was there not one Mr. Burroughs there?"

A. "Yes."

||||||||||||||||||||||||||||||||||||||||||||||||||||||||||||||||||||||||||||||||||||||||||||||||||||||||||||||||||||||||

William Chandler Is Allowed to Keep a Tavern

Taverns played important roles in the communities of early America. They provided food and lodging for travelers and places of news and entertainment for local residents. All taverns were strictly regulated as shown by this license granted to a tavern keeper in colonial Massachusetts.

Source: EARLE, ALICE MORSE. *Stage-Coach and Tavern Days*, pp. 65–66. The Macmillan Company, New York, 1927.

. . . Whereas . . . William Chandler is . . . allowed by their Majesties' Justices . . . to keep a tavern . . . known by the sign of the Horse Shoe. . . . Therefore . . . William Chandler, during the time of keeping a Public House shall not permit . . . any playing at Dice, Cards, Tables, Quoits, Loggets, Bowls, Ninepins, Billiards, or any other unlawful Game or Games in his House, yard, Garden, . . . Nor shall allow to remain in his House any person or persons not being of his own family upon Saturday nights after it is Dark, nor any time on the Sabbath Day or Evening. . . .

Nor shall allow any person to lodge or stay above one Day or Night, except those whose Name he shall deliver to some one . . . of the Constables or some one of the Officers of the Town, unless they be such as he very well knoweth, and will answer for their good conduct.

Nor shall sell any Wine or Liquors to any Indians or Negroes nor allow any apprentices or servants or any other persons to remain in his tavern tippling or drinking after nine of the Clock in the night time.

Nor buy or take to Pawn any stolen goods, nor willingly Harbor in his tavern, Barn, Stable, or Otherwhere any Rogues, Vagabonds, Thieves, nor other notorious offenders whatsoever. . . .

. . . And in his said tavern shall . . . maintain good order and Rule.

Blackbeard Loses His Head

> Pirates, especially in the waters around the southern colonies,
> frequently interfered with ships. The pirates did not always
> escape unpunished as this account, taken from a Boston news-
> paper of 1719, indicates.
> Source: *Boston News-Letter, February 16–23, 1719*. Library
> of Congress photostat, No. 775.

Boston, By Letters of the 17th of December last from North
Carolina, we are informed, That Lieutenant Robert Maynard of
his Majesty's Ship Pearl . . . with two Sloops, mann'd with Fifty
Men and small Arms, but no great Guns overtook Capt. Teach
the Pirate, called Blackbeard . . . who had ten great Guns and
Twenty one Men on Board his Sloop. . . . Maynard boarded the
Pirate ship and fought it out, hand to hand, with Pistol and Sword;
The Engagement was very desperate and bloody on both sides
and Lieutenant Maynard had Thirty five of his Men killed and
wounded in the Action, himself slightly wounded. Teach and
most of his Men were killed, the rest carryed Prisoners to Virginia . . . to be tryed there. Lt. Maynard also carrys with him
Teach's Head which he cut off, in order to get the Reward granted
by said Colony.

Ben Franklin Arrives in Philadelphia

> Benjamin Franklin was born in Boston in 1706 where he
> learned the printer's trade from his brother, James. He tells of
> his arrival in Philadelphia in 1723.
> Source: Van Doren, Carl (editor). *Benjamin Franklin's
> Autobiographical Writings*, pp. 232–235. The Viking Press, New
> York, 1945.

Arriv'd there about eight or nine o'clock on the Sunday morning, and landed at the Market-street wharf. . . . I was in my

working dress, my best cloaths being to come round by sea. I was dirty from my journey; my pockets stuff'd out with shirts and stockings, and I knew no soul nor where to look for lodging. I was fatigued with travelling . . . and want of rest. I was very hungry, and my whole stock of cash consisted of a Dutch dollar, and about a shilling in copper. . . .

Then I walked up the street, gazing about till near the market-house I met a boy with bread. I had made many a meal on bread, and, inquiring where he got it, I went immediately to the baker's he directed me to . . . and ask'd for bisket, intending such as we had in Boston; but they, it seems, were not made in Philadelphia. So . . . not knowing . . . the names of his bread, I bad him give me three-penny worth of any sort. He gave me . . . three great puffy rolls. I was surpriz'd at the quantity, but took it, and, having no room in my pockets, walk'd off with a roll under each arm, and eating the other.

Thus I went up Market-street as far as Fourth-street, passing by the door of Mr. Read, my future wife's father. . . . She, standing at the door, saw me, and thought I made, as I certainly did, a most awkward, ridiculous appearance. Then I turned and went down Chesnut-street and part of Walnut-street, eating my roll all the way, and . . . found myself again at Market-street wharf, near the boat I came in, to which I went for a draught of the river water. . . . Being filled with one of my rolls, (I) gave the other two to a woman and her child that came down the river in the boat with us, and were waiting to go farther.

Thus refreshed, I walked again up the street, which by this time had many clean-dressed people in it, who were all walking the same way. I joined them, and thereby was led into the great meeting-house of the Quakers near the market. I sat down among them, and . . . being very drowsy . . . I fell fast asleep, and continu'd so till the meeting broke up, when one was kind enough to rouse me. This was, therefore, the first house I was in, or slept in, in Philadelphia.

Walking down again toward the river, and, looking in the faces of people, I met a young Quaker man, whose countenance I lik'd, and asked him . . . where a stranger could get lodging. We were then near the sign of the Three Mariners. "Here," says he, "is one place . . . but it is not a reputable house; if thee wilt walk with me, I'll show thee a better." He brought me to the Crooked

Billet in Water-street. Here I got a dinner; and, while I was eating it, several . . . questions were asked me, as it seemed to be suspected from my youth and appearance, that I might be some runaway.

After dinner, my sleepiness return'd, and being shown to a bed, I lay down without undressing, and slept till six in the evening, was call'd to supper, went to bed again very early, and slept soundly till next morning. . . .

> [Franklin got a job with a printer named Samuel Keimer and roomed and boarded with Mr. Read, whose daughter, Deborah, he married in 1730.]

1744

A Doctor Describes the Quaker City

Dr. Alexander Hamilton, no relation of Alexander Hamilton, the famous Federalist, was a young physician educated in Scotland who came to live in Maryland. In 1744 he took a 1600-mile trip through the colonies and wrote a description which is one of our best records of colonial life at the time. Here he gives his impressions of bustling Philadelphia which was on its way to becoming the largest colonial city.

Source: BRIDENBAUGH, CARL (editor). *Gentleman's Progress: The Itinerarium of Dr. Alexander Hamilton*, pp. 18–30. University of North Carolina Press, Chapel Hill, 1948.

Wednesday, June 6, 1744. The country round the city of Philadelphia is level and pleasant. . . . The city lies betwixt the . . . Delaware and Skuylkill, the streets being laid out in rectangular squares which makes a regular, uniform plan, but . . . altogether destitute of variety.

At my entering the city, I observed the regularity of the streets, but at the same time the majority of the houses are mean and low and much decayed, the streets in general not paved, very dirty, and obstructed with rubbish and lumber (for new construction). The State House, Assembly House (now known as Independence Hall), the great church in Second Street, and Whitefield church are good buildings.

I observed several comical, grotesque faces in the inn where I put up which would have afforded a variety of hints for a painter like Hogarth. (An English artist whose caricatures were as popular in America as they were in England.) They talked at the inn upon all subjects—politics, religion, and trade—some tolerably well, but most of them ignorantly. . . .

I was shaved by a little . . . old barber who kept dancing round me and talking all the time . . . and yet did his job lightly and to a hair. He abounded in compliments and was a very civil fellow in his way. He told me he had been a journeyman for 40 . . . years, notwithstanding which, he understood how to trim gentlemen as well . . . as the best masters. . . .

Thursday, June 7. I saw one instance of industry as soon as I got up and looked out . . . my chamber window, and that was the shops open at 5 in the morning. . . .

Friday, June 8. . . . I dined at a tavern with a very mixed company of different nations and religions. There were Scots, English, Dutch, Germans, and Irish; there were Roman Catholics, Church (of England) men, Presbyterians, Quakers, Newlightmen, Methodists, Seventh day men, Moravians, Anabaptists, and one Jew. The whole company consisted of 25 planted around an oblong table in a great hall well supplied with flies. . . . The prevailing topic of conversation was politics and conjectures of a French war (King George's War in which the colonies became involved in 1744). A knot of Quakers . . . talked only about selling of flour and the low price it bore. The whole company touched a little upon religion, and high words arose among some . . . but their blood was not hot enough to quarrel. . . .

In the afternoon I went to see some ships that lay in the river. Among the rest were three vessels a fitting out for privateers. . . . At six o'clock I went to the coffee house and drank a dish of coffee. . . .

Saturday, June 9th. This morning there fell a light rain which proved very refreshing, the weather having been very hot and dry for several days. The heat in this city is excessive, the sun's rays being reflected with such power from the brick houses and from the street pavement which is brick. The people commonly use awnings of painted cloth or canvas over their shop windows and doors and, at sun set, throw buckets full of water upon the pavement which cools it. They have plenty of excellent water in this city, there being a pump at almost every 50 paces distance. There are a great number of balconies to their houses where sometimes the men sit in cool clothes and smoke.

The market in this city is perhaps the largest in North America. It is kept twice a week upon Wednesdays and Saturdays. The street where it stands, called Market Street, is large and spacious, composed of the best houses in the city.

They have but one public clock here which strikes the hour but has neither index nor dial plate. It is strange they should lack such an ornament and convenience in so large a city but the chief part of the community consisting of Quakers, they would seem to shun ornament in their public buildings as well as in their clothing. . . .

Here is no public magazine of arms nor any method of defense . . . in case of the invasion of an enemy. This is owing to the obstinacy of the Quakers in maintaining their principle of non-resistance. . . .

Tuesday, June 12. In Philadelphia one may live tolerably cheap as to articles of eating and drinking, but European goods here are extravagantly dear. Even goods of their own manufacture such as linen, woolen, and leather bear a high price. . . .

Wednesday, June 13. Early in the morning I left Philadelphia, being willing to depart that city where, because of the excessive heat, it was a pain to live and breath. . . .

1744

The Dutch Make Wampum in Albany

Dr. Hamilton continued his trip northward. He set down his impressions of all the places he visited, including Albany, New York, which at that time was almost a frontier city.
Source: BRIDENBAUGH, CARL (editor). *Gentleman's Progress: The Itinerarium of Dr. Alexander Hamilton*, pp. 71–74. University of North Carolina Press, Chapel Hill, 1948.

Monday, July 2, 1744. . . . The city of Albany lies on the west side of Hudson's River . . . about . . . 160 miles above New York. . . . This city is enclosed by a rampart or wall of wooden palisades about 10 foot high and a foot thick, being the trunks of pine trees rammed into the ground, pinned close together, and ending each in a point at top. . . . There are 5 or 6 gates to this city, the chief of which are the north and south gates. In the city are about 4,000 inhabitants, mostly Dutch or of Dutch descent.

The Dutch here keep their homes very neat and clean, both without and within. Their . . . floors are generally laid with rough plank which, in time, by constant rubbing and scrubbing becomes as smooth as if it had been planed. Their chambers and rooms are large and handsome. They have their beds generally in alcoves so that you may go through all the rooms of a great house and see never a bed. They affect pictures much, particularly those showing Bible history, with which they adorn their rooms. They set their tables much with china. Their kitchens are likewise very clean, and there they hang . . . plates and dishes all round the walls . . . having a hole drilled through the edge of the plate or dish and a loop of ribbon put into it to hang it by. . . .

They live here very frugally and plain, for the chief merit among them seems to be riches, which they spare no pains or trouble to acquire. They are a civil and hospitable people in their way but, at best, rustic and unpolished. I imagined when I first came there that there were some very rich people in the place. They talked of 30, 40, 50, and 100 thousand pounds as of nothing, but I soon found that their riches consisted more in large tracts of land than in cash.

They trade pretty much with the Indians and have their manufactorys for wampum, a good Indian commodity. It is of two sorts—the black . . . is a bead made out of the bluish black part of a clam shell. It is valued at 6 shillings . . . per 100 beads. The white is made of a conch shell from the West Indies and is not so valuable. They grind the beads to a shape upon a stone, and then with a . . . needle dipped in wax . . . they drill a hole through each bead. This trade is apparently trifling but would soon make . . . a man wealthy that could have a monopoly of it. . . . Indians because of their custom of burying quantities of it with their dead . . . will give skins or money or anything for it. The Indians, though they first taught the art of making it to the Europeans, have lost the art of making it themselves.

They live in their houses in Albany as if they were in prisons, all their doors and windows being perpetually shut. But the reason for this may be the little desire they have for conversation and society, their whole thoughts being turned upon profit and gain which necessarily makes them live retired and frugal . . . But also the excessive cold winters here obliges them in that season to keep all snug and close, and they have not summer enough to revive heat in their veins so as to make them want to air themselves. They are a healthy, long lived people, many in this city being in age near or above 100 years, and 80 is a common age. . . .

. . . Their women in general, both old and young, are the hardest favored ever I beheld. Their old women wear a comical head dress . . . short petticoats, and they stare upon one like witches. . . .

. . . .

The young men here call their sweethearts luffees, and a young fellow of 18 is reckoned a simpleton if he has not a luffee; but their women are so homely that a man must never have seen any other luffees else they would never entrap him. . . .

1747-1752

Franklin Experiments with Electricity

Benjamin Franklin earned the honorary title of "Doctor" Franklin through his scientific interests, notably his experiments with electricity. Here, in his own words and those of a contemporary, you can read of his fascination with the phenomenon of electricity.

Source: VAN DOREN, CARL (editor). *Benjamin Franklin's Autobiographical Writings*, pp. 51, 56, 69, 76, 77. The Viking Press, New York, 1945.

Letter to Peter Collinson in London

Philadelphia, August 14, 1747

Sir: I have lately written two long letters to you on the subject of electricity. . . . On some further experiments since, I have observed a phenomenon or two that I cannot at present account for on the principle laid down in those letters, and am therefore become a little diffident of my hypothesis, and ashamed that I have expressed myself in so positive a manner. In going on with these experiments how many pretty systems do we build which we soon find ourselves obliged to destroy! If there is no other use discovered of electricity, this however is something considerable, that it may help to make a vain man humble. . . .

Letter to John Lining of Charleston, South Carolina

March 18, 1755

. . . Your question, how I came first to think of proposing the experiment of drawing down the lightning in order to ascertain its sameness with the electric fluid, I cannot answer better than by giving you an extract from the minutes I used to keep of the experiments I made. . . .

"Nov. 7, 1749. Electrical fluid agrees with lightning in these particulars: 1. Giving light. 2. Colour of the light. 3. Crooked direction. 4. Swift motion. 5. Being conducted by metals. 6. Crack or noise in exploding. 7. Subsisting in water or ice. 8. Rending bodies it passes through. 9. Destroying animals. 10. Melting metals. 11. Firing inflammable substances. 12. Sulphureous smell.—The electric fluid is attracted by points.—We do not know whether this property is in lightning.—But since they agree in all the particulars wherein we can already compare them, is it not probable they agree likewise in this? Let the experiment be made. . . ."

> [Here is the experiment Franklin proposed which might prove whether lightning was attracted to "points" in the same way as the "electrical fluid."]

. . . To determine the question whether the clouds that contain lightning are electrified or not, I would propose an experiment to be tried where it may be done conveniently. On the top of some high tower or steeple, place a kind of sentry-box, big enough to contain a man and an electrical stand. From the middle of the stand let an iron rod rise and pass bending out of the door, and then upright twenty or thirty feet, pointed very sharp at the end. If the electrical stand be kept clean and dry, a man standing on it when such clouds are passing low might be electrified and (give off) sparks, the rod drawing fire to him from a cloud. If any danger to the man should be (feared) . . . let him stand on the floor of his box, and now and then bring near to the rod the loop of a wire that has one end fastened to the leads, he holding it by a wax handle; so the sparks, if the rod is electrified, will strike from the rod to the wire and not affect him.

> [The experiment Franklin proposed was carried out successfully in France on May 10, 1752. The next month, Franklin, who had not yet heard of the success of the experiment, established similar proof with his famous kite. Franklin never wrote an autobiographical account of his kite experiment, but he told the exact details to his friend, Joseph Priestley. Priestley published the story of the experiment, as follows, in his *History and Present State of Electricity*, pp. 171–172.]

June, 1752

The Doctor, having published his method of verifying his hypothesis concerning the sameness of electricity with . . . lightning, was waiting for the erection of a spire in Philadelphia to carry his views into execution . . . when it occurred to him that by means of a common kite he could have better access to the regions of thunder than by any spire whatever. Preparing, therefore, a large silk handkerchief and two cross-sticks of a proper length on which to extend it, he took the opportunity of the first approaching thunder-storm to take a walk in the fields, in which there was a shed convenient for his purpose. But, dreading the ridicule which too commonly attends unsuccessful attempts in science, he communicated his intended experiment to nobody but his son who assisted him in raising the kite.

The kite being raised, a considerable time elapsed before there was any appearance of its being electrified. One very promising cloud had passed over it without any effect, when . . . he observed some loose threads of the hempen string to stand erect and avoid one another, just as if they had been suspended on a common conductor. Struck with this promising appearance, he immediately presented his knuckle to the key, and . . . the discovery was complete. He perceived a very evident electric spark. Others succeeded, even before the string was wet, so as to put the matter past all dispute, and when the rain had wet the string he collected electric fire very copiously. This happened in June, 1752, a month after the electricians in France had verified the same theory, but before he had heard of anything they had done.

1717-1773

Passengers Describe the Grim Voyage

Normal sailing time across the Atlantic in the 1700's was from ten to thirteen weeks. Passengers faced misery, sickness, and death. Three excerpts tell the terrible details of the grim voyage across the Atlantic.

From Dublin to Boston, 1717.

Source: *Boston News-Letter, September 9–16, 1717.* Library of Congress photostat, No. 700.

Arrived here the Ship Friend's Goodwill from Dublin . . . after about Eighteen weeks passage from . . . Ireland having on board two and fifty Souls, who have sustained very great hardships on their Voyage, by Contrary Winds, being out to a very short allowance, both of Bread, Water and Meat . . . It is a Miracle they did not all perish; but God's good Providence has often been visibly seen in their preservation; first in meeting a Ship at Sea that spared them some Provisions, & then by Dolphins & Sharks they catch'd, and by Rain Water . . . on their Decks . . .

From Germany to Pennsylvania, 1750.

Source: EBEN, CARL T. (translator). *Gottlieb Mittelberger's Journey to Pennsylvania in the Year 1750.*

. . . During the voyage there is on board these ships terrible misery, stench, fumes, horror, vomiting, many kinds of sea-sickness, fever dysentery, head-ache, heat constipation, boils, scurvy, cancer, mouthrot, and the like, all of which come from old and sharply salted food and meat, also from very bad and foul water, so that many die miserably.

Add to this want of provisions, hunger, thirst, frost, heat, dampness, anxiety, want, afflictions and lamentations, together with other trouble, as . . . the lice abound so frightfully, especially on sick people, that they can be scraped off the body. The misery reaches the climax when a gale rages for 2 or 3 nights and days, so that everyone believes that the ship will go to the bottom with all human beings on board.

33

. . . Children from 1 to 7 years rarely survive the voyage; and many a time parents are compelled to see their children miserably suffer and die from hunger, thirst, and sickness, and then to see them cast into the water. I witnessed such misery in no less than 32 children in our ship, all of whom were thrown into the sea.

From Scotland to New York, 1773.

> Source: *Ezra Stiles Diary, 1770–1775.* Force Transcripts, Division of Manuscripts, Library of Congress.

About the Middle of this Mo. (December) arrived at N. York a Brig with about 200 passengers having lost about 100 (one third) on the Passage. They embarked September 17 at Dornoch . . . in Scotland about 300 Men Women & Children . . . The Captain Geo. Smith shortened their Allowance of Provisions, & so abused them that above 100 died on the Passage (which lasted three months.) Their miserable state at their arrival at N. York excited the pubc. (public) Charity. Imedy. (immediately) £80 (eighty pounds) was collected at the Presbn. Chh. (Presbyterian Church) at N. York & they were relieved.

1758

General Amherst Gives Orders at Louisbourg

> The tide began to turn in the French and Indian War when British regulars and American colonial "light troops" captured the French fort of Louisbourg on Cape Breton Island at the mouth of the Gulf of St. Lawrence. Note the careful instructions the British commander, Major General Amherst, issued to the colonials before the landing at Louisbourg.
>
> Source: "Notes and Documents" section of *Military Affairs* (the journal of the American Military Institute), Volume XXII, No. 3, Fall, 1958, pp. 146–148.

The Troops must pay exact obedience to all Orders, & they may be assured of the most impartial Justice; It is recommended to them to live in great Friendship, and Harmony amongst each other . . . as becomes Men who mean to do honour to themselves & to their Country by their behaviour.

There will be an Hospital and in time it is hoped there will be fresh meat for the sick or wounded Men; And it is not doubted but that the Commander of Corps, will in every respect have due regard to the health and welfare of their Soldiers: On the other hand the least murmur or Complaint will be check'd with great severity; And any backwardness in sight of the Enemy, will be punish'd with immediate Death.

If any man is Vilain enough to desert his Colours & go over to the Enemy, he shall . . . be hang'd with Infamy as a Traitor.

When any of our Troops are to attack the French regular forces, they are to march close up to them, discharge their pieces loaded with two Bullets, and then rush upon them with their Bayonets . . .

The Army under the Fire and Protection of the Fleet, will land perhaps, if the Wind favours, in the face of the Enemy, or we may attempt it in different parts of the Island, (so) that by dividing their force, we may be sure to succeed somewhere. When the Troops, Artillery, Stores, etc. are all landed . . . the business is half done.

. . . .

As the Air of Cape Breton is moist & foggy, there must be particular attention to the fire Arms . . . that they may be kept dry, & always fit for use, and the light infantry should fall upon some method, to secure their Arms from the Dews & Droppings of the Trees when they are in search of the Enemy.

The Commander of the light troops must teach his Corps to attack & to defend themselves judiciously . . . They must be instructed to chuse good Posts, & to lay themselves in Ambuscade to advantage: To be alert, silent, vigilant & obedient; ready at all times to turn out without the least noise, or the least Confusion. They must always march in Files & generally fight in a single rank; pushing at the Enemy when they see him in Confusion, & that the Ground favours their Efforts; Never pursue with too much eagerness, nor to give way, except in a very great inequality of Numbers.

They must avoid huddling together, & running into a Lump; In such a situation they are a fair object for their Adversaries, & not able to employ their Arms. . . .

The Commanding Officers of Regiments, Captains of Companies & other Officers, are to read & explain to their Men, all the

Orders that concern them, taking great care to inform them of every part of their duty, & shewing them upon all occasions Examples worthy of their Imitation.

1759

Washington Writes to a London Merchant

This letter reveals that, in accordance with law and custom of the times, a husband took over control of his wife's property. In addition, it shows how plantation owners did business through agents in England to whom they often were in debt.

Source: SPARKS, JARED (compiler and editor). *The Writings of George Washington*, pp. 328–329. Russell, Odiorne, and Metcalf, and Hilliard Gray and Company, 1834.

To Robert Cary, Merchant, London.

Williamsburg, 1 May, 1759.

Sir:

The enclosed is the clergyman's certificate of my marriage with Mrs. Martha Custis. . . . You will, therefore, for the future please . . . address all your letters, which relate to the affairs of the late Daniel Parke Custis, to me, as by marriage I am entitled to a third part of that estate and am invested likewise with the care of the other two-thirds by a decree of our General Court. . . .

I have many letters of yours in my possession unanswered; but at present this serves only to advise you of the above change, and at the same time to acquaint you that I shall continue to make you the same consignments of tobacco as usual, and will endeavor to increase them in proportion as I find myself and the estate benefited thereby. . . .

On the other side of this letter is an invoice of some goods, which I beg you to send me by the first ship bound either to the Potomac or Rappahannoc, as I am in immediate need of them. Let them be insured, and in case of accident, re-shipped without delay. Direct them to me at Mount Vernon, Potomac River, Virginia. . . .

I am, &c.,

George Washington

A French Visitor Hears Patrick "Henery"

No other measure so united the American colonists against Britain as did the Stamp Act. A French traveler recorded in his diary this description of the Virginia Assembly at Williamsburg considering what action to take against the Act.

Source: "Journal of a French Traveller in the Colonies, 1765," pp. 745–746 in *American Historical Review*, Vol. 26, July, 1921.

May the 30th. Set out early . . . and . . . arived at Williamsburg at 12. . . . I went imediately to the Assembly which was seting, where I was entertained with very strong debates concerning dutys that the Parlement wants to lay on the American colonys, which they call or stile stamp dutys.

Shortly after I came in, one of the members stood up and said he had read that in former times Tarquin and Julus had their Brutus, Charles had his Cromwell, and he did not doubt but some good American would stand up in favour of his Country; but says he in a more moderate manner, and was going to continue, when the Speaker of the House rose and said . . . the last that stood up had spoke traison, and was sorey to see that not one of the members of the House was loyal enough to stop him before he had gone so far.

Upon which the same member stood up again, his name is Henery, and said that if he had afronted the Speaker or the House, he was ready to ask pardon, and he would shew his loyalty to His Majesty King George the third at the expence of the last drop of his blood; but what he had said must be attributed to the interest of his country's dying liberty which he had at heart, and the heat of passion might have lead him to have said something more than he intended; but . . . if he said any thing wrong, he beged the Speaker and the House's pardon. Some other members stood up and backed him, on which that afaire was droped.

May the 31th. I returned to the Assembly to-day, and heard very hot debates stil about the stamp dutys. The whole House was for entering resolves on the records but they differed much with regard the contents or purport thereof. Some were for shewing their resentment to the highest.

One of the resolves that these proposed, was that any person that would offer to sustain that the Parlement of England had a right to impose or lay any tax or dutys whatsoever on the American colonys, without the consent of the inhabitants thereof, should be looked upon as a traitor, and deemed an enemy to his country: there were some others to the same purpose, and the majority was for entring these resolves; upon which the Governor disolved the Assembly, which hinderd their proceeding.

1767

Smith and Taite Seek Their Runaway Workers

Indentured servants and convicts sentenced to the colonies performed much of the hard but necessary work in colonial times. They were bound to work for a period of years before being freed. Some were skilled workers and if they ran away, strong efforts were made to get them back, as these advertisements show. The advertisements also show the style of dress of the colonial working class.

Source: Advertisements printed in Virginia *Gazette*, March 26 and April 16, 1767.

(1) Run away from the subscriber, in Northumberland County, two Irish convict servants named William and Hannah Daylies, tinkers by trade (menders of pots and pans), of which the woman is extremely good; they had a note of leave to go out and work in Richmond county and Hobb's Hole, the money to be paid to Job Thomas, in said county; soon after I heard they were run away. The man wore a light coloured coarse cloth frock coat, a blue striped satin jacket, and plaid one, a pair of leather breeches, a pair of Russia drill white stockings, a little brown bog wig, and his hat cocked up very sharp. He is about 5 feet eight inches high, of a sandy complexion and freckled; is a well made fellow, somewhat bow legged.

The woman had on an old stuff gown and light coloured petticoat, an under petticoat of cotton with a blue selvedge at the bottom, a blue striped satin gown like the man's jacket, two check aprons, and a pair of pale blue calimanco shoes. They both wore white shirts, with very short ruffles, and white thread stockings. They had a complete set of tinkers tools. . . . Whoever will apprehend both or either of said servants, and brings them to me shall have five pounds reward for each, and reasonable travelling charges allowed by *William Taite*.

. . . .

(2) Run away from King William court-house on the 14th of March . . . three apprentice boys, viz. James Axley, a carpenter, about 5 feet 8 inches high, and wears his own black hair cued behind; had on when he went away a gray cloth coat, without pockets or flaps, and a pair of leather breeches much daubed with turpentine.

William Arter, a carpenter, rather taller and better set than the former, of a dark complexion, has black hair, but his clothes no way remarkable.

William Kindrick, a bricklayer, which business he understands well, and is supposed to be gone with a view of carrying it on with the other boys; he is a fresh complexioned youth, wears a cap, and had on a bearskin coat with metal buttons, a dark brown waistcoat, and a pair of lead-coloured serge breeches.

It is supposed they are gone to Bedford, or into Carolina. Whoever brings the said apprentices to King William or Hanover court-houses shall have forty shillings reward for each, besides their expenses defrayed.

Francis Smith. . . .

1770

Deacon Tudor Describes
"A Most Horrid Murder"

Deacon John Tudor of Boston town wrote the following account of the "Boston Massacre" in his diary of March, 1770.
Source: *Deacon Tudor's Diary*, Boston, 1896.

March [1770]. On Monday Evening the 5th current, a few Minutes after 9 o'clock a most horrid murder was committed in King Street. . . .

March 5th. This unhappy affair began by Some Boys and young fellows throwing Snow Balls at the sentry placed at the Customhouse Door. On which 8 or 9 Soldiers Came to his assistance. Soon after a Number of people collected, when the Capt commanded the Soldiers to fire, which they did and 3 Men were Kil'd on the Spot and several Mortaly Wounded.

The Capt soon drew off his Soldiers . . . or the Consequencis mite have been terable, for on the Guns fiering the people were alarm'd & set the Bells a Ringing as if for Fire, which drew Multitudes to the place of action.

Leut. Governor Hutchinson, who was commander in Chefe . . . desired the Multitude about 10 O'Clock to . . . go home peaceable . . . but the people insisted that the Soldiers should be ordered to their Barracks 1st. . . .

Capt Preston was taken up by a warrant given to the high Sherif . . . [and sent] to Gaol . . . so aboute 4 O'clock the Town became quiet. . . .

Tuesday A. M. the inhabitants mett at Faneuil Hall & after som pertinent speches, chose a Committee of 15 Gentlemn to . . . request the immediate removeàl of the Troops . . . [The Lieut. Governor replied] that it was not in his power. . . .

March 6. The Above Reply was not satisfactory to the Inhabitants . . . [who] Adjourned to Dr. Sewill's Meetinghouse [Old South Church where they] chose a Committee to waite on the Leut. Governor to let him & the Council Know that nothing less will satisfy the people than a total & immediate removal of the Troops out of the Town.

His Honor laid before the Council the Vote of the Town. The Council [agreed and] His Honor communicated this advice . . . to Col Dalrymple . . . [who] gave his Word & honor . . . that both the Rigiments should be remov'd without delay [to Castle William].

The Comte return'd to the Town Meeting & Mr. Hancock, chairman . . . Read their Report . . . which was Received with a shoute & clap of hands, which made the Meetinghouse Ring. . . .

March 8. Agreeable to a general request of the Inhabitants, were follow'd to the Grave in succession the 4 Bodies of Saml Gray, Saml Maverick, James Caldwell & Crispus Attucks, the unhappy Victims who fell in the Bloody Massacre.

On this sorrowfull Occasion most of the shops & stores in Town were shut, all the Bells were order'd to toll a solom peal in Boston, Charleston, Cambridge & Roxbery.

The several Hearoes . . . proceeded thro' the main street, lengthened by an immense Concourse of people. So numerous as to be obliged to follow in Ranks of 4 & 6 abreast. . . .

The sorrow Visible in the Countenance . . . Surpass description; it was suppos'd that the Spectators & those that follow'd the corps amounted to 15000, som supposed 20,000 [Boston's population was 25,000]. Note: Capt Preston was tried for his Life on the affare of the above Octobr 24 1770. [John Adams was his defense attorney.] The Trial lasted 5 Days, but the Jury brought him in not Guilty.

1772

Franklin Weighs the Pros and Cons

Benjamin Franklin was indeed a most versatile man. He was a printer, author, public-spirited citizen, businessman, politician, statesman, diplomat, inventor, scientist, and common-sense philosopher. In the latter capacity, Franklin explains to a friend the method he used when faced with the necessity of making an important decision.

Source: VAN DOREN, CARL (editor). *Benjamin Franklin's Autobiographical Writings,* pp. 280–281. The Viking Press, New York, 1945.

Dear Sir: In the affair of so much importance to you wherein you ask my advice, I cannot . . . advise you *what* to determine, but if you please I will tell you *how.* When these difficult cases occur, they are difficult chiefly because while we have them under consideration, all the reasons *pro* and *con* are not present to the mind at the same time. . . .

To get over this, my way is to divide half a sheet of paper by a line into two columns; writing over the one *Pro,* and over the other *Con.* Then during three or four days' consideration I put down under the different heads short hints . . . that at different times occur to me, *for* or *against* the measure. When I have thus got them all together in one view, I endeavour to estimate their respective weights; and where I find two that seem equal, I strike them both out. If I find a reason *pro* equal to some two reasons *con*, I strike out the three. If I judge some two reasons *con* equal to some three reasons *pro*, I strike out the five; and thus proceeding I find at length where the balance lies; and if after a day or two of farther consideration, nothing new that is of importance occurs on either side, I come to a determination accordingly. And though the weight of reasons cannot be taken with the precision of algebraic quantities, yet when . . . the whole lies before me, I think I can judge better, and am less likely to make a rash step. . . . In fact, I have found great advantage from this kind of equation, in what may be called *moral* or *prudential algebra*.

Wishing sincerely that you may determine for the best, I am ever, my dear friend, yours most affectionately. . . .

Benjamin Franklin

1773

Some "Indians" Hold a Tea Party

On the night of December 16, 1773, some citizens of Boston and the surrounding countryside disguised themselves as Indians and took part in the Boston Tea Party. This account of the famous event, which led directly to the passage of the Intolerable Acts, appeared in a Boston newspaper of the time.

Source: SNYDER, LOUIS L. (editor). *A Treasury of Great Reporting*, pp. 27–28. Simon and Schuster, Inc., New York, 1949.

. . . The Indians, as they were then called, repaired to the wharf, where the ships lay that had the tea on board, and were followed by hundreds of people, to see the event of the transactions of those who made so grotesque an appearance.

They, the Indians, immediately repaired on board Captain Hall's ship, where they hoisted the chests of tea and when upon deck stove the chests and emptied the tea overboard. Having cleared this ship, they proceeded to Captain Bruce's and then to Captain Coffin's brig.

They applied themselves so dexterously to the destruction . . . that in the space of three hours they broke up 342 chests, which was the whole number in those vessels, and discharged their contents into the harbor. When the tide rose it floated the broken chests and the tea insomuch that the surface of the water was filled therewith a considerable way from the south part of the town to Dorchester Neck, and lodged on the shores.

There was the greatest care taken to prevent the tea from being stolen by the populace. One or two being detected in endeavoring to pocket a small quantity were stripped of their acquisitions and very roughly handled. It is worthy of remark that although a considerable quantity of goods were still remaining on board the vessels, no injury was sustained. Such attention to private property was observed that a small padlock belonging to the captain of one of the ships being broke, another was procured and sent to him.

The town was very quiet during the whole evening and the night following. Those persons who were from the country returned with a merry heart; and the next day joy appeared in almost every countenance, some on occasion of the destruction of the tea, others on account of the quietness with which it was effected. . . .

1775

A Corporal Disagrees with a Lady

The first account is by Amos Farnsworth, a corporal in the Massachusetts militia. It is reproduced in his own spelling.

Source: "Diary of Amos Farnsworth," Massachusetts Historical Society Proceedings, Second Series, Volume XII, pp. 83–84.

The second account is by Ann Hulton, a lady who lived in Boston but remained loyal to the British king.

Source: Reprinted by permission of the publishers from ANN HULTON: *Letters of a Loyalist Lady*, Cambridge, Mass.: Harvard University Press, copyright, 1952, by the President and Fellows of Harvard College.

(1) *Friday, June 16.* . . . At six . . . our regiment preadid and about sun-set we was drawn up and herd prayers; and about

dusk marched for Bunkers Hill under command of our own Col Prescott. . . .

Saturday, June 17. The enemy appeared to be much alarmed on Saturday morning when they discovered our operations and immediately began a heavy cannonading from a batery on Corps-Hill, Boston, and from the ships in the harbour. We with little loss continued to carry on our works till 1 o'clock when we discovered a large body of the enemy crossing Charles-River from Boston.

They landed on a point of land about a mile eastward of our intrenchment and immediately disposed their army for an attack, previous to which they set fire to the town of Charlestown. It is supposed that the enemy intended to attack us under the cover of the smoke from the burning houses, the wind favouring them in such a design. . . .

As the enemy approached, our men was not only exposed to the attack of a very numerous musketry, but to the heavy fire of the battery on Corps-Hill, 4 or 5 men of war, several armed boats or floating batteries in Mistick-River, and a number of field pieces. Notwithstanding we within the intrenchment, and at a breast work without sustained the enemy's attacks with great bravery and resolution, kiled and wounded great numbers, and repulsed them several times; and after bearing, for about 2 hours, as sever and heavy a fire as perhaps was ever known, and many having fired away all their ammunition, and having no reinforsement, althoe thare was a great boddy of men nie by, we ware over-powered by numbers and obliged to leave the intrenchment, retreating about sunset to a small distance over Charlestown Neck. . . . But I got to Cambridge that night. The town of Charlestown supposed to contain about 300 dwelling-houses, a great number of which ware large and elegant, besides 150 or 200 other buildings, are almost all laid in ashes by the barbarity and wanton cruelty of that infernal villain Thomas Gage.

(2) *Boston, June 20, 1775.* . . . Last Saturday I was a spectator of the most awful scene my eyes ever beheld.

On the morning of the 17th it was observed that the rebels had thrown up a breastwork and were preparing to open a battery upon the heights above Charlestown, from whence they might incommode the shipping and destroy the north part of Boston.

Immediately a cannonading began from the battery in the north part of the town and the ships of war on those works and on the enemy wherever they could be discovered within reach. . . .

Soon after eleven o'clock the grenadiers, light infantry, marines and two battalions marched out of their encampments and embarked in boats, and . . . were landed on a point of land eastward of Charlestown. . . . More boats arrived, and the whole advanced. . . .

On that side of the hill which was not visible from Boston, it seems very strong lines were thrown up and were occupied by many thousands of the rebels. The troops advanced with great ardor towards the intrenchments, but were much galled in the assault, both from the artillery and the small arms, and many brave officers and men were killed and wounded. As soon as they got to the intrenchments, the rebels fled, and many of them were killed in the trenches and in their flight. The marines, in marching through part of Charlestown, were fired at from the houses. . . .

Upon the firing from the houses, the town was immediately set in flames, and at four o'clock we saw the fire and the sword, all the horrors of war raging. The town was burning all night; the rebels sheltered themselves in the adjacent hills and the neighborhood of Cambridge, and the army possessed themselves of Charlestown Neck. We were exulting in seeing the flight of our enemies, but in an hour or two we had occasion to mourn and lament. . . . In the evening the streets were filled with the wounded and dying. . . . We were every moment hearing of some officer or other of our friends and acquaintance who had fallen in our defence and in supporting the honor of our country. . . .

. . . It grieves one that gentlemen, brave British soldiers, should fall by the hands of such despicable wretches as compose the banditti of the country; amongst whom there is not one that has the least pretension to be called a gentleman. They are a most rude, depraved, degenerate race, and it is a mortification to us that they speak English and can trace themselves from that stock.

Since Adams went to Philadelphia, one Warren, a rascally patriot and apothecary of this town, has had the lead in the Provincial Congress. . . . This fellow happily was killed, in coming out of the trenches the other day, where he had commanded and spirited the people to defend the lines, which, he assured them, were impregnable. You may judge what the herd must be when such a one is their leader. . . .

1776

Abigail Adams Describes a Celebration

On July 21, 1776, Mrs. John (Abigail) Adams wrote to her husband about the celebration in Boston of the Declaration of Independence. He was still in Philadelphia with the Second Continental Congress which had declared it.

Source: ADAMS, CHARLES FRANCIS (editor). *Familiar Letters of John Adams and His Wife, Abigail Adams, during the Revolution,* p. 204. New York, 1876.

Boston, 21 July, 1776

Last Thursday, after hearing a very good sermon, I went with the multitude into King Street to hear the Proclamation for Independence read and proclaimed. Some field-pieces were brought there. The troops appeared under arms, and all the inhabitants assembled there. The small-pox prevented many thousands (coming) from the country. . . . Colonel Crafts read from the balcony of the State House the proclamation. Great attention was given to every word. As soon as he ended, the cry from the balcony was, "God save our American States," and then three cheers which rent the air. The bells rang, the privateers fired, (in) the forts and batteries, the cannon were discharged, the platoons followed, and every face appeared joyful. . . . After dinner, the King's Arms were taken down from the State House and every vestige of him from every place in which it appeared, and burnt in King Street. Thus ends royal authority in this State. . . .

Samuel Downing Remembers the Revolution

Samuel Downing was one of the last surviving soldiers of the War for Independence. At the age of one hundred and two he told of his experiences to an interviewer who set down the story in the old man's words.

Source: DOWNING, SAMUEL. "Last Survivors of the Revolution," pp. 28–30 in *American Heritage*, Vol. IX, No. 3, April, 1958.

Well, the war broke out. . . . I heard say that Hopkinton (Mass.) was the enlisting place. I waited till dinner time, when I thought nobody would see me, and then I started. It was eighteen miles, and I went it pretty quick. The recruiting officer, when I told him what I'd come for, said I was too small. I told him just what I'd done. "Well," said he, "you stay here and I'll give you a letter to Col. Fifield over in Charlestown and perhaps he'll take you." So I staid with him; and when uncle and aunt came home that night they had no Sam. The next day I went and carried the letter to Col. Fifield, and he accepted me . . .

The first duty I ever did was to guard wagons from Exeter to Springfield. We played the British a trick . . . We all started off on a run . . . Pretty soon I found they were going to surprise a British wagon train. We captured it . . .

Afterwards, we were stationed in the Mohawk valley. Arnold was our fighting general, and a bloody fellow he was. He didn't care for nothing; he'd ride right in. It was "Come on, boys!" It wasn't "Go, boys!" He was as brave a man as ever lived. He was dark-skinned, with black hair, of middling height. There wasn't any waste timber on him. He was a stern looking man, but kind to his soldiers. They didn't treat him right; he ought to have had Burgoyne's sword. But he ought to have been true . . .

We heard . . . Burgoyne was coming. . . . But by and by we got Burgoyne where we wanted him, and he gave up. He saw there was no use in fighting it out. . . .

Gates was an "old granny" looking fellow. When Burgoyne came up to surrender his sword, he said to Gates, "Are you a general? You look more like a granny than you do like a general." "I be a granny," said Gates, "and I've delivered you of ten thousand men to-day."

By and by they began to talk about going to take New York. There's always policy, you know, in war. We made the British think we were coming to take the city. . . . But Washington went south to Yorktown. LaFayette laid down the white sticks, and we threw up entrenchments by them. We were right opposite Washington's headquarters. I saw him every day. . . . But you never got a smile out of him. He was a nice man. We loved him. They'd sell their lives for him. . . .

When peace was declared . . . we burnt thirteen candles in every hut, one for each State.

1777

Sally Wister Wonders whether She'll See Him Again

Young Sally Wister, educated in a Quaker girls' school, left Philadelphia with her family when the British occupied that city in September, 1777. The Wisters found refuge in a farm-house about fifteen miles outside the city. For a short time the house was headquarters for the American General Small-wood and his staff. Sally kept a journal in which she recorded for her friend Deborah Norris her feelings about the officers.

Source: MYERS, ALBERT COOK (editor). *Sally Wister's Journal, A True Narrative,* pp. 81, 83, 84, 86–88, 102–104. Ferris & Leach, Philadelphia, 1902.

[*October 19, 1777*]

. . . How new is our situation! I feel in good spirits, though surrounded by an Army, the house full of officers, the yard alive with soldiers—very peaceable sort of men, tho'. They eat like other folks, talk like them, and behave themselves with elegance; so I will not be afraid of them, that I won't.

Adieu. I am going to my chamber to dream, I suppose, of bayonets and swords, sashes, guns, and epaulets.

I dare say thee is impatient to know my sentiments of the officers. . . .

The General is tall, portly, well made. A truly martial air, the behavior and manner of a gentleman, a good understanding, and great humanity of disposition constitute [his] character. . . .

Colonel Wood . . . is one of the most amiable of men; tall and genteel, an agreeable countenance and deportment. . . .

The cause he is fighting for alone tears him from the society of an amiable wife and engaging daughter; with tears in his eyes he often mentions the sweets of domestic life.

Colonel Line is not married, so let me not be too warm in his praise, lest you suspect. He is monstrous tall and brown, but has a certain something in his face and conversation very agreeable; he . . . is sensible and humane, and a brave officer; he is only seven and twenty years old but, by a long indisposition and constant fatigue, looks vastly older, and almost worn to a skeleton, but very lively and talkative.

Capt. Furnival,—I need not say more of him than that he has, excepting one or two, the handsomest face I ever saw, a very fine person; fine light hair and a great deal of it, adds to the beauty of his face.

Well, here comes the glory, the Major, so bashful, so famous, etc. . . . I at first thought the Major cross and proud, but I was mistaken. He is about nineteen, nephew to the Gen'l, and acts as Major of brigade to him. . . . He is large in his person, manly, and (has) an engaging countenance and address.

Finley is wretched ugly, but he went away last night, so (I) shall not particularize him.

Nothing of any moment today; (some of the) officers . . . dined with us. I was dressed in my chintz, and look'd smarter than the night before.

Fourth Day, October 21st.

I just now met the Major, very reserv'd; nothing but "Good morning," or "Your servant, madam." . . .

I have heard strange things of the Major. Worth a fortune of thirty thousand pounds, independent of anybody; the Major, moreover, is vastly bashful, so much so he can hardly look at the ladies. (. . . if 'tis bashfulness only, we will drive that away.)

To-day the Militia marches, and the Gen'l and officers leave us. Heigh ho! I am very sorry; for when you have been with agreeable people, 'tis impossible not to feel regret when they bid you adieu, perhaps forever. . . .

The Major looks dull.

Second Day Noon.

About two o'clock the Gen. and Major came to bid us adieu. With daddy and mammy they shook hands very friendly; to us they bow'd politely.

Our hearts were full. I thought Major was affected.

"Good-by, Miss Sally," spoken very low. He walk'd hastily and mounted his horse. . . .

We stood at the door to take a last look. . . .

The Major turn'd his horse's head, and rode back, dismounted. "I have forgot my pistols"; pass'd us, and ran upstairs. He came swiftly back to us, as if wishing . . . to stay, (but) by duty compell'd to go. He remounted his horse.

"Farewell, ladies, till I see you again," and cantered away.

We look'd at him till the turn in the road hid him from our sight. "Amiable Major," "Clever fellow," "Good young man," was echo'd from one to the other. I wonder whether we shall ever see him again. He has our wishes for his safety.

1777-1778

A Frenchman Views Valley Forge

Although victory over Burgoyne proved to be the turning point of the War for Independence, dark days lay ahead for the patriots. A French volunteer officer, who joined Washington's troops at Valley Forge, describes the situation there.

Source: COMMAGER, HENRY STEELE, and NEVINS, ALLAN (editors). *The Heritage of America*, pp. 169–170. Little, Brown and Company, Boston, 1956.

Sand and forest, forest and sand, formed the whole way from Williamsburg to the camp at Valley Forge. I do not remember how many days I took to accomplish this difficult journey. Being badly fed . . . I walked badly, and passed at least six nights under the trees. . . . Not knowing the language, I often strayed from the right road, which was so much time and labor lost. At last, early in November, I arrived at Valley Forge.

The American army was then encamped three or four leagues from Philadelphia, which city was then occupied by the British . . . who were rapidly fulfilling the prophecy of Franklin. That celebrated man . . . (said) "It is not the British army that has taken Philadelphia, but Philadelphia that has taken the British army." The cunning old diplomat was right. . . . The British officers, who were in the city, gave themselves up to pleasure. There were continual balls and other amusements. The troops were idle and made lazy by inaction, and the generals undertook nothing all the winter.

Soon I came in sight of the American camp. My imagination had pictured an army with uniforms, the glitter of arms, standards, etc. In short, military pomp of all sorts. Instead of the imposing spectacle I expected, I saw, grouped together or standing alone, a few militiamen poorly clad, and for the most part without shoes. Many of them were badly armed, but all were well supplied with provisions, and I noticed that tea and sugar formed part of their rations. . . . In passing through the camp I also noticed soldiers wearing cotton nightcaps under their hats, and some having for cloaks or greatcoats coarse woolen blankets, exactly like those provided for the patients in our French hospitals. I learned afterwards that these were the officers and generals.

Such, in strict truth, was, at the time I came amongst them, the appearance of this armed mob, the leader of whom was . . . Washington. . . . Such were the colonists—unskilled warriors who learned in a few years how to conquer the finest troops that England could send against them. Such, also, at the beginning of the War of Independence, was the state of want in the insurgent army, and such was the scarcity of money, and the poverty of their government . . . that its notes, called Continental paper money, were nearly valueless.

George Rogers Clark Gets Secret Orders

> In 1778 and 1779 George Rogers Clark and a band of hardy Kentucky volunteers captured the British outposts of Kaskaskia, Cahokia, and Vincennes in the Illinois country. By doing so, Clark subdued the Indians and weakened British claims to what later became the Northwest Territory. Patrick Henry, at that time governor of Virginia, issued these secret orders which started Clark on his way.
> Source: *Colonel George Rogers Clark's Sketch of His Campaign in the Illinois in 1778–9 . . . and an Appendix Containing the Public and Private Instructions to Col. Clark,* pp. 96–97. Robert Clarke & Co., 1869.

In Council, Wmsbug, Jan. 2, 1778

Lieutenant Colonel George Rogers Clark:

You are to proceed with all convenient Speed to raise Seven Companies of Soldiers to consist of fifty men each officered in the usual manner & armed most properly for the Enterprise, & with this Force attack the British post at Kaskasky.

It is conjectured that there are many pieces of Cannon & military Stores to considerable amount at that place, the taking & preservation of which would be a valuable acquisition to the State. If you are so fortunate therefore as to succeed in your Expectation, you will take every possible Measure to secure the artillery & stores & whatever may advantage the State.

For the Transportation of the Troops, provisions, &c., down the Ohio, you are to apply to the Commanding Officer at Fort Pitt for Boats, &c. During the whole Transaction you are to take especial Care to keep the true Destination of your Force secret. Its success depends on this. . . .

It is earnestly desired that you show Humanity to such British Subjects and other persons as fall in your hands. If the white Inhabitants at the post & the neighbourhood will give undoubted Evidence of their attachment to this State, for it is certain they live within its limits, . . . let them be treated as fellow Citizens & their persons & property duly secured. . . . But if these people will not accede to these reasonable Demands, they must feel the

Miseries of War, under the direction of that Humanity that has hitherto distinguished Americans, & which it is expected you will ever consider as the Rule of your Conduct, & from which you are in no Instance to depart.

The Corps you are to command are to receive the pay and allowance of Militia & to act under the Laws & Regulations of this State now in Force. . . . The Inhabitants at Kaskaskia will be informed by you that in Case they accede to the offers of becoming Citizens of Virginia, a proper Garrison will be maintained among them & every attention bestowed to render their Commerce beneficial, the fairest prospects being opened to the Dominions of both France & Spain. . . .

It is in Contemplation to establish a post near the Mouth of the Ohio. Cannon will be wanted to fortify it. Part of those at Kaskasky will be easily brought thither or otherwise secured. . . .

Wishing you success, I am Sir,

Your h'ble Serv.

P. Henry

1779

John Paul Jones Replies "In the Most Determined Negative"

The struggling Americans had no formal fleet to challenge the power of the mighty British navy during the War for Independence. Yet intrepid American privateers seized many English ships. John Paul Jones persuaded the French King to outfit an old French Indiaman which he rechristened the *Bonhomme Richard*. Here is his report of his battle with the formidable British frigate *Serapis*.

Source: "Report of John Paul Jones," pp. 145–148 in *John Paul Jones Commemoration at Annapolis, April 24, 1906*. Government Printing Office, Washington, 1907.

. . . In approaching the Enemy I crowded Every possible Sail. . . . Earnest as I Was for the action, I Could not reach the

Commodore's Ship, the *Serapis*, until Seven in the evening, being then within pistol shot. When he hailed the *B. H. R.*, we answered him by firing a Whole broadside.

The battle being thus begun, Was Continued With unremitting fury. Every method was practised on both Sides to gain an advantage, and rake Each other; and I must Confess that the Enemie's Ship being much more manageable than the *B. H. R.*, gained thereby several times an advantageous situation, in spite of my best endeavours to prevent it. As I had to deal With an Enemy of *greatly Superior force*, I was under the necessity of Closing with him, to prevent the advantage Which he had over me in point of manoeuvre. It was my intention to lay the *B. H. R.* athwart the enemie's bow, but as that operation required great dexterity in the management of both Sails and helm, and Some of our braces being Shot away, it did not exactly succeed to my Wishes. The Enemie's bowsprit, however, came over the *B. H. R.'s* poop by the mizen mast, and I made both Ships fast together in that Situation, Which by the action of the Wind on the Enemie's Sails, forced her Stern close to the *B. H. R.'s* bow, so that the Ships lay Square along side of each, the yards being all entangled, and the cannon of Each Ship touching the opponent's Side.

When this position took place it Was 8 o'clock, previous to which the *B. H. R.* had received . . . eighteen pounds Shot below the water, and Leaked Very much. My battery of 12 pounders . . . Were entirely silenced and abandoned. As to the six old eighteen pounders that formed the Battery of the Lower gun-deck, they did no Service Whatever; two out of three of them burst at the first fire, and killed almost all the men Who Were stationed to manage them. . . . I had now only two pieces of Cannon, nine pounders . . . that Were not silenced. . . . I directed the fire of one . . . Cannon against the main-mast, With doubled-headed Shot, While the other . . . was exceedingly Well Served With Grape and Cannister Shot to Silence the Enemie's musquetry, and clear her decks, Which Was at last Effected. . . .

The English Commodore asked me if I demanded quarters, and I having answered him in the most determined negative, they renewed the battle with Double fury. They Were unable to Stand on the deck, but the fire of their Cannon, especially the lower battery, Which Was Entirely formed of 18 pounders, Was

54

incessant, both Ships Were Set on fire in Various places, and the Scene was dreadful beyond the reach of Language. . . .

My Situation Was really deplorable . . . and my prospect became gloomy indeed. I Would not, however, give up. . . . The Enemie's main-mast begain to shake, their firing decreased, ours Rather increased, and the British colours Were Struck at half an hour past 10 o'clock.

This prize proved to be the British Ship of War the *Serapis*, a New Ship of 44 guns, built on their most approved Construction, With two compleat batteries, one of them of 18 pounders, and Commanded by the brave Commodore Richard Pearson. I had yet two enemies to encounter. . . . I mean fire and Water. . . . The *B. H. R.* Was assailed by both. There Was five feet Water in the hould and . . . the three pumps that remained Could With difficulty only Keep the Water from gaining. . . . Fire broke out in Various parts of the Ship, in spite of all the Water that could be thrown to quench it, and at length broke out as low as the powder magazine, and Within a few inches of the powder. In that dilema, I took out the powder upon deck, ready to be thrown overboard at the Last Extremity. . . . It was 10 o'clock the next day . . . before the fire Was entirely Extinguished. With respect to the situation of the *B. H. R.* . . . a person must have been an Eye-Witness to form a just idea of the tremendous scene of Carnage, Wreck, and ruin, that Every Where appeared. Humanity Cannot but recoil from the prospect of Such . . . horror, and Lament that War Should produce Such fatal consequences. . . .

Major André Detests the Mode

Major André was the British officer who negotiated with Benedict Arnold, the American traitor, for the surrender of West Point. When the plot was discovered, Arnold escaped to the British, but André was captured and hanged as a spy. Here is an eyewitness account of André's hanging, written by a surgeon in a Massachusetts regiment.

Source: ANGLE, PAUL M. (editor). *The American Reader*, pp. 118–119. Rand McNally & Company, Chicago, 1958.

October 2, 1780

Major Andre is no more among the living. I have just witnessed his exit. It was a tragical scene of the deepest interest. . . .

The principal guard officer who was constantly in the room with the prisoner, relates that when the hour of his execution was announced to him in the morning, he received it without emotion. . . . He partook of breakfast as usual, and having shaved and dressed himself, he . . . cheerfully said to the guard officers, "I am ready at any moment, gentlemen. . . ."

The fatal hour having arrived, a large detachment of troops . . . and an immense concourse of people assembled. . . . I was so near during the solemn march to the fatal spot, as to observe every movement, and participate in every emotion which the melancholy scene was calculated to produce. Major Andre walked from the stone house, in which he had been confined, between two of our . . . officers. . . . The eyes of the immense multitude were fixed on him. . . . He betrayed no want of fortitude, but retained a complacent smile on his countenance, and politely bowed to several gentlemen whom he knew. . . .

It was his earnest desire to be shot, as being the mode of death most fitting to . . . a military man. . . . At the moment, therefore, when he suddenly came in view of the gallows, he involuntarily started backward, and made a pause.

"Why this emotion, Sir?" said an officer by his side.

Instantly recovering his composure, Andre said, "I am reconciled to my death, but I detest the mode."

While waiting and standing near the gallows, I observed some degree of nervousness in him; placing his foot on a stone, and

56

rolling it over and choking in his throat, as if attempting to swallow. So soon, however, as he perceived that things were in readiness, he stepped quickly into the wagon, and at this moment he appeared to shrink, but instantly elevating his head with firmness, he said, "It will be but a momentary pang."

(Andre) bandaged his own eyes with perfect firmness, which melted the hearts and moistened the cheeks . . . of the throng of spectators. . . . He slipped the noose over his head and adjusted it to his neck, without the assistance of the awkward executioner. Colonel Scammel now informed him that he had an opportunity to speak, if he desired it. He raised the handkerchief from his eyes and said, "I pray you to bear me witness that I meet my fate like a brave man."

The wagon being now removed from under him, he was suspended and instantly expired; it proved indeed "but a momentary pang." . . . Thus died in the bloom of life, the accomplished Major Andre, the pride of the royal army. . . .

October 19, 1781

Many Soldiers Manifest a Sullen Temper

Even though they did not sign the peace treaty until two years later, the British realized the war was lost when Cornwallis surrendered to the Allied forces at Yorktown. Thus the scene described here by James Thacher, a regimental surgeon, really meant that the thirteen United States had won their independence.

Source: ANGLE, PAUL M. (editor). *The American Reader*, pp. 128–129. Rand McNally & Company, Chicago, 1958.

At about twelve o'clock, the combined army was arranged and drawn up in two lines extending more than a mile in length. The Americans were drawn up in a line on the right side of the road, and the French occupied the left. At the head of the former, Washington . . . took his station, attended by his aids. At the head of the latter was posted the excellent Count Rochambeau and his suite. The French troops, in complete uniform, displayed a martial and noble appearance. Their band of music . . . is a delightful novelty, and produced while marching to the ground, a most enchanting effect. The Americans, though not all in uniform nor their dress so neat, yet exhibited an erect soldierly air, and every countenance beamed with satisfaction and joy. The concourse of spectators from the country was prodigious, in . . . numbers probably equal to the military, but universal silence and order prevailed.

It was about two o'clock when the captive army advanced through the line formed for their reception. Every eye was prepared to gaze on Lord Cornwallis, but he disappointed the onlookers. Pretending to be ill, he made General O'Harra his substitute as the leader of his army. This officer was followed by the conquered troops in a slow and solemn step, with shouldered arms, colors cased and drums beating. . . .

The royal troops, while marching through the line formed by the allied army, exhibited a decent and neat appearance . . . for their commander . . . directed every soldier to be furnished with a new uniform prior to the surrender. But in their line of march we saw a disorderly and unsoldierly conduct, their step was irregular, and their ranks frequently broken. . . .

Some of the officers appeared to be exceedingly chagrined when giving the word "ground arms," and . . . many of the soldiers manifested a *sullen temper*, throwing their arms on the pile with violence, as if determined to break them. . . . After having grounded their arms and divested themselves of their accoutrements, the captive troops were conducted back to Yorktown and guarded by our troops till they could be removed to the place of their destination.

Thomas Jefferson Advises His Daughter

Thomas Jefferson's wife died in 1782, leaving him to care for three small, motherless children. Jefferson took his fatherly duties seriously—perhaps too seriously—as these letters to his daughter Martha, familiarly known as Patsy, show. Patsy was about eleven years old and Jefferson had left her under the care of a widow lady named Mrs. Hopkinson while he served as a Virginia delegate to Congress under the Articles of Confederation, then meeting in Annapolis, Maryland.

Source: BOYD, JULIAN P. (editor). *The Papers of Thomas Jefferson*, Vol. VI (pp. 359–360; 416–417). Princeton University Press, Princeton, 1952.

Annapolis, Nov. 28th, 1783

My dear Patsy—After four days' journey, I arrived here without any accident, and in as good health as when I left Philadelphia. The conviction that you would be more improved in the situation I have placed you than if still with me, has solaced me on my parting with you, which my love for you had rendered a difficult thing. The acquirements which I hope you will make under the tutors I have provided for you will render you more worthy of my love; and if they cannot increase it, they will prevent its diminution.

Consider the good lady who has taken you under her roof . . . as your mother, as the only person to whom, since the loss with which heaven has been pleased to afflict you, you can now look up. . . . With respect to the distribution of your time, the following is what I should approve:

From 8. to 10. o'clock practise music.

From 10. to 1. dance one day and draw another.

From 1. to 2. draw on the day you dance, and write a letter next day.

From 3. to 4. read French.

From 4. to 5. exercise yourself in music.

From 5. till bedtime, read English, write, &c.

. . . I expect you will write me by every post. Inform me what books you read, what tunes you learn, and inclose me your best copy of every lesson in drawing. Write also one letter a week either to your Aunt Eppes, your Aunt Skipworth, your Aunt Carr, or the little lady from whom I now enclose a letter. . . . Take care that you never spell a word wrong. Always before you write a word, consider how it is spelt, and, if you do not remember it, turn to a dictionary. It produces great praise to a lady to spell well. . . .

If you love me, then strive to be good under every situation and to all living creatures, and to acquire those accomplishments which I have put in your power, and which will go far towards ensuring you the warmest love of your affectionate father,

Th: Jefferson

P. S.—keep my letters and read them at times, that you may always have present in your mind those things which will endear you to me.

> [Perhaps her fond father's program was too much for Patsy to follow, or perhaps she was merely negligent. At any rate, Jefferson wrote this letter to his daughter less than a month later.]

Annapolis, Dec. 22, 1783

My DEAR Patsy—I hoped before this to have received letters from you regularly and weekly by the post, and also to have had a letter to forward from you to one of your aunts as I desired in my letter of Nov. 28th. I am afraid you do not comply with my desires expressed in that letter. Your not writing to me every week is one instance, and your having never sent me any of your copies of Mr. Simitiere's drawing lessons is another. I shall be very much mortified and disappointed if you become inattentive to my wishes and particularly to the directions of that letter which I meant for your principal guide.

I omitted in that letter to advise you on the subject of dress, which I know you are a little apt to neglect. I do not wish you to be gayly clothed at this time of life, but that your wear should be fine of its kind. But above all things and at all times let your clothes be neat, whole, and properly put on. Do not fancy you must wear them till the dirt is visible to the eye. . . . Some ladies think they may . . . be loose and negligent of their dress in the morning. But be you, from the moment you rise till you go to bed, as cleanly and properly dressed as at the hours of dinner or tea.

A lady who has been seen as a sloven . . . in the morning, will never efface the impression she has made, with all the dress and pageantry she can afterwards involve herself in. Nothing is so disgusting to men as a want of cleanliness and delicacy in women. I hope, therefore, the moment you rise from bed, your first work will be to dress yourself in such style, as that you may be seen by any gentleman without his being able to discover a pin amiss, or any other circumstance of neatness wanting. . . .

Present my compliments to . . . Mrs. Hopkinson whose health and happiness I have much at heart. I hope you are obedient and respectful to her in every circumstance and that your manners will be such as to engage her affections. I am my Dear Patsy, yours sincerely & affectionately,

Th: Jefferson

1788

Young John Quincy Adams Studies Laws— and Ladies

John Quincy Adams, who became our sixth President in 1825, studied law in Newburyport, Massachusetts, as a young man of twenty. These excerpts from his diary reveal an equal interest in young ladies.

Source: *Life in a New England Town, 1787–1788: Diary of John Quincy Adams while a Student in the Office of Theophilus Parsons at Newburyport (Mass.)*, pp. 81–99. Little, Brown and Company, Boston, 1903.

Jan. 6. Heard Mr. Carey preach two sermons this day. . . . In the afternoon the Parson was extremely vehement . . . but he said he was not aiming at popularity. Passed the evening at Mr. Carter's. . . . Miss Sally Jenkins was there. I was pleased with her manners. She is of the middling female size and has a fine form . . . and were not the nose too much inclined to the aquiline,

61

would be very handsome. . . . She conversed not much, and indeed in the state of female education here there are very few young ladies who talk and yet preserve our admiration. . . .

Jan. 13. . . . Dined with Dr. Kilham at Dr. Swett's. We spent the afternoon and drank tea there. Mrs. Swett is handsome. . . . She has too much good breeding to know anything upon speculative subjects, and she has a proper aversion to politics. . . . Later we called in at Mrs. Emery's. This lady and her daughter converse more to my satisfaction than the generality of my female acquaintance. In their company my time passes away fast; and I am not often able to say as much.

Jan. 18. This afternoon I wrote a couple of letters . . . and as I could not finish before dark I ventured to stay in the law office till seven o'clock. I then went with Townshend to Mr. Atkin's. . . . Miss Dashwood was there, a young lady from Boston. She speaks thick and quick, which is at present all I have to say of her, except that by candlelight she looks handsome. . . .

Jan. 22. . . . Between four and five I received an invitation . . . for a party at sleighing. Though not peculiarly desirous to go I did not refuse; and at about six o'clock . . . went to Sawyer's tavern, about three miles off, and there danced till between twelve and one. The company was rather curiously sorted, but the party was agreeable. I danced with the eldest Miss Frazier, with Miss Fletcher, and with Miss Coats. . . .

Miss Coats is not in love, and is quite sociable. Her manners are not exactly what I should wish for a friend of mine; yet she is agreeable. I am not obliged with her both to make and support the conversation; and moreover, what is very much in her favor, she is an only daughter and her father has money. . . .

Jan. 23. . . . I passed the evening at Dr. Swett's. Mrs. and Miss Cazneau were there. We had some agreeable and entertaining conversation, but singing soon came on to the carpet, and then the usual nonsense succeeded. I believe I will try one of these days and see if I cannot stop the career of this . . . singing, at least for one evening. . . .

Feb. 5. . . . I passed the evening with Townshend and Amory at Dr. Smith's. The old man is very fond of telling long stories, and indeed it is quite necessary to attend to him. There are, however, two young ladies in the house, to whom we attend with much more pleasure. . . .

Feb. 14. . . . I went to the office only in the forenoon; the after part of the day being employed in rigging for the ball. I had sent a note to Miss H. Greenleaf asking her to go with me. It was late before I could get a carriage, and when I went for my lady, I found all the rest of the family were gone, which was against me again.

The ballrooms were too small,—not one-quarter of the ladies could dance at a time. . . . Townshend took cold in making the preparations for the ball, and was so unwell that at about eleven o'clock he went home, and consigned his lady, Miss L. Knight, to me. She being very agreeable was . . . I believe, more the object of my attentions than Miss Greenleaf. This cannot now be helped. . . .

Feb. 15. . . . Townshend is quite unwell; has an uncomfortable cough and sore throat. But he went with me to visit several of the ladies who were of the company last evening. . . . We stopped a few moments to see Miss Coats, who was well, and we then went to Judge Greenleaf's, where we drank tea. Here were young ladies . . . innumerable; a choice of every complexion, and probably of every disposition. . . .

Feb. 16. . . . We spent the remainder of the evening at Dr. Smith's. . . . After supper I got seated next to Miss Putnam, and entered into conversation with her. I found her inclined to flattery, a defect not uncommon among our young ladies; and I answered her in her own way, as I always do.

When a lady pays me a compliment I always consider myself indebted to her until I return one at least of equal value; and I am generally so good a creditor that I pay with large interest. I have even once or twice in my life so far surpassed a lady in that way as to silence her, and make her ashamed of attacking me with those weapons; but I never flatter a lady that I esteem. . . .

Whitney "Makes the Labor Fifty Times Less"

Eli Whitney graduated from Yale in 1792 and then went to Georgia with the intention of teaching school. While staying on the plantation of Mrs. Nathaniel Greene, widow of the famous Revolutionary War general, he was inspired to invent the cotton gin. In this letter he tells the story of one of the most important of all American inventions.

Source: COMMAGER, HENRY STEELE, and NEVINS, ALLAN (editors). *The Heritage of America*, pp. 445–446. Little, Brown and Company, Boston, 1956.

Sept. 11, 1793.

I went from N. York with the family of the late Major General Greene to Georgia . . . to their plantation about twelve miles from Savannah with an expectation of spending four or five days. . . . During this time I heard much said of the extreme difficulty of ginning cotton; that is, separating it from its seeds. There were a number of very respectable gentlemen at Mrs. Greene's who all agreed that if a machine could be invented which would clean the cotton with expedition, it would be a great thing both to the country and to the inventor. I . . . happened to be thinking on the subject and struck out a plan of a machine in my mind. . . .

In about ten days I made a little model for which I was offered, if I would give up all right and title to it, a hundred guineas. I concluded [rather] to relinquish my school and turn my attention to perfecting the machine. I made one . . . which required the labor of one man to turn it and with which one man will clean ten times as much cotton as he can in any other way before known and also cleanse it much better than in the usual mode. This machine may be turned by water or with a horse, with the greatest ease, and one man and a horse will do more than fifty men with the old machines. It makes the labor fifty times less. . . .

I returned to the northward for the purpose of having a machine made on a large scale and obtaining a patent for the invention. I went to Philadelphia soon after I arrived, made myself acquainted with the steps necessary to obtain a patent, took several of the steps, and the Secretary of State, Mr. Jefferson, agreed

to send the patent to me as soon as it could be made out. . . .
I have employed several workmen in making machines. . . .

As soon as I have got a patent in America I shall go with the
machine I am now making to Georgia, where I shall stay a few
weeks to see it at work. . . . How advantageous this business will
eventually prove to me, I cannot say. It is generally said by those
who know anything about it that I shall make a fortune by it.
I have no expectation that I shall make an independent fortune
by it but think I had better pursue it than any other business into
which I can enter. Something which cannot be foreseen may
frustrate my expectations and defeat my plan, but I am now so
sure of success that ten thousand dollars . . . would not tempt
me to give up my right and relinquish the object. I wish you,
sir, not to show this letter nor communicate anything of its contents to anybody except my brother and sister, enjoining . . .
them to keep the whole a *profound secret*.

1794

Henry Wansey Breakfasts with the Washingtons

Henry Wansey, an English cloth manufacturer, describes his
meeting with President and Mrs. Washington in 1794 while the
national capital was still in Philadelphia.

Source: NEVINS, ALLAN (editor). *American Social History:
As Recorded by British Travellers*, pp. 54, 56. Holt, Rinehart
and Winston, Inc., 1923.

June 6, 1794.

I had the honor of an interview with the President of the
United States. . . . He received me very politely, and . . . I was
asked to breakfast.

I confess, I was struck with awe and veneration, when I recol-
lected that I was now in the presence of one of the greatest men
upon earth—the GREAT WASHINGTON. . . .

The President . . . is tall and thin, but erect; rather of an engaging than a dignified presence. He appears very thoughtful,
is slow in speaking, which occasions some to conclude him re-

served, but it is rather . . . the effect of much thinking and reflection. . . . He was at this time in his sixty-third year . . . but he has very little the appearance of age, having been all his life-time so exceeding temperate.

. . . .

Mrs. Washington herself made tea and coffee for us. On the table were two small plates of sliced tongue, dry toast, bread and butter, etc., but no broiled fish, as is the general custom. Miss Custis, her granddaughter, a very pleasing young lady, of about sixteen, sat next to her, and her brother George Washington Custis, about two years older than herself. There was but little appearance of form; one servant only attended, who had no livery; a silver urn for hot water, was the only article of expense on the table.

She appears something older than the President, though, I understand, they were both born in the same year; short in stature, rather robust; very plain in her dress, wearing a very plain cap, with her grey hair closely turned up under it. . . .

After some general conversation, we rose from table, to view a model which a gentleman from Virginia . . . had brought for the inspection of the President. It was a scheme to convey vessels on navigable canals, from one lock to another . . . by means of a lever. . . .

The President has continual applications from the ingenious, as the patron of every new invention, which, good or bad, he with great patience listens to, and receives them all in a manner to make them go away satisfied.

1781–1811

Isaac Describes "A Mighty Good Master"

Isaac was born in 1775 at Monticello, Virginia. Many years later he dictated these recollections of his "old master" and of life with the Jeffersons.

Source: LOGAN, RAYFORD W. (editor). *Memoirs of a Monticello Slave: as Dictated to Charles Campbell in the 1840's by Isaac, one of Thomas Jefferson's Slaves*, pp. 21–36. University of Virginia Press, Charlottesville, 1951.

Mr. Jefferson was a tall strait-bodied man as ever you see, right square-shouldered: . . . neat a built man as ever was seen in Vaginny, I reckon or any place—a straight-up man: long face, high nose. . . .

Old master wore Vaginny cloth & a red waistcoat, all the gentlemen wore red waistcoats in dem days, & small clothes; arter dat he used to wear red breeches too. . . .

Old master was never seen to come out before breakfast—about 8 o'clock. . . . When writing he had a copyin machine: while he was a-writin he wouldn't suffer nobody to come in his room: had a dumb-waiter: when he wanted anything he had nothin to do but turn a crank & the dumb-waiter would bring him water or fruit on a plate or anything he wanted.

Old master had abundance of books: sometimes would have twenty of 'em down on the floor at once: read first one, then tother. Isaac has often wondered how old master came to have such a mighty head: read so many of them books: & when they go to him to ax him anything, he go right straight to the book & tell you all about it. He talked French & Italian. . . .

Mr. Jefferson had a clock in his kitchen at Monticello, never went into the kitchen except to wind up the clock. He never would have less than eight covers at dinner—even if nobody at table but himself. . . .

He had three fiddles: played in the arternoons & sometimes arter supper. This was in his early time: When he begin to get so old he didn't play: kept a spinnet made mostly in shape of a harpsicord: his daughter played on it. . . . Mr. Jefferson always singing when ridin or walkin: hardly see him anywhar outdoors but what he was a-singin; had a fine clear voice, sung minnits [minuets] & sich: fiddled in the parlor. Old master very kind to servants. . . .

Isaac . . . carred [carried] on the nail-business at Monticello seven years: made money at that. Mr. Jefferson had the first nail cutting machine 'twas said, that ever was in Vaginny,—sent over from England: made wrought nails & cut-nails, to shingle & lathe: sold them out of the shop. . . .

Billy Giles courted Miss Polly, old master's daughter. Isaac one morning saw him talking to her in the garden, right back of the nail-factory shop: she was lookin on de ground: All at once she wheeled round & come off. *That* was the time she turned him down. Isaac never so sorry for a man in all his life: sorry because every body thought she was going to marry him. Mr. Giles give several dollars to the servants & when he went away dat time he never come back no more. . . .

Mr. Jefferson used to hunt squirrels & partridges: kept five or six guns. . . . Old master wouldn't shoot partridges settin: said he wouldn't take advantage of em—would give em a chance for thar life: wouldn't shoot a hare settin, nuther; skeer him up fust. My old master was as neat a hand as ever you see to make keys & locks & small chains, iron & brass; he kept all kind of blacksmith and carpenter tools in a great case with shelves to it in his library —an upstairs room. Isaac went up thar constant: been up thar a thousand times: used to carry coal up thar. . . .

Mr. Jefferson never had nothing to do with horse-racing or cock-fighting: bought two race-horses once, but not in their racing day: bought em arter done runnin. One was Brimmer, a pretty horse with two white feet. . . . Tother horse was Tarkill . . . old master used him for a ridin-horse. . . .

Old master had a great many rabbits: made chains for the old buck-rabbits to keep them from killin the young ones. . . . He had dogs named Ceres, Bull, Armandy, & Claremont: most of em French dogs: he brought em over with him from France. Bull and Ceres were bull-dogs. . . .

Mr. Jefferson bowed to everybody he meet: talked wid his arms folded. Gave the boys in the nail factory a pound of meat a week, a dozen herrings, a quart of molasses & peck of meal. Give them that wukked the best a suit of red or blue: encouraged them mightily. Isaac calls him a mighty good master. . . .

Davy Crockett Takes a Wife

> Davy Crockett, Tennessee frontiersman, met Polly Findlay at
> a dance. He said he "thought she looked sweeter than sugar . . .
> and loved her almost well enough to eat her." But Polly's mother
> wanted her to marry another. Davy got his father's permission
> to marry and then went to Polly's house to get the consent of her
> parents.
> Source: BRAINERD, E. A. *The Life of David Crocket: the
> Original Humorist and Irrepressible Backwoodsman, an Autobiog-
> raphy*, pp. 40–45. A. L. Burt Company, 1902.

When I got there, the old lady appeared to be mighty wrathy
and . . . she looked at me as savage as a meat ax. The old man
appeared quite willing. . . . But I hadn't been there long, before
the old woman as good as ordered me out of her house. . . .

I . . . felt rather insulted at the old lady, and I thought I
wouldn't get married in her house. And so I told Polly that I
would come the next Thursday, and bring a horse, bridle, and
saddle for her and she must be ready to go. Her mother declared
I shouldn't have her; but I know'd I should. . . . I then said
goodby and went by the house of a justice of the peace . . . and
made a bargain with him to marry me.

When Thursday came, all necessary arrangements were made
at my father's to receive my wife; and so I took my eldest brother
and his wife; and another brother, and a single sister that I had,
and two other young men with me and cut out to her father's
house to get her. We went on . . . and when I arrived I didn't
dismount from my horse, but rode up to the door and asked the
girl if she was ready; and she said she was. I then told her to get
on the horse I was leading; and she did so. [Then Polly's mother
had a change of heart and said she would give her consent if the
young couple would be married at her house.] I agreed and we
got down and went in. I sent off then for my parson, and got
married in a short time. . . .

The next day we cut off for my father's where we met a large
company of people that had been waiting for a day and a night
for our arrival. We passed the time quite merrily, until the company broke up; and having gotten my wife I thought I . . . needed

nothing more in the whole world. But I soon found this was all a mistake—for now having a wife, I wanted everything else; and . . . I had nothing to give for it.

I remained a few days at my father's and then went back to Polly's house where, to my surprise, I found my old Irish mother-in-law in the finest humor in the world.

She gave us two . . . cows and calves, which, though it was a small marriage portion, was still better than I had expected. . . . I rented a small farm and cabin, and went to work. A friend gave me an order to a store for fifteen dollars' worth of such things as my little wife might choose. With this we fixed up pretty grand. . . . My wife had a good spinning wheel and know'd exactly how to use it. She was also a good weaver, as most of the Irish are . . . and . . . she had in a little or no time, a fine web of cloth, ready to make up; and she was good at that, too, and at almost anything else that a woman could do.

1806

Lewis Describes "An Eligant Anamal"

The famous Lewis and Clark expedition spent the winter of 1805–06 at the mouth of the Columbia River, thus strengthening later American claims to the vast Oregon Territory. Two entries from Meriwether Lewis' journal are cited below.

Source: THWAITES, REUBEN GOLD (editor). *Original Journals of the Lewis and Clark Expedition (1804–1806) by Meriwether Lewis and William Clark*, pp. 73–74, 266–274. Dodd, Mead and Company, 1904–1905.

February 15th, 1806. Fort Clatsop

. . . The horse is confined principally to the nations inhabiting the great plains of Columbia . . . and occupying the tract of country lying between the rocky Mountains and a range of Mountains [the Cascades] which pass the columbia river about the great falls. . . . in this tract of principally untimbered country so far as we know the following natives reside: the Sosone or snake Indians, the Chopunnish, Sokulks, Cutssahnims, Chymnapums, Echelutes, Eneshuh, & Chilluckkittequaws. all of whom enjoy the bennefit of that docile, generous and valuable anamal the horse, and all of them except the last three have immence numbers of them.

Their horses appear to be of an excellent race; they are lofty eligantly formed active and durable; in short many of them look like the fine English coarsers and would make a figure in any country. Some of these are (pied) with large spots of white irregularly scattered and intermixed with the black brown bey or some other dark colour, but much the larger portion are of an uniform colour with stars . . . and white feet, or in this rispect marked much like our best blooded horses in virginia, which they resemble as well in fleetness . . . as in form and colours.

the natives (allow) them to run at large in the plains, the grass of which furnishes them with their only subsistence their masters taking no trouble to lay in a winters store for them, but they even keep fat if not much used on the dry grass of the plains during the winter. no rain scarcely ever falls in these plains and the grass is short and thin. . . .

whether the horse was orrigeonaily a native of this country or not it is out of my power to determine as we cannot understand the language of the natives sufficiently to ask the question. at all events the country and climate appears well adapted to this anamal. horses are said to be found wild in many parts of this extensive plain country. the several tribes of Sosones who reside towards Mexico . . . have also a great number of mules, which among the Indians I find are much more highly prized than horses. an eligant horse may be purchased of the natives in this country for a few beads or other paltry trinkets which in the U'States would not cost more than one or two dollars. This abundance and cheapness of horses will be extremely advantageous to those who may hereafter attempt the fir trade to the East Indies by way of the Columbia river and the Pacific Ocean. the mules in the possession of the Indians are principally stolen from the Spaniards of Mexico. . . .

Friday, April 11th, 1806.

. . . the duty of getting the canoes above the rapid was by mutual consent confided to my friend Capt. C. who took with him for that purpose all the party except Bratton who is yet so weak he is unable to work, three others who were lamed by various accedents and one other to cook for the party. a few men were absolutely necessary at any rate to guard our baggage from the War-clel-lars who crouded about our camp in considerable numbers. these are the greatest theives and scoundrels we have met with. . . . one of them had the insolence to cast stones down the bank at two of the men who happened to be a little detatched from the party at the time.

on the return of the party in the evening from the head of the rapids they met with many of the natives on the road . . . two of these fellows met with John Sheilds who had delayed some time in purchasing a dog and was a considerable distance behind the party. . . . They attempted to take the dog from him and pushed him out of the road. he had nothing to defend himself with except a large knife which he drew with an intention of puting one or both of them to death before they could get themselves in readiness to use their arrows, but discovering his design they declined the combat and instantly fled through the woods.

three of this same tribe of villains . . . stole my dog this evening, and took him towards their village. I was shortly afterwards informed of this . . . by an indian who spoke the Clatsop language (some of which we had learnt from them during the winter) and sent three men in pursuit of the theives with orders if they made the least resistence or difficulty in surrendering the dog to fire on them; they overtook these fellows or reather came within sight of them at the distance of about 2 miles; the indians discovering the party in pursuit of them left the dog and fled. they also stole an ax from us, but scarcely had it in their possession before Thompson detected them and wrest it from them. we ordered the centinel to keep them out of camp, and informed them by signs that if they made any further attempts to steal our property or insulted our men we should put them to instant death.

a cheif of the Clah-clel-lah tribe informed us that these were two very bad men among the Wah-clel-lahs who had been the principal actors in these scenes of outradge of which we complained, and that it was not the wish of the nation by any means to displease us. we told him that we hoped it might be the case, but we should certainly be as good as our words if they persisted in their insolence. I am convinced that no other consideration but our numbers at this moment protects us.

72

The Cheif appeared mortified at the conduct of his people, and seemed friendly disposed toward us. as he appeared to be a man of consideration and we had reason to beleive much rispected by the neighboring tribes we thought it well to bestoe a medal of small size upon him. he appeared much gratifyed with this mark of distinction. . . .

1806

Shahaka Listens to the Great White Father

When Captain Meriwether Lewis returned to Washington he brought with him a friendly Mandan Indian chief. President Jefferson received Chief Shahaka, his wife, and child at the White House. In his welcoming speech, Jefferson tells one of his reasons for sending out the Lewis and Clark expedition and offers the Indians some good advice.

Source: TURNER, KATHERINE C. *Red Men Calling on the Great White Father*, pp. 36–37. University of Oklahoma Press, Norman, 1951.

My friends and children, we are descended from the old nations which live beyond the great water, but . . . we consider ourselves no longer of the old nations . . . but as united in one family with our red brethern here. The French, and English, and the Spaniards have now agreed . . . to retire from all the country which you and we hold between Canada and Mexico, and never more to return to it. . . . We are now your fathers; and you shall not lose by the change.

As soon as Spain had agreed to withdraw from all the waters of the Missouri and Mississippi, I felt the desire of becoming acquainted with all my red children beyond the Mississippi. . . . I wished to learn what we could do to benefit them by furnishing them the necessaries they want in exchange for their furs and peltries. I therefore sent our beloved man, Captain Lewis, . . . to go up the Missouri river to get acquainted with all the Indian nations in its neighborhood, to take them by the hand, deliver my talks to them, and to inform us in what way we could be useful to them. Your nation received him kindly, you have taken him by the hand and been friendly to him. My children . . . I thank you for the services you rendered him. . . .

My friends and children, I have now . . . important advice to give you. . . . I wish you to live in peace and friendship with one another as brethren of the same family. . . . How much better it is for neighbors to help than to hurt one another. . . . If you will cease to make war on one another, if you will live in friendship with all mankind, you can employ all your time in providing food and clothing for yourselves and your families. Your men will not be destroyed in war, and your women and children will lie down to sleep . . . without fear of being surprised by their enemies and killed or carried away. . . .

Carry my advice home to your people, and tell them . . . we wish, as a true father should do, that we may all live together as one household, and that before they strike one another, they should go to their father and let him endeavor to make up the quarrel. . . .

1807

"Many Stouthearted Sinners Were Conquered"

People on the frontiers often were too scattered to support permanently-built churches, so traveling preachers and camp meetings had to satisfy their religious needs. Worshippers came many miles and stayed several days and nights at the camp meetings, as this account of one held in Georgia testifies.

Source: A letter to the editor in the *Farmer's Gazette* (Sparta, Georgia), August 8, 1807, signed Jesse Lee.

The Methodists have lately had a Camp-Meeting in Hancock County, about three miles south of Sparta. . . . The meeting began on Tuesday, 28th July at 12 o'clock, and ended on Saturday following. We counted thirty-seven Methodist preachers at the meeting; and with the assistance of a friend I took an account of the Tents, and there were one hundred and seventy-six of them, and many of them were very large. From the number of people who attended preaching at the rising of the sun, I concluded that there were about 3000 persons . . . that lodged on the ground at night. I think the largest congregation was about 4000 hearers.

We fixed the plan to preach four times a day, at sunrise, 10 o'clock, 3 o'clock, and at night; and in general we had an exhortation after the sermon. We had 14 sermons preached at the Stage, and 9 exhortations given after the sermons were closed; besides these, there were two sermons preached at the Tents on one night, when it was not convenient to have preaching at the Stage.

The ground was laid out in a tolerable convenient place, containing 4 or 5 acres, and the Tents were pitched close to each other; yet the ground only admitted of about 120 Tents in the lines; the other Tents were pitched behind them in an irregular manner. We had plenty of springs convenient for to supply men and beasts with water.

The first day of the meeting, we had a gentle and comfortable moving of the spirit of the Lord among us; and at night it was much more powerful than before, and the meeting was kept up all night without intermission. . . .

On Wednesday at 10 o'clock the meeting was remarkably lively, and many souls were deeply wrought upon; and at the close of the sermon there was a general cry for mercy; and before night there were a good many persons who professed to get converted. That night the meeting continued all night, . . . and many souls were converted before day.

On Thursday the work revived more & spread farther than what it had done before. . . .

Friday was the greatest day of all. We had the Lord's Supper by candlelight, where several hundred communicants attended. . . . From that the work of convictions and conversions spread, and a large number were converted during the night, and there was no intermission until the breake of day—at that time many stout hearted sinners were conquered.

On Saturday morning we had preaching at the rising of the sun; and then with many tears we took leave of each other. . . .

The people in general behaved exceedingly well; and there was not a public reproof given from the pulpit during the meeting. There were a few disorderly persons who brought liquors to sell, &c. But the Magistrates took some of them with a State warrant, and bound them over to court; after this we were more quiet. This Camp-Meeting will long live in the memories of many of the people who attended it.

Sam Houston Likes the Wild Liberty
of the Red Men

Sam Houston commanded the little Texan army which defeated General Santa Anna at San Jacinto. Later he served as President of the Republic of Texas and Governor and Senator after Texas joined the Union. But when he was a boy in Tennessee, his older brothers put him to work in a store they owned. Sam hated the work and ran away to live with the Cherokee Indians. When his brothers tried to get him to come home, he explained his refusal as follows.

Source: DAY, DONALD, and ULLOM, HERBERT (editors). *The Autobiography of Sam Houston*, pp. 5–6. University of Oklahoma Press, Norman, 1954.

I stood nearly six feet tall and was straight as an Indian. When they asked me why I had left home, I replied that I preferred measuring deer tracks to tape, and that I liked the wild liberty of the Red men better than the tyranny of my own brothers. I told them to go home and leave me in peace.

My family, thinking that this was a freak from which I would soon recover, when I got tired of the Indians, gave themselves no great uneasiness about me. But week after week passed and I did not appear. At last my clothes were worn out, and I returned to be refitted. I was kindly received by my mother, and for a while my brothers treated me well. But the first act of tyranny they showed drove me to the woods again, where I passed months with my Indian mates, chasing the deer through the forest . . . and engaging in all those gay sports of the happy Indian boys. . . . It was the moulding period of life, when the heart . . . looks wistfully around on all things for light and beauty. . . .

And yet, this running wild among the Indians, sleeping on the ground, chasing wild game, living in the forests, and reading Homer's *Iliad* . . . seemed a pretty strange business, and people used to say that I would either be a great Indian chief, or die in a mad-house, or be governor of the State—for it was very certain that some dreadful thing would overtake me!

Certain it is that my early life among the Indians was a necessary portion of that wonderful training that fitted me for my destiny. There I was initiated into the profound mysteries of the red man's character, and gained a taste . . . for forest life. . . .

1809

Turnpike Charges in President Madison's Day

Modern toll roads are descendants of turnpikes of early America. But the earlier roads had a greater variety of traffic than today's highways. You can see this by examining the tolls charged on the Schenectady and Utica (New York) Turnpike, a distance of sixty-eight miles.

Source: EARLE, ALICE MORSE. *Stage-Coach and Tavern Days*, pp. 237–238. The Macmillan Company, New York, 1927.

Sheep, per score [20]..	8¢	Three horse Wagons...	15½¢
Hogs, per score	8¢	Four horse Wagons....	75¢
Cattle, per score	18¢	Five horse Wagons	87½¢
Horses, per score	18¢	(tires under six inches)	
Mules, per score.......	18¢	Six horse Wagons	$1.00
Horse and Rider	5¢	(tires under six inches)	
Tied horses, each	5¢	One horse cart	6¢
Sulkies	12½¢	Two ox cart	6¢
Chairs	12½¢	Three ox cart	8¢
Chariots	25¢	Four ox cart	10¢
Coaches	25¢	Six ox cart	14¢
Coachers	25¢	One horse sleigh	6¢
Phaetons	25¢	Two horse or ox sleigh .	6¢
Two horse Stages	12½¢	Three horse or ox sleigh	8¢
Four horse Stages	18½¢	Four horse or ox sleigh .	10¢
One horse Wagons	9¢	Five horse or ox sleigh .	12¢
Two horse Wagons	12½¢	Six horse or ox sleigh ..	14¢

Jarvis Hanks Finds His Drum Little Protection

> At the age of thirteen, Jarvis Frary Hanks enlisted as a drum-
> mer boy in a regular army regiment for service in the War of
> 1812. More than twenty years later he wrote this account of his
> experiences in the Battle of Lundy's Lane, July 25, 1814.
>   By permission of *Buffalo and Erie County Historical Society*,
> Buffalo, N. Y.

. . . On the 25th of July, occured the famous battle of Lundy's
Lane . . . nearly opposite Niagara Falls. . . . It commenced at 7
o'clock P. M. and continued till·12 at night. The enemy had . . .
planted his guns, formed his lines, and made . . . preparations to
receive us . . . Genl Brown . . . ordered Genl Scott with his
brigade to march forth and enter into engagement. . . . A solid
column was formed, which marched to the field under the influence of spirited martial music.

When that part of the column in which I was situated had
arrived within ½ a mile of the scene of action, we heard the firing
commence, and saw some of the cavalry returning wounded, and
heard the savage yell of the British Indians. I remember a trump-
eter was riding back furiously, wounded, with the blood streaming profusely down his temples & cheeks. As I was also a
musician, I felt much alarm for my own safety, not knowing
but I should be in as bad, or worse, situation in a few minutes. There was no stopping nor escape; but into battle we
must go. . . .

There was a small piece of woods thro' which we passed to
gain the open field where the battle was fought. A rail fence
divided the field from the wood. Over this fence the soldiers were
obliged to climb. . . . Many of them were shot, and fell from the
top of the fence, killed and wounded. The cannon balls, grape
shot, & musket balls flew like hailstones, and yet we were not
firing a gun. . . .

In these circumstances, I met with what I consider the most
narrow escape that I experienced while in the service. While
sitting on the fence . . . a charge of grape shot rattled around
me. . . . They cut the branches of trees over my head; . . . also

78

splintered the rails on either side and under my feet; but not so much as the hair of my head was hurt! . . .

. . . .

Every regiment has a stand of colors, consisting of two flags. The 11th, to which I belonged, had one painted on blue and one on yellow silk. . . . It is one of the first objects of contending armies, to break the centres of regiments and lines, and thus throw them into confusion. This is done as effectively as any other way by aiming at the colors, which are stationed in the centre of their respective regiments. It is thought by many that as musicians are placed in the rear of the line, they are in less danger than the soldiers. . . . But, as musicians are placed in rear of the colors, and as the aim of enemies is mainly to shoot down the flag, it seems to me that musicians are in equal danger with any other portion of the army.

During this engagement, nine different persons were shot down, under this flag. At last, this sergeant Festus Thompson took it and threw its proud folds to the breeze. He was wounded in the hip, and the staff was severed into splinters in his hand. But he again grasped it by the stump and waved it triumphantly . . . over his fellow soldiers' heads, until the close of the battle.

After many such incidents occurred . . . this memorable battle closed, by apparent consent and desire of both armies. They retreated from the scene at the same time, weary and exhausted. It has often been called a *"drawn game,"* as it was difficult to decide which inflicted or received the greatest amount of injury.

1818

Señorita Pico Is Kissed by a Pirate

Monterey was a quiet outpost in Spanish California. Like all outposts, it was subject to attack. Hypolyte Bouchard, a Frenchman, led two shiploads of pirates who raided Monterey in 1818. Maria Antonia Pico, member of a prominent Spanish family, tells of her experiences on that exciting day.

Source: LEWIS, OSCAR (compiler and annotator). *The Autobiography of the West*, pp. 51–55. Holt, Rinehart, and Winston, Inc., New York, 1958.

. . . I was sixteen years of age. A vessel brought the report to Monterey that a whole fleet of pirates were coming. Every one commenced to move. . . . My father was not at home. . . . My brother, sister, and myself went with the carts; mother was to come next day, with a servant. Night came on before we fairly started. . . . About midnight we reached a large, broken oak tree where our mother had told us to camp. We let the oxen loose to graze, and crawled under the cart. . . .

. . . I lay awake and wished my father and the men-servants had been at home. . . . While I was thinking of these things a wild, strange noise was heard approaching. . . . I knew that something must have attacked the animals. . . .

The morning was dawning when this happened, and . . . I could see a hundred feet down the cañon. An indistinct form began to be revealed there . . . a large California lion, or puma, pulling the meat from one of our oxen. . . . It grew very light before he took any notice of us where we sat under the ox-cart. As soon as he saw us he walked up . . . making a purring sound. . . . He . . . came so close that I felt his breath on me, and finally he put his nose against my ankle. I had no stockings on, only home-made shoes, and his nose felt very strange. . . . After what seemed a long time, the lion went back and lay down beside the dead ox. . . .

We lay there under the cart . . . until . . . the middle of the afternoon. . . . About three o'clock mother and José, the peon, came down from the coast way. . . . They could see the whole situation at a glance—the lion, the dead ox, the cart, and the three of us huddled together under it. José ran forward and fired two shots, wounding the lion, but he got away in the rocks. . . .

Then mother told me . . . she had forgotten a family book . . . and she wanted to ride back and obtain it. I told her I was not afraid to go; so . . . I mounted her horse, and galloped off to Monterey. After a while I heard a cannon shot, then another, and then a great many. . . . At last I reached . . . our own house, which was about a mile from the beach. . . . I ran in and found the old book. . . . But when I went out of the door, I saw my horse running off, frightened by the noise of the firing.

It was very hard to know what to do. . . . I determined to catch a horse somehow, but just as I was planning how it might be done two men came out of the bushes and spoke to me. They were armed strangers and very wild, so I fell on my knees and prayed to them to do me no harm. . . . One of them asked me . . . why I was there; so I told him. . . . He laughed and said I was a good girl, and he sent his man to catch my horse. Then . . . he came up to me and kissed me on the forehead . . . which frightened me very much. Then the man came up with my horse, and I looked at the leader of the two, and asked what he was going to do with me.

"My girl," he said, "you are more brave than some of your people were on the beach when we landed. You shall go back." He put me on my horse, and kissed my hand, and said, "Ride fast; there are others of Bouchard's men who would not treat you so well." I thanked him briefly and he added as he let go the bridle . . . that he already had two wives on board his ship, or he would have taken me there. This last made me ride in great terror and with frightful speed. . . . When I reached mother's camp I was crying. . . .

1819

A News Item Tells of the Depression of 1819

The depression of 1819 forced many poverty-stricken settlers off their land. They had no choice but to look for another place, as these two couples did.

Source: News item from the Augusta, Ga., *Chronicle*, Sept. 24, 1819.

. . . Passed through this place [Augusta, Ga.] from Greenville District, bound for Chatahouchee, a man and his wife, his son and his wife, with a cart but no horse. The man had a belt over his shoulders and he drew in the shafts—the son worked by traces tied to the ends of the shafts and assisted his father to draw the cart; the son's wife rode in the cart, and the old woman was walking, carrying a rifle and driving a cow.

A Son of Light Horse Harry Applies at West Point

Robert E. Lee received his appointment to the United States Military Academy at West Point from John C. Calhoun, who was Secretary of War. Three letters are cited in support of his application.

Source: FREEMAN, DOUGLAS SOUTHALL. *R. E. Lee*, Vol. I, pp. 39–42. Reprinted with the permission of Charles Scribner's Sons, copyright 1934, 1935, Charles Scribner's Sons.

Letter from W. H. Fitzhugh to Secretary of War Calhoun, Feb. 7, 1824

My dear Sir,

I cannot permit the young gentleman, who will hand you this letter, to make his intended application, without carrying with him, such testimony in his behalf, as a long & an intimate acquaintance both with himself and his family, justify me in giving. He is the son of Genl. Henry Lee, with whose history, you are, of course, acquainted; and who . . . certainly established, by his revolutionary services, a strong claim to the gratitude of his country. He is the son also of one of the finest women the State of Virginia has ever produced. . . .

The young gentleman, whom I have now the pleasure of introducing to you as a candidate for West-point, is her youngest son. An intimate acquaintance . . . with him, almost from his infancy, authorizes me to speak in the most unqualified terms of his amiable disposition, & his correct and gentlemanly habits. . . .

Letter from W. B. Leary, one of Robert's former teachers

Robert Lee was formerly a pupil of mine. While under my care I can vouch for his correct and gentlemanly deportment. In the various branches, of learning to which his attention has been applied, I flatter myself that his information will be found adequate to the most sanguine expectations of his friends. With me he has read all the minor classics in addition to Homer & Longinus, Tacitus & Cicero. He is well versed in arithmetic, Algebra

& Euclid. In regard to what he has read with me I am certain that when examined he will neither disappoint me or his friends.

Letter from Congressman R. S. Garnett, Feb. 16, 1824

I beg leave to recommend to your favorable attention, Master Robert Lee who is desirous to be placed in the Military academy as a cadet. He is a son of the late General Henry Lee and has strong hereditary claims on the country. I am not able to state what proficiency he has made in his studies, but testimonials will be exhibited by him in relation to this subject that I presume will prove satisfactory. He is about 18 years of age, and of excellent disposition. If he can obtain the appointment he desires, I have no doubt that he will justify the expectations which his recommendations would authorize.

1827-1828

A Sea Captain Describes Plantation Slavery

Only a minority of Southern families owned slaves and lived on plantations, yet plantation life attracted the most attention from those who visited the Old South. Captain Basil Hall, a British naval officer who toured Canada and the United States in 1827-28, here writes of slavery as he saw it on a South Carolina plantation. Few Southerners owned as many slaves as did this planter.

Source: NEVINS, ALLAN (editor). *American Social History: as Recorded by British Travellers*, pp. 154-156. Holt, Rinehart, and Winston, Inc., New York, 1931.

. . . When the negroes go to the field in the morning, it is the custom to leave such children behind as are too young to work. Accordingly, we found three dozen shining urchins collected together in a house near the center of the slave village. Over the fire hung a large pot of hominy . . . making ready for the little folks' supper. . . .

The parents and such children as are old enough to be useful go out to work at daybreak, taking their dinner with them to eat on the ground. They have another meal towards the close of day after coming home. Generally, also, they manage to cook up a breakfast; but this must be provided by themselves, out of their own earnings, during those hours which it is the custom, in all plantations, to allow the negroes to work on their own account.

It was pleasant to hear that in most parts of the South the slaves had . . . Sunday off excepting . . . at certain seasons of the year and in . . . sections of Louisiana . . . where sugar is cultivated. . . . Generally speaking the planters, who seem well aware of the advantage of not exacting too much service from their slaves, consider the day of rest as a source rather of profit than of loss.

A special task for each slave is . . . pointed out daily by the overseer; and as soon as this is completed in a proper manner, the laborer may go home to work at his own piece of ground, or tend his pigs and poultry, or play with his children. . . . [However] the work generally lasts till four or five o'clock. I often saw gangs of negroes at work till sunset.

We went into several of the slaves' huts which were . . . neat and comfortable. . . . Each hut was divided into small rooms or compartments, fitted with regular bed places; . . . they all had chimneys and doors, and some, though only a few of them, possessed the luxury of windows. I counted twenty-eight huts, occupied by one hundred and forty slaves or about five in each. This number included sixty children.

. . . .

. . . One of the greatest . . . evils of slavery arises from persons who have no control over themselves being placed . . . in command of others. Hence passion, without system, must very often take the place of patience and method; and the lash—that . . . terrible instrument of power—and one so dangerous in irresponsible hands— . . . forces obedience by the stern agony of fear. . . . The consequence, I believe, invariably is that where service is thus . . . beaten out of men, the very minimum of work, in the long run, is obtained. Judicious slave-holders, therefore, whether they be humane persons or not, generally discover . . . that the best policy . . . is to treat their slaves with as much kindness as the nature of the slave system will allow.

The gentlemen of the South sometimes assert that their slaves are . . . happier than the laboring classes in the northern parts of their own Union, and much better off than the peasantry of Eng-

land. There is no good purpose served by such arguments. . . .
It means little to talk of the poor laws of England, or the pauper-
ism in the great cities on the American coast; for, after all, such
allusions apply to a small portion only of the labouring classes.
. . . It is certainly not quite fair to compare slaves' lives with the
free New Englanders of America or the bold peasantry of Great
Britain.

1827

A Boston Editor Questions a Railroad's Value

Early railroads were regarded as dangerous and impractical.
An editorial in a Boston newspaper analyzed the prospects of a
railroad between Boston and Albany in this fashion.
Source: *Boston Courier*, June 27, 1827.

The project of a railroad from Boston to Albany is impracticable, as every one knows who knows the simplest rule of arithmetic, and the expense would be little less than the market value
of the whole of Massachusetts; and which, if practicable, every
person of common sense knows would be as useless as a railroad
from Boston to the moon.

1829

Old Hickory's Welcome, Retreat, and Escape

General Andrew Jackson was inaugurated on March 4, 1829.
This letter from Mrs. Samuel Harrison Smith of Washington to
her sister Mrs. Kirkpatrick of New Jersey, describes how the
"people en masse" responded.
Source: HUNT, GAILLARD (editor). *The First Forty Years of
Washington Society*: Portrayed by the Family Letters of Mrs.
Samuel Harrison (Margaret Bayard) Smith, pp. 291–296.
Charles Scribner's Sons, New York, 1906.

. . . I will give you an account of the inauguration in detail.

. . . The whole of the preceding day, immense crowds were coming into the city. . . . Lodgings could not be obtained, and the newcomers had to go to George Town, which soon overflowed and others had to go to Alexandria. . . .

A national salute was fired early in the morning, and ushered in the 4th of March. By ten o'clock the Avenue was crowded with carriages of every description, from the splendid Barronet and coach, down to wagons and carts, filled with women and children, some in finery and some in rags, for it was the peoples President, and all would see him; the men all walked.

We stood on the South steps of the terrace. When the appointed hour came we saw the General and his company advancing up the Avenue, slow, very slow, so impeded was his march by the crowds thronging around him. Even from a distance, he could be discerned from those who accompanied him, for he only was uncovered, the Servant in the presence of his Sovereign, the People.

The south side of the Capitol hill was literally alive with the multitude, who stood ready to receive the hero and the multitude who attended him. "There, there, that is he," exclaimed different voices. "Which?" asked others. "He with the white head," was the reply. "Ah," exclaimed others, "there is the old man and his gray hair, there is the old veteran, there is Jackson." . . .

At the moment the General entered the Portico . . . the shout that rent the air still resounds in my ears. When the speech was over, and the President made his parting bow, the barrier that had separated the people from him was broken down and they rushed up the steps all eager to shake hands with him. It was with difficulty he made his way through the Capitol and down the hill to the gateway that opens on the Avenue. Here for a moment he was stopped. The living mass was impenetrable. After a while a passage was opened, and he mounted his horse which had been provided for his return to the White House for he had walked to the Capitol. Then such a crowd as followed him! Country men, farmers, gentlemen, mounted and dismounted, boys, women and children, black and white. Carriages, wagons and carts all pursuing him to the President's house. . . .

[Mrs. Smith and her friends attended a party and then, later in the day, went to the White House.]

Some one came and informed us the crowd before the President's house was so far lessen'd that they thought we might enter. . . . But what a scene did we witness! *The Majesty of the People* had disappeared, and a rabble, a mob, of boys, negros, women, children, scrambling, fighting, romping. What a pity, what a pity! No arrangements had been made, no police officers placed on duty and the whole house had been inundated by the rabble mob. We came too late. The President, after having been *literally* nearly pressed to death and almost suffocated and torn to pieces by the people in their eagerness to shake hands with Old Hickory, had retreated through the back way and had escaped to his lodgings at Gadsby's.

Cut glass and china to the amount of several thousand dollars had been broken in the struggle to get the refreshments. Punch and other articles had been carried out in tubs and buckets . . . ice-creams, and cake, and lemonade, for 20,000 people for it is said that number were there. . . . Ladies fainted, men were seen with bloody noses and such a scene of confusion took place as is impossible to describe—those who got in could not get out by the door again, but had to scramble out of windows. . . .

This concourse had not been anticipated and therefore not provided against. Ladies and gentlemen only had been expected . . . not the people en masse. But it was the People's day and the People's President and the People would rule. . . .

1833

Black Hawk Sees His First Balloon

Black Hawk was an Indian warrior who led the Sac and Fox tribes in a brief uprising called the Black Hawk War. The Indians were soon defeated and Black Hawk, after being captured, was sent on a trip through the east so he could see how large and powerful was the United States. Here is Black Hawk's story of the trip, as dictated to an interpreter.

Source: JACKSON, DONALD (editor). *Black Hawk: An Autobiography*, pp. 167–174. University of Illinois Press, Urbana, 1955.

In a little while all were ready, and left Jefferson barracks [near St. Louis] on board of a steam boat, under charge of a young war chief, whom the White Beaver [General Henry Atkinson, commander at Jefferson Barracks] sent along as a guide to Washington. He carried with him an interpreter and one soldier. On our way up the Ohio, we passed several large villages, the names of which were explained to me. The first is called Louisville, and is a very pretty village. . . . The next is Cincinnati, which stands on the bank of the same river. This is a large and beautiful village, and seemed to be in a thriving condition. The people gathered on the bank as we passed, in great crowds, apparently anxious to see us.

On our arrival at Wheeling, the streets and river's banks were crowded with people, who flocked from every direction to see us. While we remained here, many called upon us, and treated us with kindness—no one offering to molest or misuse us. . . .

We left the steam boat here . . . and took the stage. Being unaccustomed to this mode of travelling, we soon got tired, and wished ourselves seated in a canoe on one of our own rivers. . . . We had a rough and mountainous country for several days, but had a good trail for our carriage. It is astonishing to see what labor and pains the white people have had to make this road [the Cumberland or "National" Road], as it passed over an immense number of mountains, which are generally covered with rocks and timber; yet it has been made smooth, and easy to travel upon. There are many wigwams and small villages standing on the road side. I could see nothing in the country to induce the people to live in it; and was astonished to find so many whites living on the hills! . . .

[In Maryland] we came to another road, much more wonderful than that through the mountains. They call it a *rail road!* I examined it carefully, but need not describe it, as the whites know all about it. It is the most astonishing sight I ever saw. . . . I was surprised to see so much labor and money expended to make a good road for easy travelling. I prefer riding on horseback, however, to any other way; but suppose that these people would not have gone to so much trouble and expense to make a road, if they did not prefer riding in their new fashioned carriages, which seem to run without any trouble. They certainly deserve great praise for their industry.

On our arrival at Washington, we called to see our Great

Father, the President [Andrew Jackson]. He looks as if he had seen as many winters as I have, and seems to be a *great brave!* I had very little talk with him, as he appeared to be busy, and did not seem much disposed to talk. I think he is a good man; and although he talked but little, he treated us very well. His wigwam is well furnished with every thing good and pretty, and is very strongly built. . . .

During our stay at the city, we were called upon by many of the people, who treated us well, particularly the squaws! . . . Having got a new guide, a war chief [Major Garland], we started for our own country, taking a circuitous route. . . . On our arrival at Baltimore, we were much astonished to see so large a village; but the war chief told us that we should soon see a *larger one!* This surprised us more. . . .

We left Baltimore in a steam boat, and travelled in this way to the big village, where they make *medals* and *money* [Philadelphia]. We again expressed surprise at finding this village so much larger than the one we had left; but the war chief again told us, that we would soon see another much larger than this. I had no idea that the white people had such large villages, and so many people. . . .

We next started to New York. . . . We had seen many wonderful sights on our way—large villages, the great *national road* over the mountains, the *railroads*, steam carriages, ships, steam boats, and many other things; but we were now about to witness a sight more surprising than any of these. We were told that a man was going up into the air in a balloon! We watched with anxiety to see if it could be true; and to our utter astonishment, saw him ascend in the air until the eye could no longer perceive him. Our people were all surprised, and one of our young men asked . . . if he was going up to see the Great Spirit. . . .

The chiefs were particular in showing us every thing that they thought would be pleasing or gratifying to us. We went with them to Castle-Garden to see the fireworks, which was quite an agreeable entertainment—but to the *whites* who witnessed it, less *magnificent* than the sight of one of our large *prairies* would be when on fire. . . . Every body treated us with friendship, and many with great liberality. The squaws presented us many handsome little presents, that are said to be valuable. They were very kind, very good, and very pretty—for *pale faces!* . . .

89

Having seen all the wonders of this *big village*, and being anxious to return to our people, our guide started with us for our own country. . . .

1834

A Committee Favors Free Public Schools for All

> Demands for education at public expense occurred frequently during the Jacksonian Years. In Pennsylvania, the principle of free, public schools was established by law in 1834 as a result of this report by a committee of the state legislature.
>
> Source: "Report of the Joint Committee of the Two Houses of the Pennsylvania Legislature on the Subject of a System of General Education. . . ." Harrisburg, Pa., 1834, pp. 3–6.

The number of voters in Pennsylvania, unable to read, has been computed . . . at one hundred thousand; and two thousand five hundred, grow up to be voters annually, who are equally ignorant. In a republican government, no voter should be without the rudiments of learning; for aside from political considerations, education purifies the morals, and lessens crime. Investigators who visit our jails have ascertained that more than half the convicts are unable to read. It is better to avert crime, by giving instruction to our youth, than punish them when men, as ignorant convicts.

A radical defect in our laws upon the subject of education, is that the public aid now given, and imperfectly given, is confined *to the poor*. Aware of this, your committee have taken care to exclude the word *poor*, from the bill which will accompany this report, meaning to make the system *general*; that is to say, to form an educational association between the rich, the comparatively rich, and the destitute. Let them all fare alike in the primary schools; receive the same elementary instruction; imbibe the same republican spirit, and be animated by a feeling of perfect equality. . . . It is the duty of the State to promote and foster such establishments. . . . That done, the career of each youth will depend upon himself. The State will have given the first impulse; good conduct and suitable application must do the rest. . . . Yet let them start with equal advantages, leaving no discrimination then or thereafter, but such as nature and study shall produce. . . .

But the first step is, unquestionably, the preparation of teachers; and on this highly important subject, the information collected by your committee is ample. Seminaries for the instruction of teachers, are as important as medical schools for physicians. Under the proposed system, a large supply of teachers will soon be needed and these must be properly formed for that vocation. They must be taught the art of well governing a school: they must acquire the knowledge necessary to be communicated, and the art of communicating that knowledge. . . .

. . . But how are young men to be induced to take up the business of teaching? To this your committee answer, by giving them a respectable standing in society—by making their salaries large enough to maintain them and their families. The character of a school is formed by the character of the teacher; and the respect and obedience of the pupil is regulated by the measure of respect which the master receives from the public. A shameful parsimony prevails in the remuneration of teachers. . . . The male teacher's pay, in New York, is something under twelve dollars a month; in Ohio, it is from twelve to twenty. Females, in New York, average five dollars, and in Connecticut, some women teach for seventy-five cents a week! Well paid teachers are [really] the cheapest.

1834

"Where the Weeds Grow Twenty Feet High"

American settlement in Texas began in 1821 when Moses Austin secured a charter granting lands for colonization by 200 American families. Settlers and land speculators entered the new lands in search of the kind of opportunities described in this letter by a Dr. Hoxey to a friend in Georgia.

Source: Letter printed in the *Southern Banner* (Athens, Georgia), July 19, 1834.

Cole's Settlement, Texas, April 2, 1834

Mr. Lewis S. Brown:

Dear Sir: . . . It affords me great pleasure to be able to inform you that all my enthusiastic notions of Texas are not only realized but far exceeded. . . . I have embarked, as you know largely into Texas land speculations; and could now . . . receive $30,000 profit on my investments . . . and then I really would not receive the tenth part of their value. I have seen the best lands in Alabama, Mississippi, and Louisiana and I assure you they are far inferior to the lands of Texas. I own an eleven league grant at the Falls of the Brasos River, which is the head of steamboat navigation. The fertility of the soil may be estimated by the growth of the vegetation on it; the weeds grow twenty feet high but there is no trouble to clear the land. . . . The soil of this land is at least fifty feet thick, not subject to floods, well watered with pure running streams and generally well timbered.

My lands on the San Gabriel and San Andrea are the most beautiful lands in the world for farming. They are not quite as rich as those lands on the Brasos; yet they are far superior to any in the United States. . . . Where I am now settled the country is very beautiful and healthy; the soil about four feet thick and capable of producing about two thousand pounds of cotton to the acre. I do not feel permanently settled here; but shall remove in a year or so to my lands on the San Gabriel. At present there is little or no society there, whilst the section that I am now in is thickly settled and the society as good as any in the state of Georgia or any other state. My immediate neighbors are all slave holders and cotton planters, and but for the poverty of the soil I would be willing to remain here permanently.

The emigration to Texas this year has been immense, in fact much greater than the resources of the country would support; at least two months ago nearly all the corn in Texas was consumed by emigrants, and thousands have to subsist on meat alone. . . .

Texas is the easiest country in the world for the farmer to live in; stock of no kind is ever fed and never poor. My mules and horses, although they have worked hard all the winter and spring are very fat. They have not had a grain of corn or fodder since I have been in Texas, but subsist exclusively on grass.

I know that you in the United States have very erroneous ideas about this country, particularly as regards the society and the individuals composing that society. You imagine that the country is filled with Mexicans or Spaniards; and that the American part of the population is filled with renegades from the United States; whereas there is scarcely a Mexican in Texas, the population being exclusively American; and by far the largest proportion of that number are honest, industrious and enterprising Americans. A man committing any breach against the laws of society is punished as readily and as severely here as in any part of the United States.

Our political situation with the Mexican government is a subject which is well calculated to deter Americans from coming to this country to settle—they believe that we are on the eve of a civil war; but of this there is not the remotest probability. At this time we have no taxes or any duties to pay, and hence want no better government.

> [Dr. Hoxey was a poor prophet in reporting there was not the "remotest probability" of civil war with Mexico. Within the next year the Texas War for Independence from Mexico began.]

1834

IIIIIIIIIIIIIIIIIIIIIIIIIIIIIIIIIIIIIIIIIIIIIIIIIIIIIIIIIIIIIIIIIIIIIIIIIIIIIIIIIIIIIIIIIIIIIIIIIIIIIIIIIIIIIIIIIIIIIIIII

Richard Henry Dana Begins an Epic Voyage

> By 1834, New England was changing from a commercial to an industrial area even though many ships still sailed from the larger ports. In that year, Richard Henry Dana sailed on the long voyage described in his famous sea-faring book, *Two Years before the Mast*. Here he tells of his departure.
> Source: DANA, JR., RICHARD HENRY. *Two Years before the Mast: A Personal Narrative*, pp. 1–2. Houghton Mifflin Company, Boston, 1911.

The fourteenth of August was the day fixed upon for the sailing of the brig *Pilgrim*, on her voyage from Boston, round Cape Horn, to the Western coast of North America. As she was to get under way early in the afternoon, I made my appearance on board at twelve o'clock, in full sea-rig, with my chest, containing an outfit for a two or three years' voyage . . . undertaken from a determination to cure . . . a weakness of the eyes, which had obliged me to give up my studies, and which no medical aid seemed likely to remedy.

The change from the tight frock-coat, silk cap, and kid gloves of an undergraduate at Harvard, to the loose duck trousers, checked shirt, and tarpaulin hat of a sailor . . . was soon made; and I supposed that I should pass very well for a Jack tar. But it is impossible to deceive the practiced eye in these matters; and while I thought myself to be looking as salt as Neptune himself, I was, no doubt, known for a landsman by every one on board as soon as I hove in sight.

A sailor has a peculiar cut to his clothes, and a way of wearing them which a green hand can never get. The trousers, tight round the hips, and . . . hanging long and loose round the feet, a superabundance of checked shirt, a low-crowned, well-varnished black hat, worn on the back of the head, with half a fathom of black ribbon hanging over the left eye, . . . are signs, the want of which betrays the beginner at once. Besides the points in my dress which were out of the way, doubtless my complexion and hands were quite enough to distinguish me from the regular *salt* who, with a sunburnt cheek, wide step, and rolling gait, swings his bronzed and toughtened hands . . . half-opened, as though just ready to grasp a rope.

. . . I joined the crew, and we hauled out into the stream, and came to anchor for the night. . . . I stood my first watch. I remained awake nearly all the first part of the night from fear that I might not hear when I was called; and when I went on deck, so great were my ideas of the importance of my trust, that I walked regularly fore and aft the whole length of the vessel, looking out over the bows and taffrail at each turn, and was not a little surprised at the coolness of the old seaman whom I called to take my place, in stowing himself snugly away under the longboat for a nap. That was a sufficient lookout, he thought, for a fine night, at anchor in a safe harbor.

94

1835

"Varieties of Manners" and "Odd Mortals" in Washington

> Harriet Martineau was an English writer who visited our nation's capital while it was still a crude village. She was an acute observer and a clever writer as her impressions of life in Washington show.
> Source: MARTINEAU, HARRIET. *A Retrospect of Western Travel.* Saunders and Otley, London, 1838, Vol. I, pp. 144–145, 154.

. . . The city itself is unlike any other that ever was seen, straggling out hither and thither, with a small house or two a quarter of a mile from any other. . . . In making calls "in the city," we had to cross ditches and fences and walk alternately on grass and pavements, and strike across a field to reach a street. . . .

. . . Then there was the society, singularly compounded from the largest variety of elements: foreign ambassadors, the American government, members of Congress, from Clay and Webster down to Davy Crockett . . . flippant young belles, "pious" wives dutifully attending their husbands, and groaning over the frivolities of the place; grave judges, saucy travellers, pert newspaper reporters, melancholy Indian chiefs, and timid New England ladies. . . . All this was wholly unlike anything that is to be seen in any other city in the world. . . .

It is in Washington that varieties of manners are conspicious. There the Southerners appear to the most advantage, and the New Englanders to the least; the ease and frank courtesy of the gentry of the South, with an occasional touch of arrogance, however, contrasting favourably with the cautious . . . deferential air of the members from the North. One fancies one can tell a New England member in the open air by his deprecatory walk. He seems to bear in mind perpetually that he cannot fight a duel while other people can.

The odd mortals that wander in from the western border cannot be described as a class, for no one is like anybody else. One has a neck like a crane, making an interval of inches between collar and chin. Another wears no cravat, apparently because there is no room for one. A third has his lank black hair parted accurately down the middle, and disposed in bangs in front, so that he is taken for a woman when only the head is seen in a crowd. A fourth puts an arm round the neck of a neighbour on either side as he stands, seeming afraid of his tall wirehung frame dropping to pieces if he tries to stand alone; a fifth makes something between a bow and a curtsy to everybody who comes near, and poses with a knowing air. All have shrewd faces, and are probably very fit for the business they come upon. . . .

[Miss Martineau's Description of President Jackson]

General Jackson is extremely tall and thin, with a slight stoop. . . . He has a profusion of stiff gray hair, which gives to his appearance whatever there is . . . formidable in it. His face bears usually an expression of melancholy gravity; though, when roused, the fire of passion flashes from his eyes, and his whole person looks then formidable enough. His . . . speech is slow and quiet, and his phraseology indicates that his time has not been passed among books.

1835–1842

Gjert, Johannes, and Ole Encourage Friends to Join Them

Immigrants often wrote back home offering advice to others who might want to come to America. Here are some extracts from letters written by five Norwegian immigrants.

Source: From *Land of Their Choice: The Immigrants Write Home*, pp. 22–23, 27, 37, 76, 102–103, 181. Edited by THEODORE C. BLEGEN. University of Minnesota Press, Minneapolis. Copyright 1955 by the University of Minnesota.

From Gjert G. Hovland to Torjuls A. Maeland.

Rochester, New York, 1835

. . . I do not believe that any who suffer oppression and who must rear their children in poverty could do better than to come

96

to America. But, alas, many who want to come lack the means, and many others are so stupid as to believe that it is best to live in the country where they have grown up even if they have nothing but hard bread to satisfy their hunger. It is as if they thought that those who move to a better land . . . do wrong. . . . We do not wish to live in Norway. We lived there altogether too long. Nor have I talked with any immigrant in this country who wished to return.

From Johannes Nordboe to Hans L. Rudi.

La Salle County, Illinois, 1837

This western country is far different from the eastern states. . . . That we have not been able to reach our destination before this is due to our poverty, as well as to the unfortunate sea voyage. Had we arrived without any mishaps, we should have come far enough the first year. But I am glad and thank God for things as they are. If God grants my children life and strength, and if they themselves are willing to work, they will be far more fortunate here than in Norway. . . .

From Anders Wiig to friends.

Iowa County, Wisconsin Territory, 1841

. . . As far as we know, monthly wages at the present time are these: in the northern part of Illinois for farm hands $10 to $15; for a sailor $16 to $20; for a captain, who does not have to be a navigator, from $40 to $50; for canal laborers from $12 to $20. . . .

Women, especially young girls, will be able to do relatively better. Even in Chicago, through which so many emigrants pour, Norwegian girls are in great demand. Until they have learned a little English, they get only a dollar a week, but later from $1.50 to $2.00, and because of the high regard in which women are held in this country, they are exempt from all kinds of outdoor work. . . .

From Guttorm R. Thistel to friends.

Chicago, 1844

First I want to warn all those of you who are planning to undertake the journey to America to make contracts with the skipper with whom you are emigrating. You must insist that you be

97

given at least three quarts of water a day. We got no more than one pint and almost died of thirst. It was not very good water either, for it tasted and smelled so bad that we had to throw it up.

. . . When you get to New York, you must be very cautious about changing your money into gold pieces, for many of these are false, made of both tin and glass. Again . . . you must be sure to draw up a specific contract with the skipper who offers to take you . . . through the Erie canal. Many will present themselves, but you must be careful. . . . On our trip through the canal on the canalboat we had such fine weather that we could walk on the banks of the canal alongside the boat; we gathered much fruit, especially apples, and brought it on board the boat in big sacks. You must be careful not to eat too much of this fruit, for it caused severe illness among us. . . .

From Ole Knudsen Trovatten to Tollef Olsen Juve.

Vernon, Wisconsin, 1842

. . . Every poor person who will work diligently and faithfully, can become a well-to-do man here in a short time. . . . You may take as an example myself, whose luck seemed from the beginning to be bad, for all my money . . . was stolen from me in the city of Albany. . . .

I have now been in Wisconsin about a year and a half. . . . Despite the fact that I came here empty-handed and have also been sick, I have nevertheless acquired the following property: one cow, a year-old pig, one calf, two two-year-old oxen . . . and forty acres of land, though I owe eighteen days of work on this land. . . . Though I have been sick almost half a year and have a family to take care of, still I have achieved much more than a worker can in Norway. . . .

Captain Jo Describes Mike Fink—
Half Horse Half Alligator

Many legends have grown up about Mike Fink, one of the Ohio River boatmen who carried settlers and supplies on the river before the days of the steamboat. Here is a story about Mike which appeared in 1837, about fourteen years after his death.

Source: Reprinted from *Half Horse Half Alligator: The Growth of the Mike Fink Legend* (pp. 63-64 and 262-263), edited by WALTER BLAIR and FRANKLIN J. MEINE by permission of the University of Chicago Press, Chicago, 1956.

Of all the species of mankind existing under heaven, the western boatmen deserve a distinct and separate cognomen. They are a sort of amphibious animal—kind-hearted as a Connecticut grandmother, but as rough as a Rocky Mountain bear. In high water they make the boat carry them, and in low water they are content to carry the boat—or in other words, they are ever ready to jump in and ease her over the sand-bar, then jump on board and patiently wait for the next. Spending the greater portion of their time on the water, they scarce know how to behave on shore, and feel only at home upon the deck of their craft. . . .

They have not degenerated since the days of Mike Fink, who was looked upon as the most fool-hardy and daring of his race. I have heard Captain Jo Chunk tell the story of some of his daring exploits.

"There ar'nt a man," said Captain Jo, "from Pittsburgh to New Orleans but what's heard of Mike Fink; and there aint a boatman on the river to this day, but what strives to imitate him. Before them 'ere steamers come on the river, Mike was looked up to as a kind of king among the boatmen, and he sailed a little the prettiest craft that there was to be found about these 'ere parts. Along through the warm summer afternoons, when there wa'nt nothing much to do, it used to be the fashion among the boatmen to let one hold up a tin cup in the stern of the boat, while another would knock out the bottom with a rifle ball from the bow; and the one that missed had to pay a quart for the good of the crew. Howsomever," continued Capt. Jo, "this wa'nt sport enough for Mike, and he used to bet that he could knock the tin cup off a man's head; and there was one fellow fool-hardy enough to let him do it. This was Mike's brother, who was just such another great strapping fellow as himself, but hadn't as much wit in his head as Mike had in his little finger. He was always willing to let Mike shoot the cup off his head, provided that he'd share the quart with him; and Mike would rather give him the whole of it than miss the chance of displaying his skill."

.   .   .   .

"Down there at Smithland, behind the Cumberland bar," continued Jo, "used to be Mike's headquarters; and one day when he made a bet that he'd shoot the tin cup off from a fellow's head, he happened to fire a little too quick, and lodged the ball in his brains. A man who stood a little way off, and had an old grudge against Mike, leveled his rifle and shot him dead on the spot; and this was the end of Mike Fink, the first boatman who dared to navigate a broad horn [river keelboat] down the falls of the Ohio."

1837

A Mountain Man Enjoys a Battle with the Bannocks

The "mountain men" hunted and trapped in the Rockies during the winter, then met at a designated spot to trade furs for necessary supplies in the summer. Later many of them served as guides to parties crossing the plains and mountains to California or Oregon. This account of a summer rendezvous on the Green River, in Colorado, is by Osborne Russell who was a "mountain man" in the 1830's and 1840's.

Source: RUSSELL, OSBORNE. *Journal of a Trapper, or Nine Years in the Rocky Mountains, 1834-1843*, pp. 62-64. Syms-York Co., Boise, Idaho, 1921.

Here we found the hunting parties all assembled waiting for the arrival of supplies from the States. Here presented what might be termed a mixed multitude. The whites were chiefly

Americans and Canadian French, with some Dutch, Scotch, Irish, English, half-breed and fullblood Indians of nearly every tribe of the Rocky Mountains. Some were gambling at cards, some playing the Indian game of "hand" and others horse racing, while here and there could be seen small groups collected under shady trees relating the events of the past year, all in good spirits and health, for sickness is a stranger seldom met with in these regions.

Sheep, elk, deer, buffalo and bear skins mostly supply the mountaineers with clothing, lodges, and bedding, while the meat of the same animals supply them with food. They have not the misfortune to get any of the luxuries from the civilized world but once a year, and then in such small quantities that they last but a few days.

We had not remained in this quiet manner long before something new arose for our amusement. The Bannock Indians had for several years lived with the whites on terms partly hostile, frequently stealing horses and traps, and in one instance killed two white trappers. They had taken some horses and traps from a party of French trappers who were hunting Bear River in April previous, and they were now impudent enough to come with the village of sixty lodges and encamp within three miles of us in order to trade with the whites as usual, still having the stolen property in their possession and refusing to give it up.

On the 15th of June four or five whites and two Nez Perce Indians went to their village and took the stolen horses, whilst the men were out hunting buffalo, and returned with them to our camp. About three o'clock p. m. of the same day thirty Bannocks came riding at full gallop up to the camp, armed with their war weapons. They rode into the midst and demanded the horses which the Nez Perces had taken saying they did not wish to fight with the whites. But the Nez Perces, who were only six in number, gave the horses to the whites for protection. . . . Some of the Bannocks, on seeing this, started to leave the camp. . . . Nearly all the men in camp were under arms.

Mr. Bridger [Jim Bridger, one of the most famous of the mountain men] was holding one of the stolen horses by the bridle when one of the Bannocks rushed through the crowd, seized the bridle and attempted to drag it from Mr. Bridger by force, without heeding the cocked rifles that surrounded him. . . . He was a brave Indian, but his bravery proved fatal . . . for the moment he seized the bridle two rifle balls whistled through his body. The others wheeled to run, but twelve of them were shot from their horses before they were out of reach of rifle. We then mounted horses and pursued them, destroyed and plundered their village, and followed and fought them three days, when they begged us to let them go and promised to be good Indians in future. . . .

July 5th a party arrived from the States with supplies. The cavalcade consisted of forty-five men and twenty carts drawn by mules, under the direction of Mr. Thomas Fitzpatrick, accompanied by Capt. William Stewart on another tour of the Rocky Mountains.

Joy now beamed in every countenance. Some received letters from their friends and relations; some received the public papers and news of the day; others consoled themselves with the idea of getting a blanket, a cotton shirt or a few pints of coffee and sugar to sweeten it . . . by paying 2,000 per cent profit to the traders from the States. For instance, sugar was $2 per pint, coffee the same, blankets $20 each, tobacco $2 per pound, alcohol $4 per pint, and common cotton shirts $5 each. . . . And in return trappers were paid $4 or $5 per pound for beaver.

In a few days the bustle began to subside. The furs were done up in packs ready for transportation to the States and parties were formed for the hunting the ensuing year. One party, consisting of 110 men, was destined for the Blackfoot country, under the direction of L. B. Fontanelle as commander and James Bridger as guide. I started, with five others to hunt the headwaters of the Yellowstone, Missouri, and Big Horn Rivers, a portion of the country I was particularly fond of hunting.

1839

George Strong Meets "Hell-in-Harness"

Before the nineteenth century, humans had known nothing so powerful, or so speedy, as a steam locomotive. Some of the wonder and admiration nineteenth-century Americans felt toward railroad trains can be read in this excerpt from the diary of George Templeton Strong, an educated New Yorker.

Source: NEVINS, ALLAN, and THOMAS, MILTON HALSEY (editors). *The Diary of George Templeton Strong*, Vol. I, p. 108. The Macmillan Company, New York, 1952.

July 1, 1839.

It's a great sight to see a large train get under way. I know of nothing that would more strongly impress our great-great-grandfathers with an idea of their descendants' progress in science. As to the engine, the most pithy and expressive epithet I ever heard applied to it is "Hell-in-Harness." Just imagine a locomotive rushing unexpectedly by a stranger to the invention on a dark night, whizzing and rattling and panting, with its fiery furnace gleaming in front, its chimney vomiting fiery smoke above, and its long train of cars rushing along behind like the body and tail of a gigantic dragon . . . and all darting forward at the rate of twenty miles an hour. Whew!

1841

Charles Dickens Is Impressed by the Factory Girls

Many young ladies left the rural areas of New England to work for a few years in the growing factories of that region. The factories at Lowell, Massachusetts, enjoyed an especially fine reputation for enlightened management and good working conditions. Charles Dickens, the famous English author, was greatly impressed by the high quality of the young lady workers.

Source: DICKENS, CHARLES. *American Notes for General Circulation*, pp. 78–83. Stassin and Xavier, Paris, 1842.

I was met at the station at Lowell by a gentleman intimately connected with the management of the factories there. . . . Lowell has been a manufacturing town barely twenty-one years, but is a large, populous, thriving place. . . . There are several factories in Lowell, each of which belongs to what [in England] we should term a Company of Proprietors, but what they call in America a Corporation. I went over several of these; such as a woolen factory, a carpet factory, and a cotton factory. . . .

I happened to arrive at the first factory just as the dinner-hour was over, and the girls were returning to their work. . . . They were all well-dressed . . . and that phrase necessarily includes extreme cleanliness. They had serviceable bonnets, good warm cloaks, and shawls. . . . Moreover, there were places in the mill in which they could deposit these things without injury; and there were conveniences for washing. They were healthy in appearance, many of them remarkably so, and had the manners and deportment of young women: not of degraded brutes of burden. . . .

The rooms in which they worked were as well ordered as themselves. In the windows of some there were green plants, which were trained to shade the glass; in all, there was as much fresh air, cleanliness, and comfort as the nature of the occupation would possibly admit of. . . .

The girls reside at various boarding-houses near at hand. . . . There are a few children employed in these factories, but not many. The laws of the state forbid their working more than nine months in the year, and require that they be educated during the other three. For this purpose there are schools in Lowell; and there are churches and chapels . . . in which the young women may observe that form of Worship in which they have been educated.

At some distance from the factories, and on the highest and pleasantest ground in the neighborhood, stands their hospital. . . . The weekly charge in this establishment for each patient is three dollars. . . . But no girl employed by any of the corporations is ever excluded for want of the means of payment. That they do not very often lack the means, may be gathered from the fact, that in July, 1841, no fewer than nine hundred and seventy-eight of these girls were depositors in the Lowell Savings Bank. The amount of their joint savings was estimated at one hundred thousand dollars. . . .

104

. . . There is a . . . piano in a great many of the boarding houses. . . . Nearly all these young ladies subscribe to circulating libraries. . . . They have got up among themselves a periodical called *The Lowell Offering*, "A repository of original articles, written exclusively by females actively employed in the mills."

. . . Of the merits of *The Lowell Offering* as a literary production, I will only observe, putting entirely out of sight the fact of the articles having been written by these girls after twelve hours work each day, that it will compare advantageously with a great many English publications. It is pleasant to find that many of its Tales are of the Mills and of those who work in them; that they inculcate habits of self-denial and contentment, and teach good doctrines of enlarged benevolence. A strong feeling for the beauties of nature, as displayed in the solitudes the writers have left at home, breathes through its pages like wholesome village air. . . . It has very scanty allusion to fine clothes, fine marriages, fine houses, or fine life. . . .

1843

Dorothea Dix Is "Obliged to Speak with Great Plainness"

Among the many reforms growing out of the Jacksonian Years was better understanding of the mentally ill. Dorothea Lynde Dix, although physically frail and sickly herself, gave passionate leadership to this cause, as you can see from her petition to the Massachusetts Legislature.

Source: "Memorial of Dorothea L. Dix to the Massachusetts Legislature, Boston, January, 1843."

Gentlemen:

. . . About two years ago . . . duty prompted me to visit several prisons and alms-houses in the vicinity of this metropolis. I found, near Boston, in the Jails and Asylums for the poor, a numerous class brought into unsuitable connexion with criminals and the general mass of Paupers. I refer to Idiots and Insane persons. . . . I shall be obliged to speak with great plainness, and to reveal many things revolting to the taste, and from which my woman's nature shrinks with peculiar sensitiveness. But truth is the highest consideration. *I tell what I have seen*—painful and shocking as the details often are. . . .

I come to present the strong claims of suffering humanity. I come to place before the Legislature of Massachusetts the condition of the miserable, the desolate, the outcast. I come as the advocate of helpless, forgotten, insane and idiotic men and women. . . .

I proceed, Gentlemen, briefly to call your attention to the *present* state of Insane Persons confined . . . in *cages, closets, cellars, stalls, pens! Chained, naked, beaten with rods,* and *lashed* into obedience! . . .

Men of Massachusetts, I beg, I implore, I demand, pity and protection for these. . . . Become the benefactors of your race, the just guardians of the solemn rights you hold in trust. Raise up the fallen; succour the desolate; restore the outcast; defend the helpless. . . .

It is not few but many . . . who bear unqualified testimony to this evil. A voice strong and deep comes up from every alms-house and prison in Massachusetts where the insane are or have been, protesting against such evils. . . .

Gentlemen, I commit to you this sacred cause. Your action upon this subject will affect the present and future condition of hundreds and of thousands. . . .

1844

Sam Clemens Hears the Cry, "S-t-e-a-m-boat A-comin'!"

River steamboats played an important part in the economic and social life of the United States during the nineteenth century. In this selection, Samuel L. Clemens remembers the effect of the steamboats on Hannibal, Missouri, his boyhood home on the Mississippi River.

Source: CLEMENS, SAMUEL L. *Life on the Mississippi*, pp. 32–34. Harper and Brothers, New York, 1950.

Once a day a cheap, gaudy packet arrived upward from St. Louis, and another downward from Keokuk. Before these events, the day was glorious with expectancy; after them, the day was a dead and empty thing. Not only the boys, but the whole village, felt this. After all these years I can picture that old time to myself now, just as it was then: the empty town drowsing in the sunshine of a summer's morning; the streets empty, or pretty nearly so; one or two clerks sitting in front of the Water Street stores, with their splint-bottomed chairs tilted back against the walls, chins on breasts, hats slouched over their faces, asleep . . .; a sow and a litter of pigs loafing along the sidewalk . . .; two or three lonely little freight piles scattered about the "levee"; a pile of "skids" on the slope of the stone-paved wharf, and the fragrant town drunkard asleep in the shadow of them; . . . but nobody to listen to the peaceful lapping of the great Mississippi, the majestic, the magnificent Mississippi, rolling its mile-wide tide along, shining in the sun. . . .

Presently a film of dark smoke appears . . .; instantly a Negro drayman, famous for his quick eye and prodigious voice, lifts up the cry, "S-t-e-a-m-boat a-comin'!" and the scene changes! The town drunkard stirs, the clerks wake up, and a furious clatter of drays follows, every house and store pours out a human contribution, and all in a twinkling the dead town is alive and moving. Drays, carts, men, boys, all go hurrying from many quarters to a common centre, the wharf.

Assembled there, the people fasten their eyes upon the coming boat as upon a wonder they are seeing for the first time. And the boat *is* rather a handsome sight, too. She is long and sharp and trim and pretty; she has two tall, fancy-topped chimneys, with a gilded device of some kind swung between them; a fanciful pilothouse, all glass and "gingerbread," perched on top of the "texas" deck behind them; the paddle-boxes are gorgeous with a picture or with gilded rays above the boat's name; the boiler deck, the hurricane deck, and the texas deck are fenced and ornamented with clean white railings; there is a flag gallantly flying from the jack-staff; the furnace doors are open and the fires glaring bravely; the upper decks are black with passengers; the captain stands by the big bell, calm, imposing, the envy of all; great volumes of the blackest smoke are rolling and tumbling out of the chimneys— a . . . grandeur created with a bit of pitch pine just before arriving at a town; the crew are grouped on the forecastle; the broad stage is run far out over the port bow, and an envied deck hand stands picturesquely on the end of it with a coil of rope in his hand; the pent steam is screaming through the gauge-cocks; the captain lifts his hand, a bell rings, the wheels stop; then they turn back, churning the water to foam, and the steamer is at rest.

Then such a scramble as there is to get aboard, and to get ashore, and to take in freight and to discharge freight, all at one and the same time; and such a yelling and cursing as the mates facilitate it all with! Ten minutes later the steamer is under way again, with no flag on the jack-staff and no black smoke issuing from the chimneys. After ten more minutes the town is dead again, and the town drunkard asleep by the skids once more.

1846

Irish Immigrants Strike for 87½ Cents a Day

During the 1840's and 1850's large numbers of immigrants from Ireland and Germany came to the United States. Most of them were dreadfully poor and contractors often exploited them outrageously by playing one group against another as this newspaper account of the time testifies.

Source: *New York Weekly Tribune*, May 2, 1846, p. 3, col. 3.

. . . As we understand it, a large number of Irish laborers have been at work in Winter for certain contractors for sixty-five cents per day, and the days were made pretty long at that. With this compensation, amounting to $3.90 per week, the laborers must of course live as they best could, some of them having large families to support. As the rent of any decent tenement in Brooklyn would absorb nearly the entire earnings of a laboring man at this rate, they were allowed to build miserable shanties on ground allotted them by the contractors on the plot occupied by them in performing the work.

As Spring opened and days became longer, labor more effective and employment more general, the poor laborers began to grumble at their hard lot, and at last united in an effort to improve it. They asked for 87½ cents per day (about equal to 50 in Vermont or 37½ in the West) and to have ten hours recognized as the limit of a day's work. The contractors refused to comply with their demands; whereupon the laborers struck work.

The contractors hired a cargo of freshly landed Germans to take their places, and ordered the old laborers to quit the premises, which they refused to do, and resorted to the lawless, unjustifiable step of endeavoring to drive the Germans from the work by intimidation and violence. Of course the Military were called out, the Irish overawed, the Germans protected in their work, and thus the matter stands. So far, the contractors may be said to have triumphed. . . .

1846

Susan Magoffin Travels to Santa Fe

Samuel Magoffin operated trading caravans from Independence, Missouri, to Santa Fe. He left in June, 1846, with fourteen huge wagons full of goods and a carriage for his recent bride to ride in. She was Susan Magoffin, eighteen years old, and raised on a large estate in Kentucky. Susan kept a diary in which she recorded her journey along the Santa Fe Trail.

Source: DRUMM, STELLA M. (editor). *Down the Santa Fe Trail and Into Mexico: The Diary of Susan Shelby Magoffin, 1846–1847*, pp. 2–102, *passim*. Yale University Press, New Haven, 1926.

June 11, 1846. Now the Prairie life begins! We left "the settlements" this morning. . . .

. . . After a supper at *my own table* and in *my own house* . . . I can say what few women in civilized life ever could, that the first house of his own to which my husband took me after our marriage was a *tent*. . . .

June 12. . . . Being tired of the carriage I got out and took a ramble. . . . I picked numberless flowers with which the plains are covered and threw them away to gather more. I wearied myself out at this, and as the tent was now up, I returned "home." There before supper I had a little piece of work to attend to, I

mean the feeding of my chickens. It is quite a farm house this;
poultry, dogs, cattle, mules, horses &c. . . .

Wednesday, June 17. Last night I had a wolfish kind of a
serenade! . . . Ring, my dear, good dog . . . gave one spring from
his hiding place and in a twinkling had driven the wolves off
entirely. . . .

* * * * * * *

Council Grove, 145 miles from Independence, Friday, June 19.
. . . In our travels today we stoped two miles the other side of
Council Grove at what is called Big John's Spring. . . . The
scenery around is very wild. . . . While I stood apparently very
calm and bold as Samuel got water from the clear flowing stream,
I could not suppress . . . the fear . . . of some wily savage or
hungry wolf lurking in the thick grape vines ready . . . to bounce
upon my shoulders.

Thursday, June 25. While . . . on a little stroll after dinner,
I . . . steped almost onto a large snake; it moved and frightened
me very much. Of course, I screamed and ran. . . .

* * * * * * *

Little Arkansas River, June 30. . . . About dark we came into
the mosquito regions, and I found . . . I have been complaining
all this time for *nothing;* for some two or hundred or even thousands of mosquitoes are nothing compared with what we now
encountered. . . . I drew my feet up under me, wraped my shawl
over my head, till I almost smothered with heat, and listened to
the din without. And such a noise as it was. . . . Millions upon
millions were swarming around me, and their knocking against
the carriage *reminded me of a hard rain.* . . .

After the tent was put up Magoffin came to the carriage and
told me *to run if I could,* with my shawl, bonnet and shoes on . . .
straight to the bed. When I got there they pushed me straight
in under the mosquito bar. . . . There I sat in my cage, like an
imprisoned creature frightened half to death. . . . I tried to sleep
and towards daylight succeeded. On awakening . . . I found my
forehead, arms, and feet covered with knots. . . .

[On July 4, 1846, Susan was thrown from her carriage
when it upset while descending a steep slope. She became very ill on July 17th. The caravan stopped at
Bent's Fort on the banks of the Arkansas River, where
she could be cared for. July 30th was Susan's nineteenth

110

birthday but she was too sick to enjoy it. Shortly after, she lost the baby she and her husband had been expecting. August 8 the trading caravan continued its journey. By the end of August, they were nearing Santa Fe.]

August 27, near San Miguel. We have passed through some two or three little settlements today. . . . It is truly shocking to my modesty to pass such places with gentlemen. The women go about with their arms and necks bare. . . . If they . . . cross the little creek that is near all the villages . . . they pull their dresses . . . up above their knees and paddle through the water like ducks. . . . Some of them wear leather shoes from the States, but most have buck-skin mockersins Indian style. . . . The children run about perfectly naked. . . . I . . . keep my veil drawn closely over my face all the time to hide my blushes.

[When Susan left Missouri, Santa Fe was part of Mexico. By the time she arrived, General Stephen Kearny, commanding American troops, had captured Santa Fe.]

Santa Fe, August 31, 1846. . . . I have entered the city in a year that will always be remembered by my countrymen; and under the "Star-spangled banner" too, the first American lady who had come under such auspices. . . .

1846

The Mormons Flee from Religious Persecution

After being founded by Joseph Smith in western New York, the Mormons, members of the Church of Latter-Day Saints, moved to Ohio, to Missouri, and then to Nauvoo, Illinois. Persecution caused them to leave Nauvoo early in 1846 and this contemporary newspaper account describes their departure.
Source: *Daily Missouri Republican*, St. Louis, May 13, 1846.

A few days ago, to satisfy ourselves of the actual state of affairs at Nauvoo, and to ascertain whether the Mormons were really leaving the country . . . we spent last Friday, Saturday and a portion of Sunday, in the city and surrounding country.

The city and country presents a very altered appearance since last fall. Then, the fields were covered with, or the barns contained, the crops of the season. Now, there are no crops, either growing or being planted. In many instances, the fences have been destroyed, houses have been deserted, and the whole aspect of the country is one of extreme desolation and desertion. . . . Nearly every workshop in the city has been converted into a wagon maker's shop. . . . Generally, they are providing themselves with light wagons, with strong, wide bodies, covered with cotton cloth—in some instances painted, but mostly white. These are to be met with in every direction, and contribute greatly to the singular and mournful appearance of the country.

They appear to be going in . . . companies of four to six and ten wagons, and some of them are fairly well provided with teams and provisions, but a very large portion seem poorly provided for so long a trip. . . . There are a number of women, many of whom have large families of children, inadequately provided with provisions, &c., and without the assistance or protection of any male person. How they expect to get through the journey, we cannot conceive. The Church may give them some protection and assistance, but in all preliminary preparations, and in setting out on the journey, these women seem to rely upon themselves and their children. . . .

In the midst of this scene . . . the spectator cannot fail to be struck with the lightness of heart, apparent cheerfulness, and sanguine hopes with which families bid adieu to their friends, and set on their journey. . . . The great mass go forth, sustained and cheered by the promises of their leaders and . . . a most devout conviction of the truth of their religion, and the rewards which they are to receive from heaven for their present sacrifice. . . . Their enthusiasm . . . is stimulated by songs and hymns, in which their men, women and children join, and containing allusions to their persecutions; and the names of Oregon and California, and the hopes that await them, are mingled with their religious belief and expectations.

As a stranger passes through he will find himself frequently beset, mostly by women and children, with inquiries, "Do you wish to purchase a house and lot?" "Do you wish to buy a farm?" . . . In the city, houses and lots are selling from two to five and ten hundred dollars, which must have cost the owners double that sum. They are willing to sell for cash, or oxen or cattle, or to exchange for such articles of merchandise as they can barter or carry away with them. . . . Farmers in other sections, it appears to us, would make profitable investments by exchanging their surplus stock for houses and lots in Nauvoo, or for farms. . . .

They are crossing the river every day from Nauvoo. . . . The first party, which crossed the river in February, have progressed as far as the east fork of Grand river, about 200 miles west of Nauvoo, within the Territory of Iowa. This party is called the *Camp of Israel* and have with them the Council of Twelve and most of the leading men of the Church. From the best information we could obtain, this Camp includes about 3000 souls. Between the Camp and the Mississippi river, there is said to be about 1500 wagons. . . . Allowing five or six souls to a wagon . . . it would give about seven thousand Mormons between the Mississippi and Grand river.

The first party have selected a temporary resting place on the east fork of Grand river. . . . Here they will enclose a large field . . . and leave that portion of their people who are not prepared to travel further. . . . A body of several hundred, having the stoutest teams and the most ample supply of provisions, have been sent forward with instructions to push directly across the mountains, and explore the territories of Oregon, California and Vancouver's Island, and upon their report . . . will depend where the Church will be re-established. . . .

In and about Nauvoo . . . there is every indication that . . . the Anti-Mormons . . . are satisfied that the Mormons are going, and are disposed to let them get off without further difficulty. There are, however, some . . . turbulent spirits in the county . . . and particularly some young men, who are willing, at any sacrifice, to keep up the excitement. . . . On Saturday evening . . . a number of persons assembled . . . and resolved to visit Nauvoo . . . and burn down the houses and drive out all those who had not already left. These proceedings were universally condemned by the more intelligent and respectable portion of the Anti-Mormon party. . . .

1848

The Gold Rush Leaves the Mayor
Peeling Onions

In January, 1848, James Marshall discovered gold along a branch of the American River in California's lower Sacramento Valley. Walter Colton, *Alcalde* (mayor) of Monterey, California, describes the beginnings of the "Gold Rush" when news of the discovery of gold reached his sleepy community.

Source: COLTON, REVEREND WALTER, U. S. N. *Three Years in California*, pp. 242–253. S. A. Rollo, New York, 1850.

Monday, May 29, 1848. Our town was startled out of its quiet dreams to-day, by the announcement that gold had been discovered on the American Fork. The men wondered and talked, and the women too; but neither believed. . . .

Tuesday, June 6. I determined to put an end to the suspense and sent a messenger this morning to the American Fork. He will have to ride, going and returning, some four hundred miles, but his report will be reliable. We shall then know whether this gold is a fact or a fiction. . . .

Monday, June 12. A straggler came in to-day from the American Fork, bringing a piece of yellow ore weighing an ounce. The young dashed the dirt from their eyes, and the old from their spectacles. One brought a spyglass, another an iron ladle; some wanted to melt it, others to hammer it, and a few were satisfied with smelling it. All were full of tests; and many, who could not be gratified in making their experiments, declared it a humbug. . . . They could not conceive that such a treasure could have lain there so long undiscovered. . . .

Tuesday, June 20. My messenger . . . has returned with specimens of the gold; he dismounted in a sea of upturned faces. As he drew forth the yellow lumps from his pockets and passed them around among the eager crowd, the doubts, which had lingered till now, fled. . . . The excitement produced was intense; and many were soon busy in their hasty preparations for a departure to the mines. The family who had kept house for me caught the moving fever. Husband and wife were both packing up; the blacksmith dropped his hammer, the carpenter

114

his plane, the mason his trowel, the farmer his sickle, the baker his loaf, and the tapster his bottle. All were off for the mines, some on horses, some on carts, and some on crutches, and one went in a litter. . . .

Saturday, July 15. The gold fever has reached every servant in Monterey. . . . Gen. Mason, Lieutenant Lanman, and myself eat together; we have a house, and all the utensils necessary; but our servants have run, one after another, till we are almost in despair. . . . This morning, for the fortieth time, we had to take to the kitchen and cook our own breakfast. A general of the United States Army, the commander of a man-of-war, and the Alcalde of Monterey, in a smoking kitchen, grinding coffee, toasting herring, and pealing onions! Well, . . . we shall all live just as long and be quite as fit to die.

Tuesday, July 18. Another bag of gold from the mines and another spasm in the community. It was brought down by a sailor . . . and contains three hundred and thirty-six ounces. . . . My carpenters, at work on the schoolhouse, on seeing it, threw down their saws and planes, shouldered their picks, and are off. . . . Three seamen ran from the *Warren*, forfeiting their four years' pay; and a whole platoon of soldiers left from the fort. . . .

Thursday, August 16. Four citizens of Monterey are just in from the gold mines on Feather River, where they worked in company with three others. They employed about thirty wild Indians, who are attached to the rancho owned by one of the party. They worked precisely seven weeks and three days, and have divided seventy-six thousand eight hundred and forty-four dollars—nearly eleven thousand dollars to each. . . . A man, well known to me . . . has worked on the Yuba river sixty-four days, and brought back, as the result of his individual labor, five thousand three hundred and fifty-six dollars. . . . A boy, fourteen years of age, . . . has worked . . . fifty-four days, and brought back three thousand four hundred and sixty-seven dollars. . . . A woman . . . has worked in the dry diggings forty-six days, and brought back two thousand one hundred and twenty-five dollars. Is not this enough to make a man . . . shoulder a pick? . . .

Samuel Busey Describes
"A Very Awkward Bowler"

Abraham Lincoln served one term as a Whig member of the House of Representatives from Illinois in the Thirtieth Congress, 1847–1849. While in Washington he ate his meals at Mrs. Sprigg's boardinghouse. Samuel C. Busey, a young physician who lived and ate at Mrs. Sprigg's, recalls one of Congressman Lincoln's favorite diversions.

Source: ANGLE, PAUL M. *The Lincoln Reader*. Rutgers University Press, New Brunswick, N. J., 1947.

Congressman Lincoln was very fond of bowling, and would frequently join others . . . in a match game, at the alley of James Casparis, which was near the boardinghouse. He was a very awkward bowler, but played the game with great zest and spirit, solely for exercise and amusement, and greatly to the enjoyment and entertainment of the other players and bystanders by his criticisms and funny illustrations. He accepted success and defeat with like good nature and humor, and left the alley at the conclusion of the game without a sorrow or disappointment.

When it was known that he was in the alley there would assemble numbers of people to witness the fun which was anticipated by those who knew of his fund of anecdotes and jokes. When in the alley, surrounded by a crowd of eager listeners, he indulged with great freedom in the sport of narrative. . . . His witticisms seemed for the most part to be impromptu, but he always told the anecdotes and jokes as if he . . . had heard them from someone; but they appeared very many times as if they had been made for the immediate occasion.

Congressman Lincoln was always neatly but very plainly dressed, very simple and approachable in manner, and unpretentious. He attended to his business, going promptly to the House and remaining till the session adjourned, and appeared to be familiar with the progress of legislation.

A Forty-Niner Writes to His Wife

While on their way to the California gold fields, many Forty-Niners stopped for rest and provisions in the Mormon city on the Great Salt Lake. A. P. Josselyn wrote from there to his wife, describing the Mormon haven in the wilderness as it appeared to him.

Source: MORGAN, DALE L. "Letters by Forty-Niners," in *Western Humanities Review*, Vol. 3. University of Utah, Salt Lake City, April, 1949.

City of the Great Salt Lake
Sunday, July 15th, 1849

Dear Wife:—

. . . The Mormons have had pretty hard times since they came here, but at this time they have got things pretty comfortable around them. They are just cutting their wheat, which is good; they also have corn, potatoes, etc., coming on; they also have cattle plenty; consequently cheese, butter, etc. Groceries are scarce. Coffee 50 cts. Sugar 37 cts. and other groceries in proportion. We can trade groceries for anything that they have, but they will not sell for money, for they have plenty and cannot buy what they want with it. The Mormons give very flattering accounts of the Gold Regions, and they are afraid that gold will be found in this valley. They say it will ruin them, for they would starve if they should get the gold fever bad enough to call them from their farms.

We expect to remain here until Tuesday to shoe some of our oxen. I went to hear a sermon today, and heard a very good Methodist sermon by a Mormon. They are going to have a great time here on the 24th of this month, celebrating the 2nd anniversary of the arrival of their President [Brigham Young] into this valley. They read the order of the day at the meeting to-day, and if I could get hold of it I would send it, so that you can see that they can do things up pretty strong out here. There is to be ringing of bells, firing of cannon, music from the band, &c, &c., 24 young men for something, I cannot recollect what; 24 young ladies dressed in white for something else; 24 Bishops for something else, etc. The United States Mail leaves here four times a year. It leaves next Tuesday or Wednesday, consequently you will get this letter pretty soon. You may get it sooner than the one I left at Fort Laramie, as that was to go by private conveyance.

I will now give you some kind of an idea of the Mormon City. It is laid out in an oblong square, four miles long and two miles wide; streets very wide; the size of the lots are 40 acres, and about one-half of these lots are occupied. The buildings are mostly small; they are built some of logs, but mostly of what they call dobies [adobes, or sun-dried bricks]. There are in the valley five Grist mills and eight or nine saw mills and two or three more building. Their lumber is pine and fir. They have to haul their firewood ten miles, for there is none grows in this part of the valley; consequently they have to go to the mountains for it.

When the Mormons first settled here, they put their buildings in the shape of a fort; they built two rows of buildings three-fourths of a mile in length and a fourth of a mile apart, and shut up the ends by buildings across; inside of this they had three rows of buildings at equal distances across, forming four hollow squares, into which they could take all their cattle, wagons, etc., if they should be attacked by Indians, but they have never been bothered by Indians; consequently they have spread out over the country.

The city is on a very pretty piece of ground, and if it was near a navigable stream it would be a great city, but there is no chance to get within four hundred miles of this with anything of the boat kind, and I think it is impossible to get a railroad into the valley, for it is surrounded with mountains that are almost impassable for anything. Here you can have plenty of ice all the year around, without the trouble of packing it away in ice houses; for eight miles from the city the tops of the mountains are covered with snow and ice. A few days ago I walked over snow that was ten feet deep. I could tell the depth of it by a channel that had been cut through it by the water.

A. P. Josselyn

Andrew Carnegie Starts His Climb to Fame and Fortune

Andrew Carnegie came with his impoverished parents to the United States in 1848 as a tow-headed boy of thirteen. After working for two years as a bobbin boy in a textile mill for $1.20 a week, he got his foot on the ladder of success in the way he describes here.

Source: *Autobiography of Andrew Carnegie*, pp. 35–42. Houghton Mifflin Company, Boston, 1948.

One evening, early in 1850, when I returned home from work, I was told that Mr. David Brooks, manager of the telegraph office, had asked my Uncle Hogan if he knew where a good boy could be found to act as messenger. . . . My uncle mentioned my name, and said he would see whether I would take the position. I remember so well the family council that was held. Of course I was wild with delight. No bird that ever was confined in a cage longed for freedom more than I. Mother favored, but father was disposed to deny my wish. It would prove too much for me, he said; I was too young and too small. For the two dollars and a half per week offered it was evident that a much larger boy was expected. . . . [Finally, however, Mr. Carnegie gave in and he and Andrew walked to the telegraph office.]

. . . Arrived at the door I asked father to wait outside. I insisted upon going in alone for the interview. I was led to this, perhaps, because I had by that time begun to consider myself something of an American. At first boys used to call me "Scotchie! Scotchie!" and I answered, "Yes, I'm Scotch and I am proud of the name." But in speech and in address the broad Scotch had been worn off to a slight extent, and I imagined that I could make a smarter showing alone with Mr. Brooks than if my good old Scotch father were present. . . .

The interview was successful. I took care to explain that I did not know Pittsburgh, that perhaps I would not do, would not be strong enough; but all I wanted was a trial. He asked me how soon I could come, and I said that I could stay now if I wanted. And, looking back over the circumstance, I think that answer might well be pondered by young men. It is a great mistake not to seize the opportunity. . . . Having got myself in I proposed to stay there if I could. . . .

And that is how in 1850 I got my first real start in life. From the dark cellar of the textile factory, I was lifted into paradise, yes, heaven, as it seemed to me, with newspapers, pens, pencils, and sunshine about me. There was scarcely a minute in which I could not learn something or find out how much there was to learn and how little I knew. I felt that my foot was upon the ladder and that I was bound to climb.

I had only one fear, and that was that I could not learn quickly enough the addresses of the various business houses to which messages had to be delivered. I therefore began to note the signs of these houses up one side of the street and down the other. At nights I exercised my memory by naming in succession the various firms. Before long I could shut my eyes and, beginning at the foot of a business street, call off the names of the firms in proper order along one side to the top of the street, then crossing on the other side go down in regular order to the foot again. . . .

The Pittsburgh of 1850 was very different from what it has since become. It had not yet recovered from the great fire which destroyed the entire business portion of the city on April 10, 1845. The houses were mainly of wood, a few only were of brick, and not one was fire-proof. The entire population in and around Pittsburgh was not over forty thousand. . . .

A messenger boy in those days had many pleasures. There were wholesale fruit stores, where a pocketful of apples was sometimes to be had for the prompt delivery of a message; bakers' and confectioners' shops, where sweet cakes were sometimes given to him. He met with very kind men, to whom he looked up with respect; they spoke a pleasant word and complimented him on his promptness, perhaps asked him to deliver a message on the way back to the office. I do not know a situation in which a boy is more apt to attract attention, which is all a really clever boy requires in order to rise. Wise men are always looking out for clever boys.

One great excitement of this life was the extra charge of ten cents which we were permitted to collect for messages delivered beyond a certain limit. These "dime messages," as might be expected, were anxiously watched, and quarrels arose among us as to the right of delivery. In some cases it was alleged boys had now and then taken a dime message out of turn. This was the only cause of serious trouble among us. By way of settlement I proposed that we should "pool" these messages and divide the cash equally at the end of each week. . . . I was appointed treasurer. Peace and good humor reigned ever afterwards. . . . It was my first essay in financial organization. . . .

1850

"The Senator from South Carolina Is in His Seat!"

The debates on the Compromise of 1850 were almost the last appearance on the national stage of three great Senators. They were: Henry Clay of Kentucky, Daniel Webster of Massachusetts, and John C. Calhoun of South Carolina, who was nearly dead with tuberculosis. When Webster made his famous Seventh of March speech, which did so much to win support for the Compromise, a spectator saw this touching incident.

Source: HARVEY, PETER. *Reminiscences and Anecdotes of Daniel Webster*, pp. 219–222. Little, Brown and Company, 1877.

When Mr. Webster was about to deliver his 7th of March speech, he invited me to come on to Washington to hear it. He intended to make it a great effort, the crowning address of his later public life. . . . Early on the morning of the 7th, I was sitting with him in his house, when the sergeant-at-arms of the Senate came in. He told Mr. Webster that already not only the Senate chamber itself but all the approaches to it were crowded by an eager multitude. A great speech from Mr. Webster was a national event. Mr. Webster looked at me and, in a sad voice, spoke of this being one of the last times that he should ever address listening masses on the floor of the Senate. . . . Recovering his spirits again in a moment, he turned to the sergeant-at-arms, and said:

"However crowded the Senate chamber is, I want you to be sure and save two good seats; one for Mrs. Webster, and the other for my old friend Harvey here, who has come all the way from Boston to hear my speech."

The sergeant-at-arms promised that he would do so. On going to the Senate chamber at the proper time, I found an excellent seat reserved for me, near and a little in front of the spot where Mr. Webster would stand when he made his speech. . . .

Mr. Webster had not been speaking long . . . when I saw a tall, gaunt figure, wrapped in a long, black cloak, with deep cavernous black eyes and a thick mass of snow-white hair brushed back from the large brow and falling to the shoulders, advance with slow and feeble steps through the lobby behind the Vice-president's chair, and then, aided by one of the Senators, approach and sink into a chair on the opposite side of the chamber. I looked at Mr. Webster and observed that as he spoke his face was turned the other way, so that he had not seen the almost ghostly figure come in. He went on speaking in his deep and sonorous tones; and at last came to a passage wherein he alluded to something Mr. Calhoun had once said in debate, as "the utterance of the distinguished and venerable Senator from South Carolina, who, I deeply regret, is prevented by serious illness from being in his seat to-day."

At this I glanced towards the tall, gaunt figure across the chamber. He was moving restlessly in his chair; his head and body were bent eagerly forward, and he made an effort as if trying to rise and interrupt the orator. But the effort seemed to be too much for him, for he sank back in his chair, evidently exhausted. . . .

Presently the speaker once more . . . alluded to Calhoun as "the eminent Senator from South Carolina, whom we all regret so much to miss, from such a cause, from his seat to-day."

The figure again grew restless; the hands nervously grasped both arms of his chair; the black eyes glared and shone in their eagerness; and now, half rising from his seat, and unable any longer to bear the thought that Mr. Webster should remain unconscious of his presence, he exclaimed, in a feeble and hollow voice, which yet was heard throughout the chamber:

"The Senator from South Carolina is in his seat!"

Mr. Webster turned towards him with something like a start, and when he saw that Calhoun had actually risen from the bed of death . . . to creep to the Capitol and hear his speech, he for a moment betrayed visible signs of deep emotion. Then, acknowledging this touching compliment by a bow . . . he went on with his speech.

A few days more, and Calhoun lay dead, in state, within those very walls. . . .

1852

Uncle Tom Encounters Simon Legree

Harriet Beecher Stowe's *Uncle Tom's Cabin*, first published in 1852, was very influential in hardening northern attitudes toward the extension of slavery. Indeed so powerful was its propaganda that ten years after its appearance Abraham Lincoln greeted Mrs. Stowe with the words, "So you're the little woman who wrote the book that made this great war!" This short selection tells of Tom's first encounter with his cruel master.

Source: STOWE, HARRIET BEECHER. *Uncle Tom's Cabin*, pp. 414–417. Random House, New York.

[Tom's first two owners, Mr. Shelby and Mr. St. Clare, treated their slaves decently. After St. Clare's death, however, Tom was "sent down the river" to be sold at an auction in New Orleans. There Simon Legree bought Tom and a few other slaves.]

Mr. Simon Legree, Tom's master, had purchased slaves at one place and another, in New Orleans, to the number of eight, and driven them, handcuffed, in couples of two and two, down to the good steamer *Pirate*, which lay at the levee, ready for a trip up the Red river.

Having got them fairly on board, and the boat being off, he came round . . . to take a review of them. Stopping opposite to Tom, who had been attired for sale in his best broadcloth suit, with well-starched linen and shining boots, he briefly expressed himself as follows:

"Stand up."

Tom stood up.

"Take off that stock!" and, as Tom, encumbered by his fetters, proceeded to do it, he assisted him by pulling it, with no gentle hand, from his neck, and putting it in his pocket.

Legree now turned to Tom's trunk, which, previous to this, he had been ransacking, and, taking from it a pair of old pantaloons and a dilapidated coat, which Tom had been wont to put on for his stable-work, he said, liberating Tom's hands from the handcuffs, and pointing to a recess in among the boxes. "You go there, and put these on."

Tom obeyed, and in a few moments returned.

"Take off your boots," said Mr. Legree.

Tom did so.

"There," said Mr. Legree, throwing him a pair of coarse, stout shoes, such as were common among the slaves, "put these on."

In Tom's hurried change of clothes he had not forgotten to transfer his cherished Bible to his pocket. It was well he did so; for Mr. Legree . . . proceeded deliberately to investigate the contents of Tom's pockets. He drew out a silk handkerchief, and put it into his own pocket. Several little trifles, which Tom had treasured . . . he looked upon with a contemptuous grunt, and tossed them over his shoulder into the river.

Tom's . . . hymn-book, which, in his hurry, he had forgotten, Legree now held up and turned over.

"Humph! pious, to be sure. So, what's yer name,—you belong to the church, eh?"

"Yes, Mas'r," said Tom, firmly.

"Well, I'll soon have *that* out of you. I have none o' yer bawling, praying, singing niggers on my place; so remember. Now, mind yourself," he said, with a stamp and a fierce glance of his gray eye, directed at Tom, "*I'm* your church now! You understand—you've got to be as *I* say." . . .

Simon next walked up to the place where Emmeline was sitting, chained to another woman. "Well, my dear," he said, chucking her under the chin, "keep up your spirits."

The involuntary look of horror, fright and aversion, with which the girl regarded him, did not escape his eye. He frowned fiercely. . . .

"I say, all of ye," he said, retreating a pace or two back, "look at me,—look at me,—look me right in the eye,—*straight*, now!" said he, stamping his foot at every pause.

As by a fascination, every eye was now directed to . . . Simon.

"Now," said he, doubling his great, heavy fist into something resembling a blacksmith's hammer, "d'ye see this fist? Heft it!" he said, bringing it down on Tom's hand. "Look at these yer bones! Well, I tell ye this yer fist has got as hard as iron *knocking down niggers.* I never see the nigger, yet, I couldn't bring down with one crack," said he, bringing his fist down so near to the face of Tom that he blinked and drew back. "I don't keep none o' yer cussed overseers; I does my own overseeing; and I tell you things *is* seen to. You's every one of ye got to toe the mark, I tell ye; quick,—straight,—the moment I speak. That's the way to keep in with me. Ye won't find no soft spot in me, nowhere. So, now, mind yerselves; for I don't show no mercy!" . . .

1855-1856

Charlotte Forten Experiences Integration

Charlotte Forten was the granddaughter of a free Negro who had served on board an American privateer during the American Revolution. She was raised in Philadelphia, but went to the Normal School in Salem, Massachusetts, where she made these entries in her diary.

Source: BILLINGTON, RAY ALLEN (editor). *The Journal of Charlotte L. Forten,* pp. 60–70. The Dryden Press, New York, 1953.

Saturday, March 17, 1855. This morning Mr. Edwards, Director of the Normal School, came to see me, and told me that he had no doubt of my being able to obtain a situation as teacher here if I went through the Normal School. . . . He wishes me to write to father and assure him of this. . . .

Wednesday, March 28. Received a few lines from father. To my very great joy he consents to my remaining in the Normal School. . . .

Tuesday, May 1. . . . More and more pleasant becomes my Normal School life. Yet I have made but very few acquaintances, and cannot but feel that among all my school companions there is not a single one who gives me her full and entire sympathy. My studies are my truest friends. . . .

Wednesday, May 30. Ellen and I went to Boston. Went in to the anti-slavery convention for a short time; was not able to stay long. . . . Mr. [Wendell] Phillips [a leading abolitionist] spoke beautifully.

Monday, July 16, 1855. Examination day—No further comment is needed.

Tuesday, July 17. I breathe freely—our trial is over, and happy are we to escape from the hot, crowded school-room, for it has been densely crowded all day. This evening the scholars had a pleasant meeting in the school house and the last farewells were said. . . .

Wednesday, August 1. Went with Aunt M. and a party of friends to the celebration at Abington. [This was a meeting of the Massachusetts Anti-Slavery Society, celebrating the twenty-first anniversary of the freeing of England's slaves.] Our much-loved Garrison [William Lloyd Garrison, editor and publisher of the radical anti-slavery paper, *The Liberator*] was not there. . . . His absence could not fail to be felt. But Mr. Phillips and other able speakers were there and many eloquent speeches were made. . . .

Friday, August 17. My eighteenth birthday. . . . Spent the afternoon and evening very pleasantly. . . .

Wednesday, September 12. To-day school commenced. . . . Most happy am I to return to the companionship of my studies. . . . It is pleasant to meet the scholars again; most of them greeted me cordially, and were it not for the thought . . . of the lack of *entire sympathy* even of those I know and like best, I should greatly enjoy their society.

There is one young girl and only one, Miss B., who I believe thoroughly and heartily appreciates . . . *radical* anti-slavery, and has no prejudice against color. . . . I have met girls in the school-room who have been thoroughly kind and cordial to me,—perhaps the next day met them in the street—they feared to recognize me. These I can but regard now with scorn and contempt. . . .

September 27. This evening Miss B. and I joined the Female Anti-Slavery Society. I am glad to have persuaded her to do so. She seems an earnest hearted girl, in whom I cannot help having some confidence. I can only hope and pray that she will be true, and courageous enough to meet the opposition which every friend of freedom must encounter. . . .

Friday, November 23. We are to have vacation next week—Thanksgiving week. The happy voices of the girls as they spoke of "going home" made me feel rather home-sick. But as I cannot go to either of my homes—to Canada, where father has recently moved, or to Philadelphia, I must try not to think of them. . . .

Friday, February 8, 1856. Next week we shall have our examination. I dread it, and do most heartily wish it was over!

Sunday, March 16. . . . Today we had our election for those who are to write our class poem, valedictory, and dissertation. Miss Pitman was chosen to write the dissertation; Lizzie Church the valedictory, and my unworthy self to write the poem; I most respectfully declined, but every one insists upon my doing it. . . .

Wednesday, April 2. This afternoon I had a long conversation with Mr. Edwards. . . . I desire nothing so much as some employment which shall enable me to pay my debts—I hope I shall be fortunate enough to obtain some situation as a teacher. . . .

Wednesday, June 18, 1856. Amazing, wonderful news I have heard today! It has completely astounded me. . . . I have received the offer of a situation as teacher in one of the public schools of this city,—of this conservative, aristocratic old city of Salem!!!

1856

Sergeant Bandel Describes the Sioux

Eugene Bandel was a young German immigrant who came to the United States in 1853. A year later he enlisted in the Army because he could not find suitable work. In letters to his parents in Germany he gave accurate and interesting descriptions of the land and life west of the Mississippi as he saw them in the 1850's. Here he describes the customs of the Sioux Indians, who were living in much the same way as the Indians Coronado saw more than three centuries before.

Source: BANDEL, EUGENE. *Frontier Life in the Army, 1854–1861*, pp. 93–98. Arthur H. Clark Co., California, 1932.

Lawrence, Kansas Territory, Nov. 22, 1856

Dear Parents: . . . In my last letter I promised to write you something about the Indians. . . . So let's at it! . . . As far as the authenticity of the facts . . . is concerned, everything is as I myself saw it, and you can therefore rely on its being the exact truth.

The Sioux Indians are those with whom I am best acquainted. ... Their bands extend from the upper Mississippi to the Rocky mountains, and from Canada to south of the Platte river. All are quite uncivilized, and many of them have never yet set eyes on a white man. They are said to number about twenty thousand. The men, as well as the squaws, wear their hair in long braids. ... Yet none of these Indians wears a beard. All hair on the face is pulled out by the roots, as soon as it makes its appearance, so that it never grows again.

Their clothing consists of moccasins, loin cloth, and a buffalo robe, or, if they can have it, a woolen blanket. The squaws usually wear a sort of shirt, fastened around the waist with a strap. ... In addition, ... many wear an article of clothing which they call "unska" ... for which I cannot find a fitting German name. [The "unska" are something like leggings.]

The moccasins ... are made of deer hide by the squaws, which they themselves tan, and are soled with untanned buffalo hide. They know nothing about heels. The upper portion of the moccasin is adorned with beads, obtained, as are all their necessities (such as powder, lead, muskets, calico for wearing apparel, or tin plate for their arrow points), in exchange for skins from the traders who settle among them. ... Their thread consists of the sinews of buffalo and deer, and these they split up fine enough to use for threading the tiniest of beads.

They paint their faces and eyebrows, as well as some portions of their bodies, with colors. ... All have large brass rings in their ears and around their arms. The earrings are often three to five inches in diameter, and their weight stretches the lobes of their ears to an inch in length, so that the rings touch the shoulders. Their guns are usually of a poor sort ... and only a few have even these poor guns.

All of them, however, from the boys of six years of age up, have their bows and a quiver full of arrows, and the accuracy with which they shoot is almost unbelievable. We would often let the boys, with their little bows, shoot at twenty paces ... five cent pieces off the top of posts and almost every time they did it.

... When an Indian wants a wife, he goes to her parents and inquires how much they want for their daughter and is told one horse, or so many hides or sometimes, when the girl is good-looking, two horses. ...

128

The habitations of the Indians are tents, made by the squaws of buffalo ... hides or such skins as are not valuable as furs, skillfully sewed together. Some twenty poles meeting at the top form the framework, with a hole left ... through which the smoke escapes. An opening which answers for a door is also left and is covered by an additional hide. Their fire is very small, and they always burn short pieces of dry wood to keep the smoke down. ... They say the whites are fools, since they make a big fire of green wood and are then unable to approach the fire because of the extreme heat and smoke.

When the Sioux have plenty to eat, they eat all day and ... all night also; that is, when they are not dancing, which is done in a manner and with a cry which no European can imitate. If they have nothing or little to eat ... they go buffalo hunting with their horses. They use both horses and dogs as transport animals. ... The dogs can drag almost incredibly heavy loads. These dogs are all very large and wild and are mostly half wolf. The women carry the small children on their backs, held fast by a buffalo skin. All can ride well. ...

In addition to wild game and buffalo meat, they also have some articles of food from the vegetable kingdom, such as the Indian potato. ... Then they have a wild beet similar in form to the turnip but very dry and mealy. Besides these, wild grapes grow in profusion everywhere ... the country is wooded, as well as wild plums and cherries. ... In addition, they have various sorts of berries, for which I do not know the German names. Another important item of their food is a sort of rodent called "prairie dog." These animals ... live together by the thousands and dig holes in the earth, the entrances to which look like molehills with holes in the center. When anyone approaches, they perch on these mounds and make a noise similar to the barking of a small dog; hence the name. ... The prairie dogs are a little smaller than rabbits, yet their little upstanding tails are in constant motion.

Dan'l Gets the Western Fever

Generation by generation, millions of Americans moved cease-
lessly westward. The story of this lady and her family is typical.
Source: BROWN, HARRIET CONNOR. *Grandmother Brown's
Hundred Years*, pp. 102–111. Little, Brown and Company, Boston, 1930.

We lived in Amesville, Ohio eleven years. . . . Then we sold
out and joined the Western migration. We bought a farm in Iowa
and moved there in the summer of 1856.

Dan'l had got the Western fever, and I was willing to go to
any place where I thought we might better our fortunes. . . .

It was a considerable undertaking . . . to move one's family
from Ohio to Iowa. There were no railroads to carry us across
country and we had to go by steamboat down the Hocking River
to the Ohio, down the Ohio to St. Louis, and then up the Mississippi River to Keokuk, and overland the rest of the way by
carriage. We were twenty days on the journey. But compared
with what our grandparents had had to overcome in moving from
Massachusetts to New York and Vermont, and from those places
on to Ohio, it was nothing. And then I never thought about it
being hard. I was used to things being hard.

I was very busy, those last days in Amesville, getting myself
and children ready for the journey. You may be sure that I fixed
my children up so they looked nice. Will and Charlie were nine
and seven years old . . . Lizzie past four, and Gus two. . . . They
were all rosy and in fine condition. . . .

Whenever I stopped to think, my heart was heavy at the
thought of leaving Ohio and going to such a far, strange country.
But I didn't have much time for thinking. And one thing made
it easier. My mother was going along . . . to visit Brother John,
who had settled in Minnesota. . . . Dan'l's father . . . also joined
us, and a cousin . . . so that we were a company of nine people
when gathered at the mouth of the Hocking, looking for a steamboat to carry us towards our new home in the West. . . .

Our boat was a side-wheeler . . . and was loaded to the guards
with freight. It moved very slowly. I got *so* tired before the
journey was ended. . . .

When we got to St. Louis there was a half mile of boats headed in at the wharf, and we had to wait a long time before we could land. We stopped in St. Louis long enough to buy some dishes and a cookstove. It was a good stove. . . . Made by Bridge, Beech and Company, and called the "Golden Era." Those were the years of the California gold excitement, and every door of the stove had the picture of a gold piece on it.

Finally we reached Keokuk. . . . We couldn't go above the rapids in the river. . . . So we landed at Keokuk, and Ma and I with baby and Lizzie were put into a carriage with Grandpa . . . and Cousin . . . to drive us to our farm. That was eight miles from Fort Madison and twelve miles from Burlington, which were towns of considerable size. Dan'l stayed behind in Keokuk with the little boys to look after the landing of our goods. . . . And so it was that we came to Iowa. . . .

1856

"Snowshoe Thompson" Carries the Mail

William Wright, whose pen-name was Dan de Quille, wrote many stories during the nineteenth century about the colorful persons that he knew in the western mountains and mining camps. Here he tells how people in California learned about skis.
Source: EMRICH, DUNCAN (editor). *Comstock Bonanza*, pp. 185–190. The Vanguard Press, Inc., New York, 1950.

The most remarkable and most fearless of all our Pacific Coast mountaineers was John A. Thompson, popularly known as "Snowshoe Thompson." For over twenty years he braved the winter storms, as, both by day and by night, he traversed the High Sierra. . . .

John A. Thompson was a most industrious, energetic, public-spirited, and deserving man. The early settlers on both sides of the Sierra Nevada mountains were much indebted to him, as for months during the winter season there would have been no communication between the eastern and western slopes, or between California and the older States by overland mail, but for his enterprise and daring. . . .

Early in the winter of 1856 . . . Mr. Thompson read in the papers of the trouble experienced in getting the mails across the snowy summit of the Sierra Nevada mountains. At the time, he was engaged in cutting wood. . . . What he heard and read of the difficulties encountered in the mountains, on account of the great depth of the snow, set him to thinking. When he was a boy, in Norway, snowshoes were objects as familiar to him as ordinary shoes are to the children of other lands. He determined to make a pair of snowshoes out of the oak timber he was engaged in splitting. [What Thompson called "Norwegian snowshoes" were clearly what are called "skis" today.] Although he was but ten years of age at the time he left his native land, his recollections of the shoes he had seen there were in the main correct. Nevertheless, the shoes he then made were . . . much too heavy and somewhat clumsy. They were ten feet in length, were four inches in width behind the part on which the feet rest, and in front were four inches and a quarter wide.

Having completed his snowshoes to the best of his knowledge, Thompson at once set out for Placerville in order to make experiments with them. Placerville was . . . the principal mountain town on the "Old Emigrant Road"—the road over which the mails were then carried. Being made out of green oak, Thompson's first shoes were very heavy. When he reached Placerville, he put them upon a pair of scales and found that they weighed twenty-five pounds. They were ponderous affairs, but their owner was a man of giant strength, and he was too eager to be up and doing to lose time in making another pair out of lighter wood.

Stealing away to retired places near the town, Thompson spent several days in practicing on his snowshoes. His whole soul was in the business, and he soon became so expert that he did not fear letting himself be seen in public on his snowshoes. He was so much at home on them, that he felt he would do no discredit to his native land.

When he made his first public appearance, he was already able to perform such feats as astonished all who beheld them. His were the first Norwegian snowshoes ever seen in California. At that time, the only snowshoes known were those of the Canadian pattern. [Webbed affairs, which looked like large tennis rackets.] Mounted upon his shoes—which were not unlike thin sled runners in appearance—and with his long balance-pole in his hands, he dashed down the sides of mountains at such a fearful rate of speed as to seem foolhardy. . . .

Having satisfied himself in regard to what he could do on his snowshoes, Thompson declared himself ready to undertake to transport the mails across the mountains. His first trip was made in January, 1856. He went from Placerville to Carson Valley, a distance of ninety miles. With the mail bags strapped upon his back, he glided over fields of snow that were in places from thirty to fifty feet in depth, his long Norwegian shoes bearing him safely and swiftly along upon the surface of the great drifts.

Having successfully made the trip to Carson Valley and back to Placerville, Snowshoe Thompson became a necessity, and was soon a fixed institution of the mountains. He went right ahead, and carried the mails between the two points all that winter. Through him was kept up the only land communication there was between the Atlantic States and California. All then depended upon Snowshoe Thompson, and he never failed. No matter how wild the storms that raged in the mountains, he always came through, and generally on time.

1857

J. W. Fowler, Slaveowner, Instructs His Overseers

Under the plantation slavery system, hired overseers managed the plantation and supervised the work of the slaves. Sometimes they treated slaves harshly, as did Simon Legree. But J. W. Fowler had different ideas.

Source: PHILLIPS, ULRICH B. (editor). *Documentary History of American Industrial Society*, Vol. I, pp. 112–115. Reprinted by permission of the publishers, The Arthur H. Clark Company.

State of Mississippi, Coahoma County, near Friars Point,
A. D. 1857

The health, happiness, good discipline and obedience; food, sufficient and comfortable clothing, a sufficiency of good wholesome and nutritious food for both man and beast being indispensably necessary to successful planting, as well as for reasonable dividends for the amount of capital invested, without saying anything about the master's duty to his dependants, to himself and his God—I do hereby establish the following rules and regulations for the management of my Prairie Plantation, and require an observance of the same by any and all Overseers I may at any time have in charge. . . .

Punishment must never be cruel or abusive, for it is absolutely mean and unmanly to whip a negro from mere passion or malice, and any man who can do this is entirely unworthy and unfit to have control of either man or beast.

My negroes are permitted to come to me with their complaints and grievances and in no instance shall they be punished for so doing. On examination, should I find they have been cruelly treated, it shall be considered a good and sufficient cause for the immediate discharge of the Overseer.

Prove and show by your conduct toward the negroes that you feel a kind and considerate regard for them. . . . See that their necessities are supplied, that their food and clothing be good and sufficient, their houses comfortable; and be kind and attentive to them in sickness and old age. See that the negroes are regularly fed and that their food be wholesome, nutritious and well cooked. . . .

I greatly desire that the Gospel be preached to the negroes when the services of a suitable person can be procured. This should be done on the Sabbath; day time is preferable, if convenient to the Minister. . . .

Allow such as may desire it a suitable piece of ground to raise potatoes and tobacco. They may raise chickens also with privileges of marketing the same at suitable leisure times.

There being a sufficient number of negroes on the plantation for society among themselves, they are not to be allowed to go off the plantation merely to seek society, nor on business without a permit from myself or the Overseer in charge—nor are other negroes allowed to visit the plantation.

After taking proper care of the negroes, stock, etc. the next most important duty of the Overseer is to make if practicable a sufficient quantity of corn, hay, fodder, meat, potatoes and other vegetables for the consumption of the plantation and then as much cotton as can be raised. . . .

J. W. Fowler

1858

Large Boys Fetch the Drinking Water

In mid-nineteenth century America, the "academy" flourished as a place where students could prepare for college. Although their students had to pay some tuition, many academies received some financial support from the local community. This was true of the Academy in New Braunfels, Texas, where the tuition was low, as can be seen from these academy rules passed by the Board of Trustees.

Source: KNIGHT, EDGAR W. *A Documentary History of Education in the South before 1860*, Vol. IV, pp. 60–61. University of North Carolina Press, Chapel Hill, 1953.

. . . Students of parents who do not reside within the city of New Braunfels shall be required to pay One Dollar per month as a tuition fee. Students whose parents reside within the corporation are required to pay Fifty Cents per month as a tuition fee, the said amount to be paid in advance. . . . If a student attends only part of a month, he is required to pay the tuition fee for the whole month. On the morning of the first day of each month, students are required to pay at the school house their tuition fees to the treasurer of the Academy. Should they fail to do so, they shall be required to take or send it to the treasurer within four days. After that time the treasurer is entitled to charge ten per cent commission for collecting the tuition fees at the residence of the students.

Students shall be clean and properly dressed. The teacher or professor shall reprove them if they are not. After the student has been reproved twice and has not obeyed, the teacher or professor shall notify the Committee on Instruction . . . and it shall be the Committee's duty to inform the parents or guardians of said student, and, if necessary, to take other measures.

Whenever a professor or teacher believes a student to be infected with a contagious disease, he shall notify said student . . . and said student shall be required to remain away from school so long as the disease lasts. . . .

Whenever a student has been absent from school, the professor or teacher shall be required to ascertain the cause thereof, and should a student without reasonable excuse absent himself frequently from school, the professors or teachers shall notify the trustees, whose duty it shall be to remonstrate with said student or his parents . . . and if necessary expell him from said Academy. . . .

The large boys of the class shall fetch the drinking water . . . for the classes, and if they refuse to do so, they shall be fined five cents for each time they refuse to fetch the water.

Whenever any student breaks a window pane or injures any property belonging to said Academy or to any student of said school, he shall be required to have it mended. . . .

Students who behave well at school and are studious shall be furnished by the professors or teachers with books out of the library of said Academy for their private studies, free of charge. . . .

Adopted by the Board of Trustees, March 15, 1858.

1859

John Brown Comes "To Free the Slaves"

John Brown was a controversial figure, but there can be no doubt that his raid on Harper's Ferry increased the emotional tension between North and South. A New York reporter recorded this interview with Brown immediately after his capture. Source: *The New York Herald*, October 21, 1859.

. . . When I arrived in the armory . . . Brown was answering questions put to him by Senator Mason, who had just arrived from his residence at Winchester, thirty miles distant, Colonel Faulkner, member of Congress who lives but a few miles off, Mr. Vallandigham, member of Congress of Ohio, and several other distinguished gentlemen. The following is a verbatim report of the conversation:

Mr. Mason: Can you tell us, at least, who furnished money for your expedition?

Mr. Brown: I furnished most of it myself. I cannot implicate others. . . .

Mr. Mason: . . . You killed some people passing along the streets quietly.

Mr. Brown: Well, sir, if there was anything of that kind done, it was without my knowledge. Your own citizens, who were my prisoners, will tell you that every possible means were taken to prevent it. . . . They will tell you that we allowed ourselves to be fired at repeatedly and did not return it.

A Bystander: That is not so. You killed an unarmed man at the corner of the house over there . . . and another besides.

Mr. Brown: See here, my friend, it is useless to dispute or contradict the report of your own neighbors who were my prisoners. . . .

Mr. Vallandigham: Mr. Brown, who sent you here?

Mr. Brown: No man sent me here; it was my own prompting and that of my Maker, or that of the devil, whichever you please to ascribe it to. . . .

Mr. Vallandigham: Did you get up the expedition yourself?

Mr. Brown: I did.

Mr. Mason: What was your object in coming?

Mr. Brown: We came to free the slaves, and only that.

A Young Man (in the uniform of a volunteer company): How many men in all had you?

Mr. Brown: I came to Virginia with eighteen men only, besides myself.

Volunteer: What in the world did you suppose you could do here in Virginia with that amount of men?

Mr. Brown: Young man, I don't wish to discuss that question here.

Volunteer: You could not do anything.

Mr. Brown: Well, perhaps your ideas and mine on military subjects would differ materially.

Mr. Mason: How do you justify your acts?

Mr. Brown: I think, my friend, you are guilty of a great wrong against God and humanity . . . and it would be perfectly right for anyone to interfere with you so far as to free those you willfully and wickedly hold in bondage. I do not say this insultingly. I think I did right and that others will do right who interfere with you at any time and at all times. . . .

A Bystander: Do you consider this a religious movement?

Mr. Brown: It is, in my opinion, the greatest service a man can render to God.

Bystander: Do you consider yourself an instrument in the hands of Providence?

Mr. Brown: I do. . . .

Mr. Vallandigham: Did you expect a general uprising of the slaves in case of your success?

Mr. Brown: No, sir; nor did I wish it; I expected to gather them up from time to time and set them free. . . .

Reporter . . .: I do not wish to annoy you; but if you have anything further you would like to say I will report it.

Mr. Brown: I have nothing to say, only that I claim to be here in carrying out a measure I believe perfectly justifiable, and not to act the part of an incendiary or ruffian, but to aid those suffering great wrong. . . .

Question: Brown, suppose you had every negro in the United States, what would you do with them?

Answer: Set them free. . . .

A Bystander: To set them free would sacrifice the life of every man in this community.

Mr. Brown: I do not think so.

Bystander: I know it. I think you are fanatical.

Mr. Brown: And I think you are fanatical. "Whom the gods would destroy they first make mad," and you are mad. . . .

1859

A Lady Accepts a Proposal

> *The Ladies' Guide to Perfect Gentility*, an etiquette book, published in 1859, contains this model for correct acceptance of a marriage proposal.
>
> Source: THORNWELL, EMILY, in *American Heritage*, December, 1959, p. 104.

Sir:

The attentions which you have so long and so assiduously shown to me have not escaped my notice; indeed how could they, since they were directed exclusively to me? . . . I admit the truth, that pleased and flattered by such attentions, I fondly endeavored to persuade myself that attachment toward me had formed itself in your breast.

Judge then, what must have been my feelings on reading the contents of your letter, in which you propose to pay your addresses, in a manner, the object of which cannot be mistaken—that I may regard you as my acknowledged suitor, and that you have chosen me as the most likely to contribute to your happiness in the married state.

On consulting my parents, I find that they do not object to your proposal; therefore, I have only this to add—may we still entertain the same regard which we have hitherto cherished for each other, until it shall ripen into that affection which wedlock shall sanction, and which lapse of time will not allow to fade. Believe me to be,

Yours, sincerely attached.
(Signature)

1859

No Record of the Deaths Was Kept

> The discovery of the fabulous Comstock Lode brought thousands of people to Virginia City, Nevada. In time, the city developed a rich social and cultural life, but its beginnings were crude, though energetic, as this description shows.
> Source: BROWNE, J. ROSS. "A Peep at Washoe," in *Harper's Monthly Magazine*, pp. 159-161, Vol. XXII, January, 1861.

Notwithstanding the number of physicians who had already hoisted their "shingles," there was much sickness in Virginia City, owing chiefly to exposure and dissipation, but in some measure to the bad quality of the water. . . . The water was certainly the worst ever used by man. . . . With hot saleratus [baking-soda] bread, beans fried in grease, and such drink as this, it was no wonder that scores were taken down sick from day to day.

Sickness is bad enough at the best of times, but here the condition of the sick was truly pitiable. There was scarcely a house in the place that could be regarded as affording shelter against the piercing wind; and, crowded as every tent and hovel was to its utmost capacity, it was hard even to find a vacant spot to lie down, much less sleep or rest in comfort. Many had come with barely means sufficient to defray their expenses to the diggings, in the confident belief that they would immediately strike upon "something rich"; or, if they failed in that, they could work a while on wages. But the highest wages here for common labor were three dollars a day, while meals were a dollar each, and lodgings the same. It was a favor to get work for "grub." Under such circumstances, when a poor fellow fell sick, his recovery could only be regarded as a matter of luck. No record of the deaths was kept. The mass of the emigration were strangers to each other, and it concerned nobody in particular when a man "pegged out," except to put him in a hole or somewhere out of the way.

. . . At this period there were no laws of any kind in the district for the preservation of order. Some regulations had been established to secure the rights of the claimants, but they were loose and indefinite . . . and subject to no enforcement except that of the revolver. . . . The contention was very lively. Great hopes were entertained that when Judge Cradlebaugh arrived he would hold court, and then there would be some hope of settling these conflicting claims. I must confess I did not share in the opinion that law would settle any dispute in which silver was concerned. . . .

When the snow began to clear away there was no end to the discoveries alleged to be made every day. . . . The whole country was staked off to the distance of twenty or thirty miles. Every hillside was grubbed open, and even the desert was pegged, like the sole of a boot, with stakes designating claims. . . .

In Virginia City, a man who had been at work digging a cellar found rich indications. He immediately laid claim to a whole street covered with houses. The excitement produced by this "streak of luck" was perfectly frantic. Hundreds went to work grubbing up the ground under their own and their neighbors' tents, and it was not long before the whole city seemed in a fair way of being undermined. . . . Owners of lots protested in vain.

140

. . . There was no security to personal property, or even to persons. He who turned in to sleep at night might find himself in a pit of silver by morning. . . .

It must not be supposed, from the general character of the population, that Virginia City was altogether destitute of men skilled in scientific pursuits. There were few, indeed, who did not profess to know something of geology; and as for assayers and assay offices, they were almost as numerous as barkeepers and groggeries. A tent, a furnace, half a dozen crucibles, a bottle of acid, and a hammer, generally comprised the entire establishment; but . . . the assays were always satisfactory. Silver, or indications of silver, were sure to be found in every specimen. I am confident some of these learned gentlemen in the assay business could have detected the precious metals in an Irish potato or a round of cheese for a reasonable consideration. . . .

1860

A Swiss Girl Tells of the "Handcart Pioneers"

Mormon converts from the East and from Europe traveled to the "Zion" of Salt Lake City, Utah, as cheaply as possible, for many of them were poor. Between 1856 and 1860 nearly three thousand Mormons crossed the plains by pulling handcarts and pushing wheelbarrows. Mary Ann Hafen, a Swiss immigrant, many years later wrote this girlhood remembrance of the journey across the plains by handcart.

Source: HAFEN, MARY ANN. *Recollections of a Handcart Pioneer of 1860*. Denver, 1938. Copyright 1938 by Leroy R. Hafen.

The first night out the mosquitoes gave us a hearty welcome. Father had bought a cow to take along, so we could have milk on the way. At first he tied her to the back of the cart, but she would sometimes hang back, so he thought he would make a harness and have her pull the cart while he led her. By this time mother's feet were so swollen that she could not wear shoes, but had to wrap her feet with cloth. Father thought that by having

141

the cow pull the cart mother might ride. This worked well for some time.

One day a group of Indians came riding up on horses. Their jingling trinkets, dragging poles and strange appearance frightened the cow and sent her chasing off with the cart and children. We were afraid that the children might be killed, but the cow fell into a deep gully and the cart turned upside down. Although the children were under the trunk and bedding, they were unhurt, but after that father did not hitch the cow to the cart again. He let three Danish boys take her to hitch to their cart. Then the Danish boys, each in turn, would help father pull our cart.

Even when it rained the company did not stop traveling. A cover on the handcart shielded the two younger children. The rest of us found it more comfortable moving than standing still in the drizzle. In fording streams the men often carried the children and weaker women across on their backs. The company stopped over on Sundays for rest, and meetings were held for spiritual guidance and comfort. At night, when the handcarts were drawn up in a circle and the fires were lighted, the camp looked quite happy. Singing, music and speeches by the leaders cheered everyone. . . .

At times we met or were passed by the overland stage coach with its passengers and mail bags and drawn by four fine horses. When the Pony Express dashed past it seemed almost like the wind racing over the prairie.

Our provisions began to get low. One day a herd of buffalo ran past and the men of our company shot two of them. Such a feast as we had when they were dressed. Each family was given a piece of meat to take along. My brother John, who pushed at the back of the cart, used to tell how hungry he was all the time and how tired he got from pushing. He said he felt that if he could just sit down for a few minutes he would feel so much better. But instead, father would ask if he couldn't push a little harder. . . .

When we got that chunk of buffalo meat father put it in the handcart. My brother John remembered that it was the fore part of the week and that father said we would save it for Sunday dinner. John said, "I was so very hungry and the meat smelled so good to me while pushing at the handcart that I could not resist. I had a little pocket knife and with it I cut off a piece or two each half day. Although I expected a severe whipping when father found it out, I cut off little pieces each day. I would chew them so long that they got white and perfectly tasteless. When father came to get the meat he asked me if I had been cutting off some of it. I said 'Yes, I was so hungry I could not let it alone.' Instead of giving me a scolding or whipping, father turned away and wiped tears from his eyes."

Even when we were on short rations, if we met a band of Indians the captain of our company would give them some of the provisions so the Indians would let us go by in safety. Food finally became so low that word was sent to Salt Lake City and in about two weeks fresh supplies arrived.

At last, when we reached the top of Emigration Canyon, overlooking Salt Lake City, on that September day, 1860, the whole company stopped to look down through the valley. Some yelled and tossed their hats in the air. A shout of joy arose at the thought that our long trip was over, that we had at last reached Zion, the place of rest. We all gave thanks to God for helping us safely over plains and mountains to our destination.

When we arrived at the city we were welcomed by the people who came out carrying baskets of fruit and other kinds of good things to eat. Even though we could not understand their language, they made us feel that we were among friends.

1861

A War Correspondent Describes Two Presidents

William Howard Russell was a war correspondent for the London *Times* who observed both the North and South during the early hectic months of 1861. In his diary he recorded these impressions on meeting President Lincoln and, a while later, President Jefferson Davis of the Confederate States of America.

Source: RUSSELL, WILLIAM HOWARD, edited and introduced by FLETCHER PRATT. *My Diary North and South*, pp. 22–24, 93–94. Copyright, 1954, by Fletcher Pratt. Reprinted by permission of Harper & Brothers.

March 27th.

[Russell met Lincoln at the White House, where Secretary of State Seward had taken him.]

. . . Soon afterward there entered, with a shambling, loose, irregular, almost unsteady gait, a tall, lank, lean man, considerably over six feet in height, with stooping shoulders, long pendulous arms, terminating in hands of extraordinary dimensions, which, however, were far exceeded in proportion by his feet. He was dressed in an ill-fitting, wrinkled suit of black. . . . Round his neck a rope of black silk was knotted in a large bulb, with flying ends projecting beyond the collar of his coat; his turned-down shirt-collar disclosed a sinewy muscular yellow neck, and above that . . . rose the strange quaint face and head, covered with its thatch of wild republican hair, of President Lincoln.

The impression produced by the size of his extremities, and by his flapping and wide projecting ears, may be removed by the appearance of kindliness, sagacity, and the awkward friendliness of his face. The mouth is absolutely prodigious. The lips, straggling and extending almost from óne line of black beard to the other, are only kept in order by two deep furrows from the nostril to the chin. The nose itself—a prominent organ—stands out from the face with an inquiring anxious air, as though it were sniffing for some good thing in the wind. The eyes, dark, full, and deeply set, are penetrating, but full of an expression which amounts to tenderness. . . . One would say that, although the mouth was made to enjoy a joke, it could also utter the severest sentence which the head could dictate, but that Mr. Lincoln would be . . . willing to temper justice with mercy. . . .

Mr. Seward took me by the hand and said—"Mr. President, allow me to present to you Mr. Russell of the London *Times.*" On which Mr. Lincoln put out his hand in a very friendly manner, and said, "Mr. Russell, I am very glad to make your acquaintance, and to see you in this country. The London *Times* is one of the greatest powers in the world—in fact, I don't know anything which has much more power—except perhaps the Mississippi. I am glad to know you. . . ." Conversation ensued for some minutes, which the President enlivened by two or three peculiar little sallies, and I left agreeably impressed with his shrewdness, humour, and natural sagacity.

144

May 9th.

[Russell met President Davis in the first capital of the Confederacy at Montgomery, Alabama. He was introduced by a Mr. Wigfall.]

. . . We walked straight upstairs to a small hall which was surrounded by doors. . . . On one of these was written simply, "The President." Mr. Wigfall went in, and after a moment returned and said, "The President will be glad to see you; walk in, sir." When I entered, the President was engaged with four gentlemen. . . . Shaking hands with each, he . . . bowed them and Mr. Wigfall out, and turning to me said, "Mr. Russell, I am glad to welcome you here. . . ." He then requested me to sit down close to his own chair at his office-table, and proceeded to speak on general matters. . . .

I had an opportunity of observing the President very closely. He did not impress me as favorably as I had expected, though he is certainly a very different looking man from Mr. Lincoln. He is like a gentleman—has a slight, light figure, little exceeding middle height, and holds himself erect and straight. He was dressed in a rustic suit of slate-coloured stuff, with a black silk handkerchief round his neck; his manner is plain, and rather reserved and drastic. His head is well-formed with a fine full forehead, square and high, covered with innumerable fine lines and wrinkles. His features are regular, though the cheek-bones are too high, and the jaws too hollow to be handsome. The lips are thin, flexible, and curved, the chin square, well-defined; the nose very regular, with wide nostrils; and the eyes deep set, large and full. One seems nearly blind, and is partly covered with a film. . . . Wonderful to relate, he does not chew tobacco, and is neat and clean-looking, with hair trimmed and boots brushed. The expression of his face is anxious, he has a very haggard, care-worn, and pain-drawn look, though no trace of anything but the utmost confidence and greatest decision could be detected in his conversation. . . .

I mentioned that I had seen great military preparations through the South, and was astonished at the speed with which the people sprang to arms. "Yes, sir," he remarked, . . . "they laugh at us because of our fondness for military titles and displays. . . . But the fact is, we are a military people. . . . We are not less military because we have had no great standing armies. But perhaps we are the only people in the world where gentlemen go to a military academy, who do not intend to follow the profession of arms."

1861

Major Anderson Reports on Evacuation

After the Union defenders of Fort Sumter surrendered, a South Carolina vessel transported Major Anderson and the fort's garrison to the United States ship *Baltic*, which was waiting just outside Charleston harbor. While the *Baltic* steamed north to New York, Major Anderson wrote the following short dispatch to the United States War Department.

Source: *The War of the Rebellion: A Compilation of the Official Records of the Union and Confederate Armies*, Series I, Vol. I, p. 12. The Government Printing Office, Washington, 1880.

Steamship *Baltic,* off Sandy Hook,
Thursday, April 18, 1861

Hon. S. Cameron, Secretary of War, Washington, D. C.:

Sir:—Having defended Fort Sumter for thirty-four hours, until the quarters were entirely burned, the main gates destroyed by fire, the gorge wall seriously injured, the magazine surrounded by flames, and its door closed from the effect of the heat, four barrels and three cartridges of powder only being available, and no provisions but pork remaining, I accepted terms of evacuation, offered by General Beauregard . . . and marched out of the fort, Sunday afternoon, the 14th instant, with colors flying and drums beating, bringing away company and private property, and saluting my flag with fifty guns.

Robert Anderson,
Major First Artillery

Mrs. Witherspoon Is Murdered by Her Slaves

Most slaves remained quietly at work while the war which was to bring them freedom progressed. Nevertheless some slave-holders feared that their slaves would revolt. That this some-times happened, is shown by the diary of Mrs. Mary Boykin Chesnut, of South Carolina.

Source: CHESNUT, MARY BOYKIN, edited by BEN AMES WIL-LIAMS. *A Diary from Dixie*, pp. 139–147. Houghton Mifflin Company, Boston, 1949.

September 21st. Last night when the mail came in, I was seated near the lamp. Mr. Chesnut, lying on a sofa at a little distance, called out to me: "Look at my letters and tell me whom they are from." I began to read one of them aloud. It was from Mary Witherspoon, and I broke down; horror and amazement was too much for me. Poor cousin Betsey Witherspoon was mur-dered! She did not die peacefully in her bed, as we supposed, but was murdered by . . . her Negroes. I remember when Dr. Keith was murdered by his Negroes. . . .

September 24th. The men who went to Society Hill, the With-erspoon home, have come home again with nothing very definite. William and Cousin Betsey's old maid, Rhody, are in jail; strong suspicion but as yet no proof of their guilt. The neighborhood is in a ferment. Evans and Wallace say these Negroes ought to be burnt. Lynching proposed! But it is all idle talk. They will be tried as the law directs, and not otherwise. John Witherspoon will not allow anything wrong or violent to be done. He has a detective there from Charleston. . . .

October 7th. . . . And now comes back on us that bloody story that haunts me night and day, Mrs. Witherspoon's murder. The man William, who was the master spirit of the gang, once ran away and was brought back from somewhere west; and then his master and himself had a reconciliation and the master hence-forth made a pet of him. The night preceding the murder, John Witherspoon went over to his mother's to tell her of some of William's and Rhody's misdeeds. While their mistress was away from home, they had given a ball fifteen miles away from Society Hill. To that place they had taken their mistress's china, silver, house linen, etc. After his conversation with his mother, as he rode out of the gate, John shook his whip at William and said: "Tomorrow I mean to come here and give every one of you a thrashing." . . .

Mrs. Edwards, who was a sister of Mrs. Witherspoon, some-time ago was found dead in her bed. It is thought this suggested their plan of action to the Negroes. What more likely than she should die as her sister had done! When John went off, William said: "Listen to me and there will be no punishment here to-morrow." They made their plan, and then all of them went to sleep, William remaining awake to stir up the others at the proper hour.

[This is the story one later confessed.] After John went away that night, Rhody and William made a great fuss. They were furious at Mars' John threatening them. . . . William said: "Mars' John more than apt to do what he say he will do, but you all follow what I say and he'll have something else to think of. . . . If ole Marster was alive now, what would he say to talk of whipping us!" Rhody always kept the key to the house to let herself in every morning, so they arranged to go in at twelve, and then William watched and the others slept. . . . They smothered her with a counterpane from a bed in the entry. They had no trouble the first time, because they found her asleep and "done it all 'fore she waked." But after Rhody took her keys and went into the trunk and got a clean night gown—for they had spoiled the one she had on—she came to! Then she begged them hard for life. . . . But Rhody stopped her mouth with the counter-pane, and William held her head and hands down, and the other two sat on her legs. . . .

That innocent old lady and her gray hair moved them not a jot. Fancy how we feel. I am sure I will never sleep again without this nightmare of horror haunting me.

"Prices So High That Nobody Can See Them"

George Cary Eggleston was born in Indiana but educated in Virginia where he stayed to fight for the Confederacy. His written recollections contain this description of finances and prices under the Confederate government.

Source: EGGLESTON, GEORGE CARY. *A Rebel's Recollections*, pp. 95–102. Indiana University Press, Bloomington, 1959. Reissue of this book with an introduction by DAVID DONALD is now available from the Indiana University Press.

. . . The financial system adopted by the Confederate government was singularly simple and free from technicalities. It consisted chiefly in the issue of treasury notes enough to meet all the expenses of the government, and in the present advanced state of the art of printing there was but one difficulty . . . namely, the impossibility of having the notes signed in the Treasury Department, as fast as they were needed. There happened, however, to be several thousand young ladies in Richmond willing to accept light and remunerative employment at their homes. . . . As it was really a matter of small moment whose name the notes bore, they were given out in sheets to these young ladies, who signed and returned them for a consideration. I shall not undertake to guess how many Confederate treasury notes were issued. Indeed I am . . . informed by a gentleman who was high in office in the Treasury Department that even the secretary himself did not . . . know. . . .

We knew only that money was astonishingly abundant. Provisions fell short sometimes, and the supply of clothing was not always as large as we should have liked, but nobody found it difficult to get money enough. . . . And to some extent the abundance of the currency really seemed to atone for its extreme badness. Going the rounds of the pickets on the coast of South Carolina, one day in 1863, I heard a conversation between a Confederate and a Union soldier, stationed on opposite sides of a little inlet, in the course of which this point was brought out.

Union Soldier. Aren't times rather hard over there, Johny?

Confederate Soldier. Not at all. We've all the necessaries of life.

U. S. Yes; but how about luxuries? You never see any coffee nowadays, do you?

C. S. Plenty of it.

U. S. Isn't it pretty high?

C. S. Forty dollars a pound, that's all.

U. S. Whew! Don't you call that high?

C. S. Well, perhaps it is a trifle uppish, but then you never saw money so plentiful as it is with us. We hardly know what to do with it, and don't mind paying high prices for things we want.

And that was the universal feeling. Money was so easily got, and its value was so utterly uncertain, that we were never able to determine what was a fair price for anything. We fell into the habit of paying whatever was asked, knowing that tomorrow we should have to pay more. . . .

A facetious friend used to say prices were so high that nobody could see them. . . . He held, however, that the difference between the old and the new order of things was a trifling one. "Before the war," he said, "I went to market with the money in my pocket, and brought back my purchases in a basket. Now I take the money in the basket, and bring the things home in my pocket." . . .

I am sometimes asked at what time prices attained their highest point in the Confederacy, and I find that memory fails to answer the question satisfactorily. . . . The financial condition got steadily worse to the end. I believe the highest price, relatively, I ever saw paid, was for a pair of boots. A cavalry officer, entering a little country store, found there one pair of boots that fitted him. He inquired the price. "Two hundred dollars," said the merchant. A five hundred dollar bill was offered, but the merchant, having no smaller bills, could not change it. "Never mind," said the cavalier, "I'll take the boots anyhow. Keep the change. I never let a little matter of three hundred dollars stand in the way of a trade."

That was on the day before Lee's surrender, but it would not have been an impossible occurrence at any time during the preceding year. The money was of so little value that we parted with it gladly whenever it would purchase anything at all desirable. I cheerfully paid five dollars for a little salt, at Petersburg, in August, 1864, and being thirsty drank my last two dollars in a half-pint of cider.

150

An Eight-Year-Old Takes Over the White House

> Noah Brooks was a newspaper correspondent and close friend
> of President Lincoln during the war years in Washington.   To
> Brooks we are indebted for this intimate description of the close
> relationship between Abraham Lincoln and his youngest son,
> Thomas, better known by his nickname of "Tad."
>
> Source: BROOKS, NOAH, edited with an introduction by HER-
> BERT MITGANG. *Washington in Lincoln's Time*, pp. 246-250.
> Copyright 1958 by Herbert Mitgang. Reprinted by permission
> of Holt, Rinehart and Winston, Inc.

For many years before Lincoln became President, there had
been no children living in the White House. Buchanan was un-
married, and Pierce was childless when he took up his residence
in the Executive Mansion. Although the great house . . . never
could be made to assume an air of domesticity, the three boys of
the Lincoln family did much to invest the historic building with
a phase of human interest which it did not have before. . . .

When the Lincoln family took up their abode in the White
House, Robert, the eldest of the three children, was not quite
eighteen years old. He had been admitted to Harvard College
in 1860, and was away from home during a greater part of the
time thereafter. . . . The second son, Willie, a bright and cheery
lad, greatly beloved by his parents, was a little past ten years
old when the family entered the White House. He died in
February, 1862, while the black shadows rested on many another
American home. Tad was eight years old when he was taken to
Washington with the rest of the family. He had a curious im-
pediment in his speech which rather heightened the effect of his
droll sayings; and the difficulty which he had in pronouncing his
own name gave him the odd nickname by which he was always
known. . . .

Perhaps it was heaviness of grief at the loss of Willie that made
it well-nigh impossible for Lincoln to treat Tad's innumerable
escapades with severity. While the family lived in Washington,
the lad was allowed his own way almost without check. . . .
But I am bound to say that Tad . . . was never anything else,
while I knew him, but a boisterous, rollicking, and absolutely

151

real boy. . . . He was a big-hearted and fresh-faced youngster, and when he went away from the White House, after his father's tragic end, he carried with him . . . the same boyish frankness and simplicity that he took into it.

Very soon after he began life in the White House, Tad learned what an office-seeker was. All day long, unless the President was absent from the building, the office-seekers lined the upper corridors and passages; and sometimes the lines extended all the way down the stairs and nearly to the main entrance. When other diversions failed him, Tad liked to go around among these waiting place-hunters and institute inquiries on his own account. He would ask what they wanted, how long they had been there, and how much longer they proposed to wait. Some of these men came day after day, and for many successive days; with these Tad became acquainted, and to them he would give much sympathetic advice in his own whimsical but sincere way. Once he mounted guard at the foot of the public staircase, and exacted toll of all who passed up. "Five cents for the benefit of the Sanitary Fund," he explained to the visitors, who were not unwilling to have a friend at court for so small a price. . . .

Everything that Tad did was done with a certain rush and rude strength which were peculiar to him. I was once sitting with the President in the library, when Tad tore into the room in search of something, and, having found it, he threw himself on his father like a small thunderbolt, gave him one wild, fierce hug, and, without a word, fled from the room before his father could put out his hand to detain him. With all his boyish roughness, Tad had a warm heart and a tender conscience. He abhorred falsehood as he did books and study. Tutors came and went, like changes of the moon. None stayed long enough to learn much about the boy; but he knew them before they had been one day in the house. "Let him run," his father would say; "there's time enough yet for him to learn his letters and get pokey. Bob was just such a little rascal, and now he is a very decent boy." . . .

. . . His father took great interest in everything that concerned Tad, and when the long day's work was done, and the little chap had related to the President all that had moved him or had taken up his attention during the daylight hours, and had finally fallen asleep under a drowsy cross-examination, the weary father would turn once more to his desk, and work on into

the night. . . . Then, shouldering the sleeping child, the man
for whom millions of good men and women nightly prayed took
his way through the silent corridors and passages to his boy's
bed-chamber. . . .

1862

"What on Earth Will Josephine Skinner Say?"

> Louisa May Alcott, later to be the author of the classic *Little
> Women*, volunteered as a nurse during the war. She had been
> on duty only a few days when her hospital received the wounded
> after the bloody battle of Fredericksburg.
> Source: ALCOTT, LOUISA MAY. *Hospital Sketches*, pp. 54-64.
> Published in the American Century Series by Hill and Wang,
> Inc.

"They've come! They've come! Hurry up ladies—you're
wanted."

"Who have come? The Rebels?"

This sudden summons in the gray dawn was somewhat start-
ling to a three days' nurse like myself . . . but my room-mate
took it more coolly, and . . . answered my bewildered question,—

"Bless you, no, child; it's the wounded from Fredericksburg;
forty ambulances are at the door, and we shall have our hands
full in fifteen minutes."

"What shall we have to do?"

"Wash, dress, feed, warm and nurse them for the next three
months, I dare say. . . . Now you will begin to see hospital life
in earnest." . . .

[Miss Alcott went to her ward]

The sight of several stretchers, each with its legless, armless,
or desperately wounded occupant, entering my ward, admonished
me that I was there to work. . . . Forty beds were prepared,
many already tenanted by tired men who fell down anywhere,
and drowsed till the smell of food aroused them. Round the great
stove was gathered the dreariest group I ever saw—ragged, gaunt

and pale, mud to the knees, with bloody bandages untouched since put on days before; many bundled up in blankets, coats being lost or useless; and all wearing that disheartened look which proclaimed defeat. . . . Presently, Miss Blank . . . put basin, sponge, towels, and a block of brown soap into my hands, with these appalling directions:

"Come, my dear, begin to wash as fast as you can. Tell them to take off socks, coats and shirts, scrub them well, put on clean shirts, and the attendants will finish them off, and lay them in bed."

If she had requested me to shave them all, or dance a hornpipe on the stove funnel, I should have been less staggered; but to scrub some dozen men at a moment's notice was really—really——. However, there was no time for nonsense, and, having resolved when I came to do everything I was bid, I . . . clutched my soap manfully, and, assuming a business-like air, made a dab at the first dirty specimen I saw. . . .

I chanced to light on a withered old Irishman, wounded in the head. . . . He was so overpowered by the honor of having a lady wash him . . . that he did nothing but roll up his eyes, and bless me, in an irresistible style which was too much for my sense of the ludicrous; so we laughed together. When I knelt down to take off his shoes, he "flopped" also and wouldn't hear of my touching "them dirty craters. May your bed above be aisy, darlin', for the day's work ye are doon!—Whoosh! there ye are, and bedad, it's hard tellin' which is the dirtiest, the fut or the shoe." It was; and if he hadn't helped me, I should have gone on pulling, under the impression that 'the "fut" was a boot, for trousers, socks, shoes, and legs were a mass of mud. This comical tableau produced a general grin, at which . . . I took heart and scrubbed away like any tidy parent on a Saturday night. Some of them took the performance like sleepy children, leaning their tired heads against me as I worked, others looked grimly scandalized, and several of the roughest blushed like bashful girls. One wore a soiled little bag about his neck, and, as I moved it, to bathe his wounded chest, I said,

"Your talisman didn't save you, did it?"

"Well, I reckon it did, marm, for that shot would a gone a couple a inches deeper but for my old mammy's camphor bag," answered the cheerful philosopher.

154

Another, with a gunshot wound through the cheek, asked for a mirror, and when I brought one, regarded his swollen face with a sad expression, as he muttered—

"I vow to gosh, that's too bad! I warn't a bad looking chap before, and now I'm done for. Won't there be a thunderin' scar? And what on earth will Josephine Skinner say?"

He looked up at me with his one eye so appealingly, that . . . I assured him that if Josephine was a girl of sense, she would admire the honorable scar . . . for all women thought a wound the best decoration a brave soldier could wear. . . .

The next scrubbee was a nice looking lad, with a curly brown mane. . . . He lay on a bed, with one leg gone, and the right arm so shattered that it must evidently follow; yet the little Sergeant was as merry as if his afflictions were not worth lamenting over, and when a drop or two of salt water mingled with my suds at the sight of this strong young body, so marred and maimed, the boy looked up, with a brave smile, though there was a little quiver of the lips, as he said,

"Now don't you fret yourself about me, miss; I'm first rate here, for it's nice to lie still on this bed after knocking about in those confounded ambulances, that shake what there is left of a fellow to jelly. I never was in one of these places before, and think this cleaning up a jolly thing for us, though I'm afraid it isn't for you ladies."

1862

Lincoln Fulfills a Promise Made to His Maker

Although the Battle of Antietam was not a clear-cut Union victory, Lincoln decided it was the success he had been awaiting before issuing his Proclamation of Emancipation. Five days later he called his Cabinet together and took the actions Secretary of the Treasury Chase here records in his diary.

Source: DONALD, DAVID (editor). *Inside Lincoln's Cabinet: The Civil War Diaries of Salmon P. Chase*, pp. 149–151. Longmans, Green and Co., New York, 1954.

Sept. 22 (1862) *Monday. . . .* State Department messenger came with notice to Heads of Departments to meet at 12. . . . Went to White House.

All the members of the Cabinet were in attendance. There was some general talk; and the President mentioned that Artemus Ward had sent him his book. [Artemus Ward was the pen-name of Charles Farrar Browne, a humorous writer of the day, whose style of humor appealed greatly to Abraham Lincoln.] Proposed to read a chapter which he thought very funny. Read it, and seemed to enjoy it very much. . . . The Chapter was "High-handed Outrage at Utica."

The President then took a graver tone and said:

"Gentlemen: I have, as you are aware, thought a great deal about the relation of this war to Slavery; and you all remember that, several weeks ago, I read to you an Order I had prepared on this subject, which, on account of objections made by some of you, was not issued. Ever since then, my mind has been much occupied with this subject, and I have thought all along that the time for acting on it might very probably come. I think the time has come now. I wish it were a better time. I wish that we were in a better condition. The action of the army against the rebels has not been quite what I should have best liked. But they have been driven out of Maryland, and Pennsylvania is no longer in danger of invasion. When the rebel army was at Frederick, I determined, as soon as it should be driven out of Maryland, to issue a Proclamation of Emancipation such as I thought most likely to be useful. I said nothing to any one; but I made the promise to myself, and . . . to my Maker. The rebel army is now driven out, and I am going to fulfill that promise.

"I have got you together to hear what I have written down. I do not wish your advice about the main matter—for that I have determined for myself. This I say without intending any thing but respect for any one of you. But I already know the views of each on this question. They have been heretofore expressed, and I have considered them as thoroughly and carefully as I can. What I have written is that which my reflections have determined me to say. If there is anything in the expressions I use, or in any other minor matter, which anyone of you thinks had best be changed, I shall be glad to receive the suggestions.

"One other observation I will make. I know very well that

many others might, in this matter, as in others, do better than I can; and if I were satisfied that the public confidence was more fully possessed by any one of them than by me, and knew of any Constitutional way in which he could be put in my place, he should have it. I would gladly yield it to him. But though I believe that I have not so much of the confidence of the people as I had some time ago, I do not know that, all things considered, any other person has more; and, however this may be, there is no way in which I can have any other man put where I am. I am here. I must do the best I can, and bear the responsibility of taking the course which I feel I ought to take."

The President then proceeded to read his Emancipation Proclamation, making remarks on the several parts as he went on, and showing that he had fully considered the whole subject, in all the lights under which it had been presented to him. . . .

[There then followed some discussion of minor changes in the Proclamation, which Lincoln readily agreed to. It was then issued as a preliminary Proclamation. The formal and definite Proclamation of Emancipation came on January 1, 1863.]

1862

The Monitor *Meets the* Merrimac

On March 9, 1862, the *Monitor* and the *Merrimac* at Hampton Roads, Virginia fought the world's first battle between ironclad vessels. Lieutenant S. Dana Greene, who assumed command of the *Monitor* when Captain John L. Worden was blinded by a direct hit on the pilot house, wrote this account a few days after the engagement in a letter to his family.

Source: GREENE, LIEUTENANT S. DANA. "An Eyewitness Account: 'I fired the first gun and thus commenced the great battle.'" *American Heritage*, June, 1957, pp. 13 and 102–103.

[On Thursday, March 6, the *Monitor* left New York harbor and was towed most of the way to Hampton Roads by the steamer *Seth Low*. It was a difficult trip and the officers and small crew of the *Monitor* got little sleep or rest. But the *Monitor* was needed to protect Union wooden ships from the ironclad *Merrimac*.]

. . . When about 1/3 way between Fortress Monroe and Cape Henry we spoke to a pilot boat and were told that the *Cumberland* was sunk, and the *Congress* on fire, and had surrendered to the *Merrimac*. We did not credit it at first, but as we approached . . . we could see the fine old *Congress* burning brightly, and we knew it must be so. Sadly indeed did we feel to think those 2 fine old vessels had gone to their last homes with so many of their brave crews. Our hearts were so very full and we vowed vengeance on the *Merrimac*, if it should ever be our lot to fall in with her.

At 9 P. M. [Saturday, March 8] we anchored near the Frigate *Roanoke*, the flag ship. . . . Captain Worden immediately went on board, and received orders to proceed to Newport News, and protect the *Minnesota* . . . from the *Merrimac*. . . . At 1 A. M. we anchored near the *Minnesota*. . . . At daylight we discovered the *Merrimac* at anchor, with several vessels under Sewells Point. We immediately made every preparation for battle. At 8 A. M. on Sunday the *Merrimac* got under weigh accompanied by several steamers and steered direct for the *Minnesota* and when a mile distant she fired 2 guns at the *Minnesota*. By this time our anchor was up, the men at quarters, the guns loaded, and everything ready for action.

As the *Merrimac* came closer the Captn passed the word to commence firing. I . . . fired the first gun and thus commenced the great battle between the *Monitor* & *Merrimac*.

Now mark the condition our men were in. Since Friday morning 48 hours, they had had no rest, and very little food, as we could not conveniently cook. They had been hard at work all night, had nothing to eat for breakfast except hard bread, and were thoroughly worn out. As for myself I had not slept a wink for 51 hours, and had been on my feet almost constantly. But after the first gun was fired we forgot all fatigue, hard work, and everything else—& went to work fighting as hard as men ever fought.

We loaded and fired as fast as we could—I pointed and fired the guns myself. Every shot I would ask the Captain the effect, and the majority of them were encouraging. The Captn. was in the Pilot House directing the movements of the vessel. . . .

Five times during the engagement we touched each other. . . . Once she tried to run us down with her iron prow, but did no damage whatever. After fighting 2 hours, we hauled off for half an hour to hoist our shot into the gun Tower. Then at it we went again as hard as we could. The shot, shell, grape, cannister, musket, and rifle, balls flew about in every direction, but did us no damage. Our tower was struck several times, and though the noise was pretty loud, it did not affect us any. . . .

At about 11:30 the Captn. sent for me. I went forward, & there he stood at the foot of the ladder of the Pilot House. His face was perfectly black with powder & iron & he was apparently perfectly blind. I asked him what was the matter. He said a shot had struck the Pilot House exactly opposite his eyes, and blinded him. . . . He told me to take charge of the ship, and use my own discretion. I led him to his room, and laid him on the sofa, and then took his position.

On examining the Pilot house, I found the iron hatch on top had been knocked about $\frac{1}{2}$ way off, & the second iron log from the top on the forward side was completely cracked through. We still continued firing, the tower being under the direction of Stimers. . . . I knew if another shot should strike our pilot house in the same place, our steering apparutus would be disabled, & we would be at the mercy of the batteries on Sewells point. The *Merrimac* was retreating towards the latter place. We had strict orders to act on the defensive, and *protect the Minnesota.*

. . . Our pilot house was damaged, & we had strict orders not to follow the *Merrimac* up. Therefore after the *Merrimac* had retreated, I went to the *Minnesota*, and remained by her. . . .

The fight was over now. . . . My men & myself were perfectly black with smoke, and powder. All my underclothes were perfectly black, and my person in the same condition. As we ran alongside the *Minnesota*, Secretary Fox [Assistant Secretary of the Navy Gustavus V. Fox] hailed us, & told us we had fought the greatest naval battle on record, and behaved as gallant as men could. He saw the whole fight.

I felt proud and happy then Mother, and felt fully repaid for all I had suffered. When our noble Captn. heard the *Merrimac* had retreated he said he was happy & willing to die since he had saved the *Minnesota*. . . .

General Lee Takes the Blame at Gettysburg

> The gallant charge of troops led by General Pickett on the
> third day of the Battle of Gettysburg has often been called the
> "High Tide of the Confederacy." Colonel Fremantle, a British
> military observer with Lee's army, tells here how he missed
> witnessing the charge but saw what happened afterward.
> Source: LORD, WALTER (editor). *The Fremantle Diary:
> Being the Journal of Lieutenant Colonel James Arthur Lyon
> Fremantle, Coldstream Guards, on his Three Months in the
> Southern States*, pp. 211–215. Little, Brown and Company, Bos-
> ton, 1954.

July 3rd. The distance between the Confederate guns and the
Yankee position . . . was at least a mile, quite open, gently un-
dulating, and exposed to artillery the whole distance. This was
the ground which had to be crossed in today's attack. Pickett's
division, which had just come up, was to bear the brunt in
Longstreet's attack. . . .

. . . Finding that to see the actual fighting it was absolutely
necessary to go into the thick of the thing, I determined to make
my way to General Longstreet. It was then about two-thirty.
After passing General Lee and his staff, I rode on through the
woods in the direction in which I had left Longstreet.

I soon began to meet many wounded men returning from the
front. . . . The farther I got, the greater became the number of
the wounded. . . . Some were walking alone on crutches composed of two rifles, others supported by men less badly wounded
than themselves, and others were carried on stretchers by the
ambulance corps. . . . They were still under a heavy fire; the
shells were continually bringing down great limbs of trees
and carrying further destruction amongst this melancholy procession. . . .

When I got close to General Longstreet, I saw one of his regiments advancing through the woods in good order. So, thinking
I was just in time to see the attack, I remarked to the General
that "I wouldn't have missed this for anything." Longstreet was
seated at the top of a . . . fence at the edge of the wood and
looking perfectly calm and imperturbed. He replied, laughing:

"The devil you wouldn't! I would like to have missed it very much; we've attacked and been repulsed; look there!"

For the first time I then had a view of the open space between the two positions and saw it covered with Confederates, slowly and sulkily returning toward us in small . . . parties, under a heavy fire of artillery. . . . The General told me that Pickett's division had succeeded in carrying the enemy's position and capturing his guns, but after remaining there twenty minutes, it had been forced to retire. . . .

Soon afterward I joined General Lee, who had in the meanwhile come to the front on becoming aware of the disaster. If Longstreet's conduct was admirable, that of Lee was perfectly sublime. He was engaged in rallying and in encouraging the broken troops. . . . His face, which is always placid and cheerful, did not show signs of the slightest disappointment, care, or annoyance. . . . He was addressing to every soldier he met a few words of encouragement, such as: "All this will come right in the end; we'll talk it over afterwards; but in the meantime, all good men must rally. We want all good and true men just now," etc. He spoke to all the wounded men that passed him, and the slightly wounded he exhorted to "bind up their hurts and take up a musket" in this emergency. Very few failed to answer his appeal, and I saw many badly wounded men take off their hats and cheer him.

He said to me, "This has been a sad day for us, Colonel—a sad day; but we can't expect always to gain victories." . . . I saw General Willcox . . . come up to him and explain, almost crying, the state of his brigade. General Lee immediately shook hands with him and said cheerfully: "Never mind, General, all this has been MY fault—it is I that have lost this fight, and you must help me out of it in the best way you can."

In this way I saw General Lee encourage and reanimate his somewhat dispirited troops and magnanimously take upon his own shoulders the whole weight of the repulse. It was impossible to look at him or to listen to him without feeling the strongest admiration. . . .

Caves Are the Fashion at Vicksburg

Union shelling forced Confederate non-combatants to live in caves during the Siege of Vicksburg, May 18–July 4, 1863. Mrs. Mary Ann Loughborough, wife of a Confederate officer, published her story of the siege and of life in the caves the year after Vicksburg surrendered.

Source: JONES, KATHERINE M. *Heroines of Dixie*, pp. 232–235. Copyright © 1955 by the Bobbs-Merrill Company, Inc., New York, reprinted by special permission of the publishers.

. . . The cave we inhabited was about five squares from the levee. A great many had been made in a hill immediately beyond us . . . and near this hill we could see most of the shells fall. Caves were the fashion—the rage—over besieged Vicksburg. Negroes, who understood their business, hired themselves out to dig them, at from thirty to fifty dollars, according to size. Many persons, considering different localities unsafe, would sell them to others, who had been less fortunate, or less provident. . . . So great was the demand for cave workmen, that a new branch of industry sprang up and became popular. . . .

Even the . . . animals seemed to share the general fear of a sudden and frightful death. The dogs would be seen in the midst of the noise to gallop up the street, and then to return, as if fear had maddened them. On hearing the descent of a shell, they would dart aside—then, as it exploded, sit down and howl in the most pitiful manner. There were many walking the street, apparently without homes. . . .

The horses, belonging to the officers, and fastened to the trees near the tents, would frequently strain the halter to its full length, rearing high in the air, with a loud snort of terror, as a shell would explode near. I could hear them in the night cry out in the midst of the uproar, ending in a low, plaintive whinny of fear. . . .

The hill opposite our cave might be called "death's point" from the number of animals that had been killed in eating the grass on the sides and summit. In all directions I could see the turf turned up, from the shells that have gone ploughing into the earth. Horses or mules that are tempted to mount the hill by the promise of grass that grows profusely there, invariably come limping down wounded, to die at the base, or are brought down dead from the summit.

A certain number of mules are killed each day by the commissaries, and are issued to the men, all of whom prefer the fresh meat, though it be of mule, to the bacon and salt rations that they have eaten so long a time without change. There have already been some cases of scurvy; the soldiers have a horror of the disease; therefore, I suppose, the mule meat is all the more welcome. Indeed, I petitioned . . . to have some served on our table. . . .

It was astonishing how the young officers kept up their spirits, frequently singing quartets . . . amid the pattering of Minié balls; and I often heard gay peals of laughter from headquarters, as the officers that had spent the day, and perhaps the night, previous in the rifle pits, would collect to make out reports. . . .

News came that one of the forts to the left of us had been undermined and blown up, killing sixty men; then of the death of the gallant Colonel Irwin, of Missouri; and again, the next day, of the death of the brave old General Green, of Missouri.

We were now swiftly nearing the end of our siege life: the rations had nearly all been given out. For the last few days I had been sick. . . . My little one had swung in her hammock, reduced in strength, with a low fever flushing in her face. . . . A soldier brought up, one morning, a little jaybird, as a plaything for the child. After playing with it for a short time, she turned wearily away. "Miss Mary," said the servant, "she's hungry; let me make her some soup from the bird." At first I refused: the poor little plaything should not die; then, as I thought of the child, I half consented. With the utmost haste, the servant disappeared; and the next time she appeared, it was with a cup of soup, and a little plate, on which lay the white meat of the poor little bird.

On Saturday a painful calm prevailed: there had been a truce proclaimed; and so long had the constant firing been kept up, that the stillness now was absolutely oppressive. . . . I put on my bonnet and sallied forth beyond the terrace, for the first time since I entered. . . .

I could now see how very near to the rifle pits my cave lay: only a small ravine between the two hills separated us. . . . No one knew, or seemed to know, why a truce had been made; but all believed that a treaty of surrender was pending. . . .

The next morning, M—— came up, with a pale face, saying: "It's

163

all over! The white flag floats from our forts! Vicksburg has surrendered!" . . .

After the surrender, an old gray-headed soldier, in passing on
the hill near the cave, stopped, and, touching his hat, said:

"It's a sad day this, madam; I little thought we'd come to it,
when we first stopped in the intrenchments. I hope you'll yet be
happy, madam, after all the trouble you've seen."

1863

John Torrey Meets a Mob on Fifth Avenue

Shortly after the Battle of Gettysburg, dissatisfied Irish Democrats rioted in New York City in protest against the draft. They
attacked rich people, Negroes, government officials, and well-
known Republicans. John Torrey, who worked in the United
States Treasury office in New York, tells of the riots in letters
to Asa Gray, a professor at Harvard University.

Source: DUPREE, A. HUNTER, and FISHEL, JR., LESLIE H.
(editors). "An Eyewitness Account of the New York Draft Riots,
July, 1863," *The Mississippi Valley Historical Review*, December,
1960, pp. 475–479.

July 13th, 1863. . . . We have had great riots in New York today
& they are still in progress. They were reported to us at the
Treasury office about noon. . . . Fresh accounts came in every
half hour & some of our Treasury officers . . . were alarmed. . . .
This afternoon . . . Mr. Mason came in & said that he saw a mob
stop two 3rd Avenue cars and take out some negroes & maltreat
them. This decided me to return home, so as to protect my
colored servants. I could go neither by the 3rd nor 6th Avenues,
as the cars had stopped. Taking the 4th Av. I found the streets
full of people. After getting off at 34th Street I found the whole
roadway & side walks filled with some rough fellows, & some
equally rough women, who were tearing up rails, cutting down
telegraph poles, & setting fire to buildings. . . .

The mob . . . came to our house, wishing to know if a Republican lived there. . . . They were going to burn [Columbia Col-
lege] Pres. King's house, as he was rich, & a decided Republican.

164

. . . The furious bareheaded and coatless men assembled under our windows & shouted aloud for Jeff. Davis! [Toward evening, the rioting quieted down in his neighborhood, so Torrey took a walk down 5th Avenue to survey the situation. There he found another mob, threatening to burn a rich man's house.] I conversed with one of the ring-leaders who told me they would burn the whole city before they got through. He said they were to take Wall St. in hand tomorrow! . . . Strange to say the military were nowhere to be seen at my latest investigation. There may be bloody times tomorrow.

Wednesday, July 15. You doubtless learn from the newspapers that our city is still in the power of a brutal mob. We were not molested on Monday night, & I slept well. . . . [Most of the horse cars and busses in the city have stopped running. There are many rumors of killings, rioting, burning, and other destruction of property.]

This morning I was obliged to ride down to the office in a hired coach. . . . At our office there had been no disturbance in the night. Indeed the people there were "spoiling for a fight." They had a battery of about 25 rifle barrels, carrying 3 balls each, & mounted on a gun-carriage. It could be loaded & fired with rapidity. We had also 10-inch shells, to be lighted & thrown out of the windows. . . .

Walking home we found that a large number of soldiers . . . are moving about. [Many of these soldiers had been sent by General Meade from Gettysburg.] The worst mobs are on the 1st & 2nd & 7th Avenues. Many have been killed there. [Police estimated that more than one thousand people were killed in the riots. Property damage amounted to over one million dollars.] Thieves are going about in gangs, calling at houses, & demanding money—threatening the torch if denied. They have been across the street this afternoon, & I saw them myself. . . .

This evening there was a great light north of us—and I found, on looking with a spyglass, that it was from the burning of a fine bridge over the Harlem valley, used by one of the railroads. There was some cannon-firing in the 1st Avenue, with what result I don't know.

The city looks very strangely. Nothing in Broadway but a few coaches. Most of the stores closed, but the side walks are full of people, & not a few ladies are out. . . .

Thursday, July 16. The cars are running this morning, but the stores are closed in the greater part of the 3rd Avenue. . . . [Marines are stationed at the Treasury office and the 7th Regiment is at its armory, ready to go wherever needed.] We feel that our chief danger is past. . . . We were in the most dangerous part of the city, & have been kept more or less anxious on account of our colored servants, but I trust we shall not be driven from our home. A friend . . . who visits us almost every week, & is known to be an abolitionist, had his house smashed up yesterday. . . .

1864

Private Tracy Describes the "Dead Line"

Both northern and southern prisoner-of-war camps were grim and unhealthy places, but the prison camp known as Andersonville, in Georgia, gained a particularly unpleasant reputation. You can see why by reading the testimony of Private Prescott Tracy, of New York, who was an exchanged prisoner from Andersonville in 1864.

Source: HARWELL, RICHARD B. (editor). *The Union Reader*, pp. 284–291. Longmans, Green and Co., Inc., New York, 1958.

On entering the Stockade Prison we found it crowded with twenty-eight thousand of our fellow-soldiers. By *crowded* I mean that it was difficult to move in any direction without jostling and being jostled. This prison is an open space . . . without trees or shelter of any kind. . . . The fence is made of upright trunks of trees, about twenty feet high, near the top of which are small platforms, where the guards are stationed. Twenty feet inside and parallel to the fence is a light railing, forming the "dead line," beyond which the projection of a foot or finger is sure to bring the deadly bullet of the sentinel.

Through the ground . . . runs or rather creeps a stream . . . varying from five to six feet in width, the water about ankle deep, and near the middle of the enclosure, spreading out into a swamp of about six acres. . . . Before entering this enclosure, the stream, or more properly sewer, passes through the camp of the guards, receiving from this source, and others farther up, a large amount of the vilest material. . . . The water is of a dark color, and an ordinary glass would collect a thick sediment. This was our only drinking and cooking water. It was our custom to filter it as best we could, through our remnants of haversacks, shirts and blouses. . . .

. . . The rebel authorities never removed any filth. There was seldom any visitation by the officers in charge. Two surgeons were at one time sent by President Davis to inspect the camp, but a walk through a small section gave them all the information they desired, and we never saw them again. . . .

Our only shelter from the sun and rain and night dews was what we could make by stretching over us our coats or scraps of blankets, which a few had, but generally there was no attempt by day or night to protect ourselves.

The rations consisted of eight ounces of corn bread, the cob being ground with the kernel, and generally sour, two ounces of condemned pork, offensive in appearance and smell. . . . To the best of my knowledge, information and belief, our ration was . . . a starving one, it being either too foul to be touched or too raw to be digested. . . .

The clothing of the men was miserable in the extreme. Very few had shoes of any kind, not two thousand had coats and pants, and those were late comers. More than one-half were indecently exposed, and many were naked.

. . . The "dead line" bullet, already referred to, spared no offender. One poor fellow, just from Sherman's army—his name was Roberts—was trying to wash his face near the "dead-line" railing, when he slipped . . . and fell with his head just outside the fatal border. We shouted to him, but it was too late—"another guard would have a furlough," the men said. It was a common belief among our men, arising from statements made by the guard, that General Winder, in command, issued an order that anyone of the guard who should shoot a Yankee outside of the "dead-line" should have a month's furlough, but there probably was no truth in this. About two a day were thus shot, some being cases of suicide, brought on by mental depression or physical misery, the poor fellows throwing themselves, or madly rushing outside the "line." . . .

Some few weeks before being released, I was ordered to act as clerk in the hospital. This consists simply of a few scattered trees and . . . tents, and is in charge of Dr. White, an excellent and considerate man, with very limited means, but doing all in his power for his patients. . . . I have seen one hundred and fifty bodies waiting passage to the "dead house," to be buried with those who died in the hospital. The average of deaths through the earlier months was thirty a day: at the time I left, the average was over one hundred and thirty, and one day the record showed one hundred and forty-six.

The proportion of deaths from starvation . . . I cannot state; but to the best of my knowledge, information and belief, there were scores every month. We could, at any time, point out many for whom such a fate was inevitable, as they lay or feebly walked, mere skeletons. . . . For example: in some cases the inner edges of the two bones of the arms, between the elbow and the wrist, with the intermediate blood vessels, were plainly visible when held toward the light. . . .

The number in camp when I left was nearly thirty-five thousand, and daily increasing. The number in hospital was about five thousand. . . .

1864

"In the Name of Humanity, How Is She to Get Along?"

The rapid rise in the cost of living during the Civil War brought protests such as this one on behalf of the printers in New York city.
Source: *The Printer*, New York, July, 1864, p. 102.

We have "gone through the mill," and "know whereof we speak," and are satisfied that no family embracing four children can exist in comfort on less than the following:

One bag of flour	$1.40
Small measure of potatoes, daily, at 13¢ per day .	.91
One quarter of a pound of tea	.32
One pound of coffee (mixed or adulterated—can't afford better)	.35
Three and a half pounds of sugar	.80
Meats for the week	$3.00
Two bushels of coal	$1.20
Four pounds of butter	$1.60
Two pounds of lard	.38
Kerosene	.20
Soap, starch, pepper, salt, vinegar, etc.	.75
Vegetables	.50
Dried apples (to promote the health of children)	.25
Sundries	.44
Rent	$4.00
Total	$16.10

Every old housekeeper is aware that, in addition to the above, there are numberless calls for three cents here, and five cents there, and that an additional dollar might squarely be added to our estimate. But we will suppose the printer's wife to be as firm as a rock on the subject of expenses, and that she *will* keep within the absolute necessities; and even then, in the name of humanity, how is she to get along? The average wages of all branches of printers in this city is sixteen dollars per week—the average family consists of the number stated. How, then, are these families to subsist, if . . . every dollar is consumed for food and house-rent? Wearing apparel has trebled in price, and not one dollar is left from the weekly wage to procure a supply. Every workman's family is short of house-linens, underclothing, shoes, etc.; and the fortunate printer that has more than one suit to his back, or whose wife can boast of more than a change of calicoes, can scarcely be found.

It may be objected that our estimate of weekly expenses is too high—that the rent item can be reduced. But let any family man carefully inspect the items, and he will be satisfied they cannot be reduced, except on the half-ration principle. As to rent, if the printer takes his family into a crowded tenement house, he may possibly save a little—only to be doubly swallowed up in doctor's bills, and the general health of his wife and children materially affected.

But where is the remedy?

The remedy consists in one of two courses. Either the workman must have his wages . . . increased, or be paid in the gold standard of four years ago. The average value of sixteen dollars now paid is really only eight dollars; and what printer was expected to support a family on that pittance four years ago?

The old-fashioned eleven dollars a week, gold standard, enabled the workman to live. At the present value of paper money, the minimum wages must be twenty-two dollars to place the journeyman in the position he formerly occupied at eleven dollars per week. It matters little which way it is done, so long as the receipts are made equal to the expenditures. Only let it be done, and let the employers feel and acknowledge that the increase is reasonable and called for by the peculiar circumstances of the times.

1865-1866

Georgians Describe "The Great Robber"

John Trowbridge visited the desolated South in 1865 and 1866, then published a book about what he saw. Here he tells of Sherman's march through Georgia.

Source: TROWBRIDGE, JOHN T., edited with an introduction by Gordon Carroll. *The Desolate South, 1865–1866; A Picture of the Battlefields and of the Devastated Confederacy*, pp. 253–257. Duell, Sloan and Pearce, New York, 1956.

According to a tradition which I found current in middle Georgia, General Sherman remarked, while on his grand march through the state, that he had his gloves on as yet, but that he would take them off in South Carolina. . . . At mention of this, however, many good Georgians . . . blazed with indignation: "If he had his gloves on here, I should like to know what he did with his gloves off!" A Confederate brigadier general said to me:

"One could track the line of Sherman's march all through Georgia and South Carolina by the fires on the horizon. He burned the ginhouses, cotton presses, railroad depots, bridges, freighthouses and unoccupied dwellings, with some that were occupied. He stripped our people of everything. He deserves to be called the great robber of the nineteenth century. . . ."

The citizens talked with equal freedom of the doings of the "Great Robber." A gentleman of Jones County said:

"I had a noble field of corn, not yet harvested. Old Sherman came along and turned his droves of cattle right into it, and in the morning there was no more corn there than there is on the back of my hand. His devils robbed me of all my flour and bacon and corn meal. They took all the pillow-slips, . . . dresses, . . . sheets and bed quilts they could find in the house to tie their plunder in. You couldn't hide anything but they'd find it."

A lady living near Milledgeville was the president of a soldiers'-aid society. At the time of Sherman's visit she had in her house a box full of stockings knit by patriotic ladies for the feet of the brave defenders of their country. This box she buried in a field which was afterwards ploughed, in order to obliterate all marks of concealment. A squadron of cavalry arriving at this field formed in line, charged over it, and discovered the box by a hollow sound it gave forth under the hoofs. The box was straightway brought to light, to the joy of many a stockingless invader, who had the fair ladies of Milledgeville to thank for his warm feet that winter.

Sherman's field orders show that it was not his intention to permit indiscriminate destruction and plundering. Yet these orders appear to have been interpreted very liberally. A regiment was usually sent ahead with instructions to guard private dwellings; but as soon as the guards were removed, a legion of stragglers and Negroes rushed in to pillage; and . . . in some cases even the guards pilfered industriously. . . .

"The Federal Army generally behaved very well in this state," said a Confederate officer. "The destruction of railroads, mills, and ginhouses, if designed to cripple us, was perfectly justifiable. But you did have as mean a set of stragglers following your army as ever broke jail. . . . Your fellows hung several men in my neighborhood to make 'em tell where their money was. Some gave it up after a little hanging; but I know one man who went to the limb three times, and saved his money and his life too.

Another man had three hundred dollars in gold hid in his garden. He is very fat; weighs, I suppose, two hundred and fifty pounds. He held out till they got the rope around his neck, then he caved in. 'I'm dogged,' says he, 'if I'm going to risk my weight on a rope just for a little money!'"

Sherman's invasion cannot properly be called a raid. . . . Sherman had under his command four infantry corps and a corps of cavalry, pursuing different routes, their . . . tracks sometimes crossing each other, braiding a belt of devastation from twenty-five to fifty miles in breadth, and upwards of six hundred miles in extent. The flanking parties driving the light-footed Rebel cavalry before them; bridges fired by the fugitives; pontoon trains hurrying to the front of the advancing columns when streams were to be crossed; the hasty corduroying of bad roads; the jubilant foraging parties sweeping the surrounding country of whatever was needful to support life and vigor in those immense crawling and bristling creatures called army corps; the amazing quantity and variety of plunder collected together on the routes of the wagon trains . . . the ripping up of railroads; the burning and plundering of plantations; the encampment at evening; the kindling of fires; the sudden disappearance of fences and the equally sudden springing up of shelter-tents, like mushrooms, all over the ground; the sleep of the vast, silent, guarded hosts; and the hilarious awakening to the toil and adventures of a new day—such are the scenes of this momentous expedition, which painters, historians, romancers will in future labor to conceive and portray.

Warned by the flying cavalry, and the smoke and flames of plantations on the horizon, the panic-stricken inhabitants thought only of saving their property and their lives from the invaders. Many fled from their homes carrying the most valuable of their possessions, or those which could be most conveniently removed. Mules, horses, cattle, sheep, hogs were driven wildly across the country, avoiding one foraging party perhaps only to fall into the hands of another. The mother caught up her infant; the father, mounting, took his terrified boy upon the back of his horse behind him; the old man clutched his moneybag and ran; not even the poultry, not even the dogs were forgotten; men and women shouldered their household stuffs, and abandoned their houses to the mercies of the soldiers, whose waving banners and bright steel were already appearing on the distant hilltops.

172

1865

A Teen-Ager Sees "A Horrid Sight!"

Emma LeConte was seventeen when Sherman's march
prompted these entries in her diary. She lived in Columbia,
South Carolina, where her father had taught chemistry at South
Carolina College.

Source: MIERS, EARL SCHENCK (editor). *When the World
Ended: The Diary of Emma LeConte*, pp. 8–42, *passim.* Oxford
University Press, New York, 1957.

Jan. 4, 1865. . . . I am constantly thinking of the time when
Columbia will be given up to the enemy. The horrible picture is
constantly before my mind. They have promised to show no
mercy in this State. . . .

Jan. 21. . . . Everyone seems to feel that Columbia is doomed.
Aunt Josie thinks we had all better run off . . . and camp in the
woods of North Carolina till danger is over. . . .

Oh, what times to live in! Who knows what may become of
us in ten days! . . . Nothing could surprise me now, unless some
wonderful help should break in upon our trouble and give us the
independence we have been longing and fighting for all these
sad years. Even my books fail to keep my attention. . . .

Jan. 23. . . . It may be of interest some day to recall the poor
style in which we lived during the war, so I shall make a few
notes. My underclothing is of coarse unbleached homespun, such
as we gave the negroes formerly, only much coarser. My stockings I knit myself, and my shoes are of heavy calfskin. My
dresses are two calicoes (the last one bought cost sixteen dollars
a yard), a homespun of black and white plaid, and . . . a couple
of old silks, carefully preserved for great occasions. . . . The
homespun cost about eight or ten dollars a yard—calico is twenty
to thirty dollars a yard now, and going higher from week to
week. My shoes are one hundred and fifty dollars a pair. In two
or three months, these prices will be doubled.

We live tolerably poorly. Two meals a day. Two plates of
bread for breakfast. . . . Corn itself is forty dollars a bushel.
Dinner consists of a very small piece of meat, generally beef, a
few potatoes and a dish of hominy and a pone of corn bread.

We have no reason to complain, so many families are so worse off. Many have not tasted meat for months, and we, too, having a cow, are able to have butter. Wood is hard to get at one hundred dollars a load. We keep but one fire in the dining room where we sit. We have been fortunate in having gas (lights) thus far . . . but now and then it is cut off and we burn tallow candles at two dollars apiece. We never have sweet things now, and even molasses candy is a rarity seldom to be thought of.

Jan. 27. . . . How dreadfully sick I am of this war. Truly we girls, whose lot it is to grow up in these times, are unfortunate! It commenced when I was thirteen, and I am now seventeen and no prospect yet of its ending. No pleasure, no enjoyment— nothing but rigid economy and hard work—nothing but the stern realities of life. These which should come later are made familiar to us at an age when only gladness should surround us. . . .

Feb. 14. . . . What a panic the whole town is in! I have not been out of the house myself, but Father says the intensest excitement prevails on the streets. The Yankees are reported a few miles off on the other side of the river. How strong no one seems to know.

Feb. 16. How can the terror and excitement of today be described! . . . The breakfast hour passed in comparative calm. About nine o'clock we were sitting in the dining room. . . . "Wouldn't it be dreadful if they should shell the city?" someone said. "They would not do that," replied Mother, "for they have not demanded its surrender." Scarcely had the words passed her lips when Jane, the nurse, rushed in crying out that they were shelling. We ran to the front door just in time to hear a shell go whirring past. It fell and exploded not far off. This was so unexpected. I do not know why, but in all my list of anticipated horrors I somehow had not thought of a bombardment. If I had only looked for it, I wouldn't have been so frightened. . . .

The shelling was discontinued for an hour or two and then renewed with so much fury that we unanimously resolved to adjourn to the basement and abandon the upper rooms. . . .

10 o'clock p. m. (The rest of the family) is trying to sleep. I don't think I shall attempt it. . . . Perhaps the Yankees may be in to-night—yet I do not feel as frightened as I thought I would be. . . .

Feb. 17. One o'clock p. m. Well, they are here. I was sitting

174

in the back parlor when I heard the shouting of troops. I was at the front door in a moment. Jane came running and crying, "Oh, Miss Emma, they've come at last!" She said they were then marching down Main Street, before them flying a panic-stricken crowd of women and children who seemed crazy. . . . I ran upstairs to my bedroom windows just in time to see the U. S. flag run up over the State House. Oh, what a horrid sight! What a degradation! After four long years of bloodshed and hatred, now to float there at last! That hateful symbol of despotism! I do not think I could possibly describe my feelings. I know I could not look at it. I left the window and went back downstairs to Mother. . . .

1865

Grant Tells of Lee's Surrender

On April 9, 1865, General Lee surrendered his exhausted Army of Northern Virginia to Lieutenant General U. S. Grant at Appomattox Court House, Virginia. Lee wrote no memoirs, but Grant told this story in his memoirs, written twenty years later.

Source: *Personal Memoirs of U. S. Grant,* Vol. II, pp. 489–95. Charles L. Webster & Company, New York, 1885.

When I had left camp that morning I had not expected (the surrender) so soon and consequently was in rough garb. I was without a sword, as I usually was when on horseback on the field, and wore a soldier's blouse for a coat, with the shoulder straps of my rank to indicate to the army who I was. When I went into the house [of Mr. McLean] I found General Lee. We greeted each other, and after shaking hands took our seats. I had my staff with me, a good portion of whom were in the room during the whole of the interview.

What General Lee's feelings were I do not know. As he was a man of much dignity, with an impassable face, it was impossible to say whether he felt inwardly glad that the end had finally come, or felt sad over the result, and was too manly to show it.

Whatever his feelings, they were entirely concealed from my observation; but my own feelings . . . were sad and depressed. I felt like anything rather than rejoicing at the downfall of a foe who had fought so long and valiantly, and had suffered so much for a cause, though that cause was, I believe, one of the worst for which a people ever fought. . . .

General Lee was dressed in a full uniform which was entirely new, and was wearing a sword of considerable value . . . an entirely different sword from the one that would ordinarily be worn in the field. In my rough traveling suit, the uniform of a private with the straps of a lieutenant-general, I must have contrasted very strangely with a man so handsomely dressed, six feet high and of faultless form. But this was not a matter that I thought of until afterwards.

We soon fell into a conversation about old army times. He remarked that he remembered me very well in the old army; and I told him that . . . I remembered him perfectly, but from the difference in our rank and years (there being about sixteen years' difference in our ages), I had thought it very likely that I had not attracted his attention. . . . Our conversation grew so pleasant that I almost forgot the object of our meeting. After the conversation had run on in this style for some time, General Lee called my attention to the object of our meeting . . . by suggesting that the terms I proposed to give his army ought to be written out. I called to General Parker, secretary on my staff, for writing materials, and commenced writing out the . . . terms.

[The terms provided that the Army of Northern Virginia should surrender and not take up arms again during the continuance of the war, but that officers could keep their side arms, horses, and private baggage.]

. . . When (General Lee) read over that part of the terms about side arms, horses, and private property of the officers, he remarked with some feeling, I thought, that this would have a happy effect upon his army.

Then, after a little further conversation, General Lee remarked to me again that . . . in their army the cavalrymen and artillerists owned their own horses; and he asked if he was to understand that the men who so owned their horses were to be permitted to retain them. I told him that as the terms were written they

176

would not; that only the officers were permitted to take their private property. . . .

I then said to him that I thought this would be about the last battle of the war—I sincerely hoped so; and I said further I took it that most of the men in the ranks were small farmers. The whole country had been so raided by the two armies that it was doubtful whether they would be able to put in a crop to carry themselves and their families through the next winter without the aid of the horses they were then riding. The United States did not want them and I would, therefore . . . let every man of the Confederate army who claimed to own a horse or a mule take the animal to his home. Lee remarked again that this would have a happy effect. . . .

The much talked of surrendering of Lee's sword and my handing it back, this and much more that has been said about it is the purest romance. The word sword or side arms was not mentioned by either of us until I wrote it in the terms. . . .

General Lee, after all was completed and before taking his leave, remarked that his army was in a very bad condition for want of food . . . that his men had been living for some days on parched corn exclusively, and that he would have to ask me for rations. . . . I told him "certainly," and asked for how many men he wanted rations. His answer was "about twenty-five thousand." I authorized him to send . . . to Appomattox Station, two or three miles away, where he could have, out of the trains we had stopped, all the provisions wanted. . . .

When news of the surrender first reached our lines our men commenced firing a salute of a hundred guns in honor of the victory. I at once sent word . . . to have it stopped. The Confederates were now our prisoners, and we did not want to exult over their downfall. . . .

Gideon Welles Describes Lincoln's Last Hours

Lincoln's Secretary of the Navy kept a diary throughout the war years. In it he recorded many of history's most dramatic moments, including this description of Lincoln's death.

Source: BEALE, HOWARD K. (editor). *The Diary of Gideon Welles*, Vol. II, pp. 283–288. W. W. Norton & Co., Inc., New York, 1960.

I had retired to bed about half past ten on the evening of the 14th of April and was just getting asleep when . . . my wife said some one was at our door. . . . I arose at once and raised a window, when my messenger, James Smith, called to me that Mr. Lincoln . . . had been shot. . . .

I immediately dressed myself and, against the earnest remonstrance of appeals of my wife, went directly to Mr. Seward's whose residence was on the east side of the square, mine being on the north. . . .

[There Welles met Secretary of War Stanton who told him Seward and his son had been attacked by an assassin and it began to appear that there was a plot afoot to kill off all the leaders of the Union government.]

As we descended the stairs, I asked Stanton what he had heard in regard to the President that was reliable. He said the President was shot at Ford's Theater, that he had seen a man who was present and had witnessed the occurrence. I said I would go immediately to the White House. Stanton told me the President was not there but was at the theater. "Then," said I, "let us go immediately there." He said that was his intention and asked me, if I had not a carriage, to go with him. . . . The streets were full of people. Not only the sidewalks but the carriage-way was to some extent occupied, all or nearly all hurrying toward Tenth Street. When we entered that street we found it pretty closely packed.

The President had been carried across the street from the theater to the house of a Mr. Peterson. We entered by ascending a flight of steps . . . and passing through a long hall to the rear where the President lay extended on a bed, breathing heavily. Several surgeons were present, at least six. . . . I inquired of Doctor Hall, as I entered, the true condition of the President. He replied the President was dead, to all intents, although he might live three hours or perhaps longer.

The giant sufferer lay extended diagonally across the bed, which was not long enough for him. . . . His large arms, which were occasionally exposed, were of a size which one would scarce have expected from his spare appearance. His slow, full respiration lifted the clothes with each breath that he took. His features were calm and striking. I had never seen them appear to better advantage than for the first hour . . . that I was there. . . .

. . . The room was small and overcrowded. The surgeons and members of the cabinet were as many as should have been in the room, but there were many more, and the hall and other rooms in the front . . . were full. One of these rooms was occupied by Mrs. Lincoln and her attendants. . . . About once an hour Mrs. Lincoln would come to the bedside of her dying husband and with lamentation and tears remain until overcome by emotion.

A door which opened upon a porch . . . and also the windows were kept open for fresh air. The night was dark, cloudy, and damp, and about six it began to rain. I remained in the room until then . . . listening to the heavy groans and witnessing the wasting life of the good and great man who was expiring before me.

About 6 A. M. I experienced a feeling of faintness . . . and took a short walk in the open air. It was a dark and gloomy morning, and rain set in before I returned to the house some fifteen minutes later. Large groups of people were gathered . . . all anxious and solicitous. Some one or more from each group stepped forward as I passed to inquire into the condition of the President and to ask if there was no hope. Intense grief was on every countenance when I replied that the President could survive but a short time. . . .

A little before seven I went into the room where the dying President was rapidly drawing near the closing moments. His wife soon after made her last visit to him. . . . Robert, his son, stood with several others at the head of the bed. He bore himself well but on two occasions gave way to overpowering grief and sobbed aloud. . . . The respiration of the President became suspended at intervals and at last entirely ceased. . . .

179

1865

A Yankee Meets a Rebel Miss

The writer of this revealing incident was Sidney Andrews, a northern reporter who toured the South a few months after the war ended. The encounter took place on a train between Charleston and Orangeburg, South Carolina.

Source: ANDREWS, SIDNEY. *The South since the War: as Shown by 14 Weeks of Travel and Observation in Georgia and the Carolinas*, pp. 12–14. Ticknor & Fields, Boston, 1866.

We left Charleston at seven and a half o'clock in the morning. . . . In front of me sat a good-looking young woman, of about twenty-two, I judged. Hearing her very plainly say that she was going to Orangeburg, I determined to ask her about the town and its hotel accommodations.

"Yes, I live there," she said.

"Is there a hotel in the town, or any place at which a person can stop?"

"O yes, there's a hotel," she said; and after a pause, she added, "but it's hardly such a place as a gentleman would choose, I think."

She spoke pleasantly enough, and, having answered my question, might have dropped the conversation; instead of which, she went on to say that persons who had occasion to stop in town for some days frequently took a room at a private house, and were much better suited than at the hotel. I did the only thing I well could do,—the thing that it was perfectly natural I should do. I asked her if she could mention one or two private houses at which I might ask for accommodations, if the hotel proved unendurable. I fully expected that she would say her mother sometimes accommodated gentlemen; and I may as well admit that I had determined what reply I should make to that announcement.

Instead, however, she turned in her seat so as to face me, and said, with considerable vim, "Are you a Yankee?"

The question surprised me; and I simply answered, "From the North."

"By what right do you presume to speak to me, sir?" she asked, in a clear and snapping tone, that caught the ears and eyes of most of the passengers.

The strangeness of the question, no less than the remarkable change in her manner, coupled with the fact that I knew myself to be under the observation of thirty or more persons of Southern birth and feeling, embarrassed me to such degree that I could only stammer, "By the right which I supposed a gentleman always had to ask a lady a civil question."

"Well, sir, I don't choose to talk with you." And she settled herself sharply into her seat, jerked her little body into a very upright position, and squared her shoulders in a very positive manner,—while I sat flushed and confused.

What should I do about it? That was a question I asked myself twenty times per hour for the next thirty miles. I was seriously inclined to apologize, though I hardly knew for what; but didn't for I feared the little Rebel might snub me again, if I gave her an opportunity. In front of her sat a young man who had been a captain in the Rebel army. Him she soon engaged in conversation, and they cheered the slow miles with most lively chat. . . . I could have borne her indignation quite easily; but each individual in the car soon made me aware that my Yankee baseness was well known. . . .

The forenoon wore away, and the crazy old engine dragged itself along. Little Miss was vivacious and entertaining; the ex-officer was evidently in a cheerful frame of mind; I sat alternating between repentance and indignation. Finally the whistle sounded for Branchville.

Missy rose in her seat, shook out her skirts, drew on her small thread glove, turned to me,—mind you, not to the ex-officer, but to me,—and asked me if I would be good enough to hand out her basket for her.

Here was another surprise. Queer creatures, these little Rebels, said I to myself, as I followed her, carrying the not heavy basket. She didn't stop when we reached the platform of the station-house, but walked on toward its upper end; and I followed, demurely, but wonderingly. Fifteen or twenty yards away from the car, she suddenly stopped, and turned quickly upon me with "Thank you; I want to apologize to you; I was rude."

And here was the greatest surprise of all! It caught me in confusion; but I managed to say something to the effect that perhaps I was too forward in asking the question I did.

"No, you were not. It was right that you should ask it, and I was rude to answer you so uncivilly. But you caught me at a disadvantage; I hadn't spoken to a Federal since Sumter was taken."

"Well, it didn't hurt you very much, did it?" said I. Whereat she laughed and I laughed, and then the engine whistled.

"I'm going to stop here a day or two," she remarked; and then, "You'll shake hands, won't you?" as I started for the car. So we shook hands, and I left her standing on the platform.

1865

"Come Down Here and Help Us Build"

> Northern businessmen, northern capital, and northern ideas invaded the South after the war. These, with the help of energetic southerners, created the "New South."
>
> Source: ANDREWS, SIDNEY. *The South since the War: as Shown by 14 Weeks of Travel and Observation in Georgia and the Carolinas*, pp. 1–4. Ticknor & Fields, Boston, 1866.

A city of ruins, of desolation, of vacant houses, of widowed women, of rotting wharves, of deserted warehouses, of weed-wild gardens, of miles of grass-grown streets, of acres of pitiful barrenness—that is Charleston wherein Rebellion loftily reared its head five years ago. . . .

We can never again have the Charleston of the decade previous to the war. . . . Five millions of dollars could not restore the ruin of these past four years; and that sum is . . . far beyond the command of the city. . . . Yet, after all, Charleston was Charleston because of the hearts of its people. Now one marks how few young men there are, how generally the young women are dressed in black. The flower of their proud aristocracy is buried on scores of battle-fields. If it were possible to restore the broad acres of crumbling ruins to their foretime style and uses, there would even then be but the dead body of Charleston.

The Charleston of 1875 will doubtless be proud in wealth and intellect and rich in grace and culture. . . . Yet the place has not in itself recuperative power for such a result. The material on which to build that fair structure does not here exist, and, as I am told by dozens, cannot be found in the State. If Northern capital and Northern energy do not come here, the ruin, they say, must remain a ruin. . . .

It was noted on the steamship by which I came from New York that . . . our passengers were from Charleston and from Massachusetts. We had nearly as many Boston men as Charleston men. . . .

Of Massachusetts men, some are already in business here, and others came on to "see the lay of the land," as one of them said. "That's all right," observed an ex-Rebel captain in one of our after-dinner chats,—"that's all right; let's have Massachusetts and South Carolina brought together, for they are the only two States that amount to anything."

"I hate all you Yankees most heartily in a general sort of way," remarked another of these Southerners; "but I find you clever enough personally, and I expect it'll be a good thing for us to have you come down here with your money, though it'll go against the grain with us pretty badly."

There are many Northern men here already, though one cannot say that there is much Northern society, for the men are either without families or have left them at home. Walking out yesterday with a . . . Charlestonian . . . he pointed out to me the various "Northern houses"; and I shall not exaggerate if I say that this classification appeared to include at least half the stores on each of the principal streets. "The presence of these men," said he, "was at first very distasteful to our people, and they are not liked any too well now; but we know they are doing a good work for the city."

I fell into some talk with him concerning the political situation. . . . When I asked him what should be done, he answered: "You Northern people are making a great mistake in your treatment of the South. We are thoroughly whipped; we give up slavery forever; and now we want you to quit reproaching us. Let us–back into the Union, and then come down here and help us build up the country."

Sam Clemens Writes of Cats and Centipedes

Samuel Clemens had not yet gained his great reputation as a
writer when he visited Hawaii in 1866, thirty-two years before
the islands were annexed by the United States. But he was well
on his way as this selection testifies.

Source: CLEMENS, SAMUEL L. *Roughing It*, Vol. II, pp. 176–
180. Harper and Brothers, New York.

On a certain bright morning the Islands hove in sight, lying
low on the lonely sea, and everybody climbed to the upper deck
to look. After two thousand miles of watery solitude the vision
was a welcome one. As we approached, the imposing promontory
of Diamond Head rose up out of the ocean, its rugged front softened by the hazy distance, and presently the details of the land
began to make themselves manifest; first the line of beach; then
the plumed cocoanut trees of the tropics; then cabins of the natives; then the white town of Honolulu, said to contain between
twelve and fifteen thousand inhabitants, spread over a dead level;
with streets from twenty to thirty feet wide, solid and level as a
floor, most of them straight as a line and few as crooked as a
corkscrew.

The further I traveled through the town the better I liked it.
Every step revealed a new contrast—disclosed something I was
unaccustomed to. In place of the grand mud-colored brown
fronts of San Francisco, I saw dwellings built of straw, adobes,
and cream-colored pebble-and-shell conglomerated coral, cut into
oblong blocks and laid in cement; also a great number of neat
white cottages, with green window-shutters; in place of front
yards like billiard-tables with iron fences around them, I saw
these homes surrounded by ample yards, thickly clad with green
grass, and shaded by tall trees, through whose dense foliage the
sun could scarcely penetrate. . . . I saw luxurious banks and
thickets of flowers, fresh as a meadow after a rain, and glowing
with the richest colors. . . . I saw huge-bodied, wide-spreading
forest trees, with strange names and stranger appearance—trees
that cast a shadow like a thunder-cloud, and were able to stand
alone without being tied to green poles. . . . I saw cats—Tom

184

cats, Mary-Ann cats, long-tailed cats, bob-tailed cats, blind cats, one-eyed cats, wall-eyed cats, cross-eyed cats, gray cats, black cats, white cats, yellow cats, striped cats, spotted cats, tame cats, wild cats, individual cats, groups of cats, platoons of cats, companies of cats, regiments of cats, armies of cats, multitudes of cats, millions of cats, and all of them sleek, fat, lazy, and sound asleep. . . .

. . . Instead of wretched cobblestone pavements, I walked on a firm foundation of coral, built up from the bottom of the sea by the absurd but persevering insect of that name, with a light layer of lava and cinders overlying the coral, belched up out of fathomless perdition long ago through the seared and blackened crater that stands dead and harmless in the distance now. Instead of cramped and crowded street cars, I met . . . native women sweeping by, free as the wind, on fleet horses . . . with gaudy riding-sashes streaming like banners behind them. . . . I breathed the balmy fragrance of jasmine, oleander, and the Pride of India. In place of the hurry and bustle and noisy confusion of San Francisco, I moved in the midst of a summer calm. . . . When the sun sunk down . . . it was . . . luxury to sit in the perfumed air and forget that there was any world but these enchanted islands.

It was such ecstasy to dream and dream—till you got a bite. A scorpion bite. Then the first duty was to get up out of the grass and kill the scorpion; and the next to bathe the bitten place with alcohol . . . and the next to resolve to keep out of the grass in the future. Then came an adjournment to the bedchamber and the pastime of writing up the day's journal with one hand and the destruction of mosquitoes with the other—a whole community of them at a slap. . . . Then to bed and become a promenade for a centipede with forty-two legs on a side and every foot hot enough to burn a hole through a rawhide. More soaking with alcohol, and a resolution to examine the bed before entering it, in future. Then wait, and suffer, till all the mosquitoes in the neighborhood have crawled in under the bar, then slip out quickly, and shut them in and sleep peacefully on the floor till morning. Meantime it is comforting to curse the tropics in occasional wakeful intervals. . . .

Kelley Keeps Step with the Music of the Age

Oliver H. Kelley founded the Patrons of Husbandry, better known as the Grange, in 1867. As he wrote in this circular, sent to farmers throughout the country, his objectives for the Grange were social and economic, rather than political. Nevertheless, in the 1870's, the Granges did become the basis for farmers' political parties.

Source: KELLEY, OLIVER H. *Patrons of Husbandry*, pp. 125–130.

National Grange, Washington, D. C.
September, 1868.

In response to numerous inquiries in regard to the organization and objects of our Order, this circular is issued. The Order was organized . . . by a number of distinguished agriculturists of various states of the Union, at Washington, in December, 1867, and since then has met with most encouraging success, giving assurance that it will soon become one of the most useful and powerful organizations in the United States. Its grand object is not only improvement in husbandry, but to increase the general happiness, wealth and prosperity of the country. It is founded upon the axioms that the products of the soil comprise the basis of all wealth; that individual happiness depends upon general prosperity, and that the wealth of a country depends upon the general intelligence and mental culture of the producing classes. . . .

Women are admitted into our Order, as well as young persons of both sexes over the ages of sixteen and eighteen respectively. In its proceedings a love for rural life will be encouraged, the desire for excitement and amusement, so prevalent in youth, will be gratified. . . . Not, however, in frivolities . . . but by directing attention to the wonder-workings of nature, and leading the mind to enjoy and appreciate that never-ending delight which follows useful studies, relating to the animal, vegetable and mineral kingdoms. . . .

We ignore all political or religious discussions in the Order. . . . Its objects . . . are to advance education, to elevate and dignify the occupation of the farmer, and to protect its members against the numerous combinations by which their interests are injuriously affected. There is no association that secures so many advantages to its members as this. . . .

In the meetings of this Order, all but members are excluded, and there is in its proceedings a symbolized Ritual, pleasing, beautiful and appropriate, which is designed not only to charm the fancy, but to cultivate and enlarge the mind, and purify the heart, having, at the same time, strict adaptation to rural pursuits.

It is an order in which all persons will find innocent recreation and valuable instruction, pecuniary profit and mutual protection. . . .

Among other advantages which may be derived from the Order can be mentioned: systematic arrangements for procuring and disseminating information relative to crops, demand and supply, prices, markets and transportation throughout the country; and for the establishment of depots for the sale of special and general products in the cities; also for the purchase and exchange of stock, seeds, and desired varieties of plants and trees; and for the purpose of procuring help at home or from abroad, and situations for persons seeking employment; also for ascertaining and testing the merits of newly invented farming implements . . . and for detecting and exposing those that are unworthy; and for protecting by all available means, the farming interests from fraud and deception of every kind.

In conclusion, we desire that agricultural societies shall keep step with the music of the age, and keep pace with improvements in the reaping machine and steam engine. In this Order we expect to accomplish these results. Every Grange is in intimate relation with its neighboring Granges, and these with the State Grange, and the State Granges are in unity with the National Grange. Valuable information and benefits enjoyed by one are communicated to all. The old style of Farmers' Clubs, like the old sickle and flail, were very good in their day, but they are of the past, and are too far behind all other enterprises in the progress of civilization. Hence the necessity of this new Order.

O. H. Kelley, Secretary of the National Grange

A Visitor Thinks Our Girls Eat Too Much Pie

The Reverend David Macrae, from Scotland, visited the
United States in the late 1860's and wrote down the following
delightful impressions of American women.

Source: MACRAE, DAVID. *The Americans at Home*, pp. 39–43.
Reprinted by permission of E. P. Dutton & Company, Inc.

. . . I found many women discharging public functions which
have in Britain been monopolized by men. In New Jersey I found
a lady "Doctoress" Fowler, acting as a public physician, with the
reputation of being the most skillful, and having the largest and
most lucrative practice in the district. . . . In different parts of
the country I heard ladies delivering public lectures—one of them,
Miss Anna Dickinson, amongst the most popular in the States. In
Massachusetts I heard of a female . . . clergy*woman* . . . the
Rev. Olympia Brown, who has a good congregation. . . . I heard
of "another of the same," the Rev. Miss Chapin, pastor of the
Milwaukee Society. . . .

At Albany, in the State Normal School, I found a dark-eyed
young lady, not long out of her teens, officiating as a professor
of mathematics . . . and watching a whiskered student considerably older than herself demonstrate a proposition on the blackboard, correcting him whenever he went wrong. In Chicago
when I was there the *Legal News* was edited by a lady; and another lady was acting on the Board of Examiners for the Chicago
High School. But these cases, though more common than in
Britain, are still few and far between. . . . American women, as a
rule, are just as gentle, as kind, as agreeable, as affectionate, and
as lovely as our own. . . .

American girls, however, . . . are generally *too* pale and thin.
. . . The American girls themselves, I think, are nervous about
their thinness, for they are constantly having themselves weighed,
and every ounce of increase is hailed with delight. . . . I asked
one beautiful Connecticut girl, whom I met in Pennsylvania, how
she liked the change. "Oh, immensely!" she said, "I have gained
eighteen pounds . . . since last April." It sounds very odd to a
stranger. Every girl knows her own weight to within an ounce or
two, and is ready to mention it at a moment's notice. . . .

But to return to the complexion. This paleness in the American girls, though often beautiful, is too universal; an eye from the old country begins to long for a rosy check. . . . My private impression is . . . the peculiar paleness of the . . . girls connects itself with too much . . . pie. I have strong convictions on this subject of pie. Not to speak of mere paleness, I don't see how the Americans can . . . live to the age they do, considering the amount of pie they eat, and the rapidity with which they generally eat it. I rarely sat down to dinner in America . . . without finding pie . . . often of several kinds, on the table. . . . Everybody partook of it, down to the . . . baby. Pie seems indispensable. . . . I believe the prohibition of pie would precipitate a revolution. . . .

Paleness and pie notwithstanding, the American girls are very delightful. And in one point they fairly surpass the majority of English girls—they are all educated and well informed. . . . The admirable educational system . . . covering the whole area of society, has given them education whether they are rich or poor, has furnished them with a great deal of general information, and has quickened their desire for more. An American girl will talk with you about anything, and . . . seem to feel interest in it. Their tendency is perhaps to talk too much, and . . . it seemed to me sometimes to make no perceptible difference whether they knew anything of the subject they talked about or not. But they usually know a little of everything; and their general intelligence and vivacity make them very delightful companions.

Before I went to America, I had an impression that American ladies spent time on intellectual pursuits to the neglect of household duties. I did not find it so. Comparing class with class they are quite as good housekeepers as I have seen anywhere. They had need to be, for service at present is in a very wretched condition in America; so much so that middle-class families . . . often dispense with servants altogether. The young American ladies are taught to make beds as well as demonstrate propositions in geometry, and their mental efforts never interfere with the perfection of their pies. Samuel Johnson used to say that a man would rather that his wife should be able to cook a good dinner than read Greek. But he does not seem to have anticipated a time when a woman could learn to do both.

A Scotsman Meets Democracy Aboard
an Iron Horse

Because of the vast distances to be covered and because of
the spirit of democracy, railroad travel in the United States
developed differently from railroad travel in Britain. The Reverend David Macrae comments on some of these differences.
Source: MACRAE, DAVID. *The Americans at Home*, pp. 455-
460. Published by E. P. Dutton & Co., Inc., and reprinted with
their permission.

. . . It seems to me that America, in some of her railway . . .
comforts has left the rest of the world behind. On one of the
Western lines, I travelled several hundreds of miles in a train
where, by the payment of a few extra dollars, you secure a beautiful little parlour and bedroom all to yourself. . . . It is like a
little travelling hotel. These . . . are only found as yet on a few
of the longest and most traveled lines. But almost every train
that runs by night in Canada or the States carries a sleeping car,
where the payment of an extra dollar secures you a tolerably
comfortable berth, in which . . . you may sleep as soundly as you
would in your own bed at home.

To understand this and many of the other peculiarities of railway travelling in America, it is necessary to remember that the
. . . "cars" are not divided into compartments like ours, with
doors at the side. You enter by a door opening from a little platform at the end, and find yourself in what seems a long narrow
room with a passage down the middle, and sixteen or twenty
little cross sofas on each side. . . . If you find the one you first
enter full, you can step along the passage, and out upon the little
platform at the other end, from which you can step . . . to the
platform of the next car, and so, if you like, thread the whole
train.

This construction clears the way for almost all the conveniences
that make railway travelling in America so much pleasanter and
less fatiguing than in Britain. There is a stove at one end of
every car, and a fountain at the other. If you feel cold, you can
go and heat yourself at the stove; if you feel thirsty, you can

go to the fountain and have a drink. . . . The same arrangement allows you, if you want a smoke, to pass forward when you please to the smoking car; or, if night comes on, to pass rearward to the sleeping car. It also allows the conductor to pass through and examine or collect the tickets without any stoppage of the train: and allows the "train-boy" to pass to and fro, selling such articles as travellers may be supposed to want. . . .

In cars constructed like this there is of course no separation of classes. . . . In the ordinary cars, which charge about the same as British second class . . . all classes are together. The Irish servant-girl pays the same fare as the Vice-President of the United States, and takes her seat beside him. Everyone has a cushioned seat, a carpet, a rail for his feet, an ornamental rack for his luggage, and a lattice blind to screen him from the sun. . . .

There are inconveniences connected with this state of things, but they are far fewer than I had been led to expect. . . . While the privacy that is possible in Britain is impossible here . . . this mingling of all classes . . . is one of the ways in which the people, high and low, are being educated for the new form of society to which the world is moving. . . . One notices in these American cars that the millionaire, finding that the laborer can sit on the same seat and claim equal rights, learns to be accommodating, and to take his seat not as a millionaire but as a man. . . . The laborer finding that he is amongst ladies and gentlemen, and is expected to act like a gentleman himself, becomes polite. . . . Of course men and masses of men are not refined in a day, but the process of education is going on.

1869

A Workman Meets an Unknown Knight

Uriah Stephens, a tailor from Philadelphia, founded the Loyal Order of the Knights of Labor as a secret society in 1869. He wrote this secret initiation ceremony, which explains the Order's objectives and the reasons for its secrecy when first founded. Source: An undated manual of the Knights of Labor.

Opening Service: Precisely at the hour for opening, the Master Workman . . . shall give one rap and say, "All persons not entitled to sit with us will please retire." After a short pause he will say, "The proper Officer will satisfy himself that all present are entitled to sit with us. . . ."

Initiation: (The Assistant Unknown Knight meets the candidate in the vestibule.)

Ass't. Unknown Knight: Do you believe in God, the Creator and Universal Father of All?

Candidate: I do.

Ass't. Unknown Knight: Do you obey the Universal Ordinance of God, in gaining your bread by the sweat of your brow?

Candidate: I do.

Ass't. Unknown Knight: Are you willing to take a solemn vow binding you to Secrecy, Obedience, and Mutual Assistance?

Candidate: I am.

(The candidate is turned over to the Unknown Knight who brings him into the main room. There the Master Workman has formed the Assembly of Knights in a circle, with an opening through which the Unknown Knight and the candidate enter.)

Unknown Knight: Master Workman, Mr. (candidate's name) has satisfactorily answered all inquiries and now desires to be covered with our shield and admitted to fellowship in this noble and holy Order.

Master Workman: (After a short pause and amid perfect silence) Place him in the center and administer the vow.

The Candidate's Vow: I, ——— ———, do truly and solemnly swear (or affirm) that I will never reveal, by word, act . . . or implication . . . the name or object of this Order (or) the name . . . of any member . . . (or) its signs, mysteries, arts, privileges or benefits. . . .

I do truly and solemnly promise that I will to the best of my ability, defend the life, interest, reputation, and family of all true members of this Order, help and assist all employed and unemployed, unfortunate, or distressed Brothers to procure employment, secure just remuneration, relieve their distress and counsel others to aid them. . . .

192

All this I swear without reservation or evasion. . . . So help me God, and keep me steadfast to the end.

(The Unknown Knight then takes the candidate to the Worthy Foreman for instruction.)

Unknown Knight: Worthy Foreman, by permission of this Assembly . . . and the command of the Master Workman, I present to you Mr. —— ——, for instruction.

Worthy Foreman: In the beginning God ordained that man should labor, not as a curse, but as a blessing; not as a punishment, but as a means of development. . . . By labor is brought forth the kindly fruits of the earth in rich abundance. . . . Labor is noble and holy. . . . To defend it from degradation; to divest it of the evils to body, mind, and estate which ignorance and greed have imposed; to rescue the toiler from the grasp of the selfish is a work worthy of the noblest and best of our race. Without your seeking, without even your knowledge, you have been selected from among your fellows for that exalted purpose. Are you willing to accept the responsibility and . . . labor with what ability you possess, for the triumph of these principles among men?

(If the candidate answers affirmatively, the Unknown Knight and the Worthy Foreman take him back to the Master Workman.)

Worthy Foreman: Master Workman, I present Mr. —— —— as a fitting and worthy person to receive the honor of fellowship with this noble and holy Order.

Master Workman: (taking the candidate's hand) On behalf of the toiling millions of earth, I welcome you to this Sanctuary, dedicated to the service of God, by serving humanity. Open and public associations having failed . . . to protect or advance the interest of labor, we have lawfully constituted this Assembly. Hid from public view, covered by an impenetrable veil of secrecy (not to promote or shield wrong doing) but to shield ourselves and you, from persecution and wrong . . . when we endeavor to secure the just reward of our toil.

In using this power of organized effort and co-operation, we but imitate the example of capital heretofore set in numberless instances. In all the . . . branches of trade, capital has its combinations, and whether intended or not, it crushes the manly hopes of labor and tramples poor humanity in the dust. We mean no conflict with legitimate enterprise, no antagonism to necessary capital, but men in their haste and greed, blinded by self interest, overlook the interests of others, and sometimes even violate the rights of those they deem helpless.

We mean to uphold the dignity of labor, to affirm the nobility of all who live in accordance with the ordinance of God, "in the sweat of thy brow shalt thou eat bread." We mean to create a healthy public opinion on the subject of labor . . . and the justice of its receiving a full, just share of the values or capital it has created. We shall with all our strength, support laws made to harmonize the interests of labor and capital . . . and also those laws which tend to lighten the exhaustiveness of toil.

We shall use every lawful and honorable means to procure and retain employment for one another, coupled with just and fair remuneration, and should accident or misfortune befall one of our number, render such aid as lies within our power to give, without inquiring his country or his creed; and, without approving of general strikes . . . yet should it become justly necessary to enjoin an oppressor, we will protect and aid any of our members who thereby may suffer loss, and as opportunity offers, extend a helping hand to all branches of honorable toil. . . .

Your duties and obligations, your privileges and benefits you will learn as you mingle with, and become acquainted in, the noble and holy Order of the K_____ of L____. (The name of the organization was always given by secret signs and never pronounced by the members.)

1869

The Irish and Chinese Meet on Promontory Hill

Alexander Toponce was the author of this colorful eyewitness account of the historic occasion when the rails were joined to unite America's east and west coast by railroad.

Source: TOPONCE, KATIE. *Reminiscences of Alexander Toponce, Pioneer*, pp. 177–179. Century Printing Company, Salt Lake City, Utah, 1923.

I saw the Golden Spike driven at Promontory, Utah, on May 10, 1869. I had a beef contract to furnish meat to the construction camps. . . . The Golden Spike could have been driven a couple of weeks earlier than it was. But the two companies had settled on Promontory as the meeting place some days prior to the actual meeting. . . .

If the Union Pacific had crowded their work as hard as the Central Pacific did in the last two weeks the Golden Spike would have been driven a good many miles to the west. The Union Pacific employed white labor, largely Irish, and the Central Pacific had Chinese labor. The Irish and Chinese met on Promontory Hill. . . .

On the last day only about 100 feet of rails were laid, and everybody tried to have a hand in the work. I took a shovel from an Irishman, and threw a shovel full of dirt on the ties just to tell about it afterward. . . .

It was a very hilarious occasion; everybody had all they wanted to drink all the time. Some of the participants got "sloppy" and these were not all Irish and Chinese by any means.

California furnished the Golden Spike. Governor Tuttle of Nevada furnished one of silver. Governor Stanford . . . presented one of gold, silver, and iron from Arizona. The last tie was of California laurel.

When they came to drive the last spike, Governor Stanford, president of the Central Pacific, took the sledge, and the first time he struck he missed the spike and hit the rail.

What a howl went up! Irish, Chinese, Mexicans, and everybody yelled with delight. Everybody slapped everybody else on the back and yelled, "He missed it. Yee!" The engineers blew the whistles and rang their bells. Then Stanford tried it again and tapped the spike and the telegraph operators had fixed their instruments so that the tap was reported in all the offices, east and west, and set bells to tapping in hundreds of towns and cities. . . .

Then Vice President T. C. Durant of the Union Pacific took up the sledge and he missed the spike the first time. Then everybody slapped everybody else again and yelled, "He missed it, too. Yow!"

It was a great occasion, everyone carried off souvenirs and there are enough splinters of the last tie in museums to make a good bonfire. When the connection was finally made the Union Pacific and the Central Pacific engineers ran their engines up until their pilots touched. Then the engineers shook hands and had their pictures taken and each broke a bottle of champagne on the pilot of the other's engine and had their pictures taken again. . . .

Both before and after the spike driving ceremony there were speeches, which were cheered heartily. I do not remember what any of the speakers said now, but I do remember that there was a great abundance of champagne.

1870's and 1880's

A Cowboy Describes the Long Drive

Cattlemen on the western plains did not fence their cattle in. Instead, they allowed them to graze free on the government-owned grass lands. Each spring cowboy outfits got together and sorted out their cattle in a spring round up, a description of which follows.

Source: WESTERMEIER, CLIFFORD P. (editor and compiler). *Trailing the Cowboy: His Life and Lore as Told by Frontier Journalists*, pp. 64–69. The Caxton Printers, Ltd., Caldwell, Idaho, 1955.

Branding is the most important feature of ranch life. . . . Each owner . . . has his brands, such as 7K, LX, LIT, etc. These brands are on the left or right side of the animal. In addition, ranchers marked their cattle with distinctive marks on the animals' ears. The purpose of an earmark is greater safety to owners, but also it is a labor-saver to the cowboys. Brands are difficult to see when crowded into herds, but both ears are . . . pointed forward as soon as one attracts the animals' attention. This enables a rider, as he moves through a herd searching for the cattle of a certain brand, to find his animals with ease. . . .

Each outfit takes an assigned post and all together make a line along the southern border of the range . . . sometimes a distance of one hundred and fifty miles. Then the round up begins, all moving to the north, covering the entire country, and bringing the cattle along much on the same principle that a room is swept. . . . This is hard work on horses, and a cowboy generally saddles three of his seven ponies each day, reserving the best one for hard and unusual work during dark and stormy nights. . . .

The purpose of bringing all the cattle as far northward as possible is to keep them on the proper range. Cattle in any voluntary movement of their own never work north and but seldom and slightly to the east or west. Every storm, however, coming as storms do from the north, sends the cattle to the south and unless turned back yearly . . . the cattle of the entire Western country, from the Yellowstone south, would in time pack themselves into . . . southern Texas between the Rio Grande and the Gulf.

An outfit from the beginning of the round up points to some corral or branding pen. On its arrival there the marking of the calves begins. A branding pen . . . is circular in form and made of twelve foot timbers stuck endwise in the ground. . . . There is one opening through which the cattle are driven. . . . As many of the cows and calves as will fill the corral are forced through the entrance and locked in, and then the fires are lighted. . . . Every calf is branded with the brand on its mother, the roper calling the brand to the men at the fires, as he rides up dragging the victim. As fast as a penful is branded it is turned loose on the range and the pen is refilled from the herd. The work is continued until completed when the outfit again moves northward and resumes the further collection and branding of the cattle until the range has been completely and thoroughly combed. . . .

All through the blistering, sunburned day, the bunch of cattle, guarded by the men . . ., crawl slowly to the north. . . . At night a gently sloping hillside is picked to bed the cattle on. The range boss, assisted by the riders . . . rounds up and stops the herd. . . . Nine riders are divided into three guards of three men each—the first to ride herd until eleven o'clock, the second going on until three o'clock and the third holding the herd until morning.

"It looks like it might be a bad night," says the range boss, "so you all better ketch up and saddle your night ponies and be ready to go on herd any minute."

Supper of bacon, biscuit and canned sweet corn is over and every man's best horse, brought up and saddled, is left to wait any necessity which may arise. By eight o'clock each tired rider not on herd is asleep in his blankets. Two hours go by. . . . Suddenly a flash of lightning blazes in the northwest and soon a dull rumble of thunder follows. . . .

All hands are roused out and, grumbling . . . ride to the herd. A stampede must be avoided for with so many grazing cattle in a herd it would be doubly disastrous. The riders . . . go circling about the herd . . . accompanying their efforts with whistle, song and shout. Meanwhile the rain begins. . . . The lightning grows brighter. . . . The thunder . . . has grown into a constant, never ending roar, and the frightened herd with heads upraised and glaring eyes push about, ready on the instant to stampede. This would mean serious business, this turning $100,000 worth of cattle loose in pitch darkness, to break their scampering legs and frightened necks over precipice and rock. So the boys crowd upon the herd, still circling it, riding harder and singing louder than ever.

At last morning breaks and the storm . . . dies away. The herd again is composed and the tired boys . . . come riding up to breakfast.

1870

Hamlin Gets His Face Washed in the Snow

Hamlin Garland wrote in realistic fashion of everyday farm life on the midwestern prairies and plains as it was from the 1860's to about 1900. This selection from his autobiography, *A Son of the Middle Border*, describes the type of one-room school in which millions of midwestern farm boys and girls got their formal education in the late nineteenth century.

Source: GARLAND, HAMLIN. *A Son of the Middle Border*, pp. 95–97. The Macmillan Company, New York, 1923.

The school-house which was to be the center of our social life stood on the bare prairie . . . and like thousands of other similar buildings in the west, had not a leaf to shade it in summer nor a branch to break the winds of savage winter. "There's been a good deal of talk about setting out a wind-break," neighbor Button explained to us, "but nothing has as yet been done." It was merely a square pine box painted a glaring white on the outside and a desolate drab within; at least drab was the original color, but the benches were mainly so greasy and hacked that original intentions were obscured. It had two doors on the eastern end and three windows on each side.

A long square stove, . . . a wooden chair, and a rude table in one corner, for the use of the teacher, completed the movable furniture. The walls were roughly plastered and the windows had no curtains. . . .

With what fear, what excitement we approached the door on that first day. . . . All the scholars were strange to me except Albert and Cyrus Button, and I was prepared for rough treatment. However, the experience was not so harsh as I had feared. True, Rangely Field did throw me down and wash my face in snow, and Jack Sweet tripped me up once or twice, but I bore these indignities with such grace and dignity as I could command, and soon made a place for myself among the boys. . . .

I cannot remember much of that first winter of school. It was not an experience to remember for its charm. Not one line of grace, not one touch of color relieved the room's bare walls or softened its harsh windows. Perhaps this very barrenness gave to the poetry in our readers an appeal that seems magical, certainly it threw over the faces of Frances Babcock and Mary Abbie Gammons a lovelier halo. They were "the big girls" of the school, that is to say, they were seventeen or eighteen years old. Frances was the special terror of the teacher, a pale and studious pigeon-toed young man who was preparing for college.

In spite of the cold, the boys played open air games all winter. "Dog and Deer," "Dare Gool" and "Fox and Geese" were our favorite diversions, and the wonder is that we did not all die of pneumonia, for we battled so furiously during each recess that we often came in wet with perspiration and coughing so hard that for several minutes recitations were quite impossible. But we were a hardy lot and none of us seemed the worse for our colds.

There was not much chivalry in the school—quite the contrary, for it was dominated by two or three big rough boys and the rest of us took our tone from them. To protect a girl, to shield her . . . required a good deal of bravery and few of us were strong enough to do it. Girls were foolish, ridiculous creatures, set apart to be laughed at or preyed upon at will. To shame them was a great joke. How far I shared in these barbarities I cannot say but that I did share in them I know, for I had very little to do with my sister Harriet after crossing the school-house yard. She kept to her tribe as I to mine.

1871

A Grand Jury Condemns the Ku Klux Klan

Southern whites' opposition to Reconstruction sometimes took the form of secret societies, such as the Ku Klux Klan. Congress outlawed the Klan in 1871, partly because of reports from federal grand juries, like this one in South Carolina.

Source: HART, ALBERT BUSHNELL (editor). *American History Told by Contemporaries*, Vol. IV, pp. 495–497. The Macmillan Company, New York, 1950.

To the Judges of the United States Circuit Court:

In closing the labors of the present term, the grand jury beg leave to submit the following . . .: During the whole session we have been engaged in investigations of the most grave and extraordinary character—investigations of the crimes committed by the organization known as the Ku Klux Klan. The evidence . . . has been voluminous, gathered from the victims themselves and their families, as well as those who belong to the Klan and participated in its crimes. The jury has been shocked . . . at the number and character of the atrocities committed, producing a state of terror and a sense of utter insecurity among a large portion of the people, especially the colored population. The evidence produced before us has established the following facts:

1. That there has existed in 1868, in many counties of the State, an organization known as the "Ku Klux Klan" . . . which embraces in its membership a large proportion of the white population of every profession and class.

2. That this Klan is bound together by an oath, administered to its members at the time of their initiation into the order, of which the following is a copy:

200

"I, (name), before the immaculate Judge of Heaven and Earth, and upon the Holy Evangelists of Almighty God, do, of my own free will and accord, subscribe to the following sacredly binding obligation:

"1. We are on the side of justice, humanity, and constitutional liberty, as bequeathed to us in its purity by our forefathers.

"2. We oppose and reject the principles of the radical party.

"3. We pledge mutual aid to each other in sickness, distress, and pecuniary embarrassment.

"4. Female friends, widows, and their households, shall ever be special objects of our regard and protection.

"Any member divulging, or causing to be divulged, any of the foregoing obligations, shall meet the fearful penalty and traitor's doom, which is Death! Death! Death!"

That in addition to this oath the Klan has a constitution and by-laws, which provides, among other things, that each member shall furnish himself with a pistol, a Ku Klux gown, and a signal instrument. That the operations of the Klan were executed in the night, and were invariably directed against members of the Republican party by warnings to leave the country, by whippings, and by murder.

3. That in large portions of the counties of York, Union, and Spartanburgh . . . the civil law has been set at defiance, and ceased to afford any protection to the citizens.

4. That the Klan, in carrying out the purposes for which it was organized and armed, inflicted . . . vengeance on the colored citizens of these counties, by breaking into their houses at the dead of night, dragging them from their beds, torturing them in the most inhuman manner, and in many instances murdering them; and this, mainly, on account of their political affiliations. . . .

5. That for this condition of things, for all these violations of law and order, and the sacred rights of citizens, many of the leading men of these counties were responsible. It was proven that large numbers of the most prominent citizens were members of the order. . . .

The jury has been appalled as much at the number of outrages as at their character, it appearing that eleven murders and over six hundred whippings have been committed in York County alone. Our investigation in regard to the other counties named has been less full; but it is believed, from the testimony, that an equal or greater number has been committed in Union, and that the number is not greatly less in Spartanburgh and Laurens.

We are of the opinion that the most vigorous prosecution of the parties implicated in these crimes is imperatively demanded; that without this there is great danger that these outrages will be continued, and that there will be no security to our fellow-citizens of African descent.

We would say further, that unless the strong arm of the Government is interposed to punish these crimes . . ., there is every reason to believe that an organized and determined attempt at retaliation will be made, which can only result in a state of anarchy and bloodshed too horrible to contemplate.

1871

Europeans Are Invited to a Grand Buffalo Hunt

> An estimated 15,000,000 buffaloes roamed the Great Plains at one time. By 1885, the buffaloes were nearly extinct, destroyed by hunters for food, clothing, profit, and sport. Many European sportsmen came to hunt buffalo and other big game in the American West. Posters such as the following, which appeared in England, attracted them.
>
> Source: FAULKNER, VIRGINIA (compiler and editor). *Roundup: A Nebraska Reader*, p. 51. University of Nebraska Press, Lincoln, 1957.

GRAND BUFFALO HUNT

A Grand Buffalo Hunt will be held in September next, on the prairies of NEBRASKA AND COLORADO, United States, and through the magnificent valley of the Republican River, the rich . . . feeding grounds of the buffalo. The valley of the Republican River possesses some of the most varied and magnificent scenery in America, the wild pastures are rich in grasses, and it is most beautifully wooded and watered by clear streams and rivulets. The southern portion of Nebraska, through which the Republican Valley passes, will bear comparison either for climate, soil, or picturesque scenery with any country.

The Burlington and Missouri-River Railroad Company own some millions of acres of land . . . and will aid and assist this Hunting Party in every way, in order that the Sportsmen of England may see the Western Country . . . Mr. Charles S. Dawson, who left England last April, has made arrangements with a corps of Western Hunters, Trappers, and Scouts, of the Western Frontier of the United States, for a Grand Hunt on the plains of Nebraska and Colorado, and in the valley of the Republican River, where Buffalo, Elk, Antelope, Red Deer, Beaver, Otter, Wild Turkey, Prairie Chicken, &c., abound in large numbers; the Buffalo in herds of from 3,000 to 10,000. THERE ARE NO HOSTILE INDIANS IN NEBRASKA WHATEVER; friendly chiefs of the Otoes, Pawnees, &c., will accompany the party.

Sportsmen will be provided with army tents and beds during the Hunt, and everything generally found in a first-class Hotel. There will be servants to take care of the horses, and in fact all arrangements have been made to give the Hunting party the greatest amount of pleasure with the least possible trouble. Wagons will be provided for the conveyance of any trophies of the chase, such as Buffalo Skins, Elk Horns and Antlers in limited quantity.

> FARE—*For the Round Trip of about Seven Weeks including every expense, except Wines, Liquors, Cigars, Guns, Rifles, and Ammunition, 90 Guineas.*
>
> The arrangements will be such as to admit of Ladies joining the party, but the charge for Ladies will be 100 Guineas each.

For further particulars apply to

**THE BURLINGTON AND MISSOURI-RIVER
RAILROAD COMPANY**

Booker T. Washington Passes His Entrance Exam

> Booker T. Washington was born a slave a few years before the Civil War and grew to be the best-known leader of his race. Here he tells the story of how he determined to go to college while working in the mines at Malden, West Virginia.
>
> Source: WASHINGTON, BOOKER T. *Up from Slavery*, pp. 42–53, *passim*. Doubleday & Company, Inc., New York, 1951.

One day, while at work in the coal-mine, I happened to over-hear two miners talking about a great school for coloured people somewhere in Virginia. This was the first time that I had ever heard anything about any kind of school or college that was more pretentious than the little coloured school in our town. . . .

As they went on describing the school, it seemed to me that it must be the greatest place on earth, and not even Heaven presented more attractions for me at that time than did the Hampton Normal and Agricultural Institute in Virginia, about which these men were talking. I resolved at once to go to that school, although I had no idea where it was, or how many miles away, or how I was going to reach it. . . .

In the fall of 1872 I determined to make an effort to get there. . . . I do not think that anyone thoroughly sympathized with me in my ambition . . . unless it was my mother, and she was troubled with a grave fear that I was starting out on a "wild-goose chase." . . . Perhaps the thing that touched and pleased me most in connection with my starting for Hampton was the interest that many of the older coloured people took in the matter. They had spent the best days of their lives in slavery, and hardly expected to see the time when they would see a member of their race leave home to attend a boarding-school. Some of these older people would give me a nickel, others a quarter, or a handkerchief.

Finally the great day came, and I started for Hampton. I had only a small, cheap satchel that contained what few articles of clothing I could get. . . . The distance from Malden to Hampton is about five hundred miles. I had not been away from home many hours before it began to grow painfully evident that I did not have enough money to pay my fare to Hampton. . . . By walking, begging rides both in wagons and in the railroad cars, in some way, after a number of days, I reached the city of Richmond, Virginia, about eighty-two miles from Hampton. . . . When I reached Richmond, I was completely out of money. . . .

I must have walked the streets till after mid-night. At last I became so exhausted that I could walk no longer. . . . Just about the time when I reached extreme physical exhaustion, I came upon a portion of a street where the board sidewalk was considerably elevated. I waited for a few minutes, till I was sure that no passers-by could see me, and then crept under the sidewalk and lay for the night upon the ground, with my satchel of clothing for a pillow.

The next morning . . . I was extremely hungry, because it had been a long time since I had had sufficient food. As soon as it became light enough for me to see my surroundings I noticed that I was near a large ship, and that this ship seemed to be unloading a cargo of pig iron. I went at once to the vessel and asked the captain to permit me to help unload the vessel in order to get money for food. The captain . . . consented. I worked long enough to earn money for my breakfast, and it seems to me . . . to have been about the best breakfast that I have ever eaten.

My work pleased the captain so well that he told me if I desired I could continue working for a small amount per day. This I was very glad to do and I continued working on this vessel for a number of days. In order to economize in every way possible, so as to be sure to reach Hampton in a reasonable time, I continued to sleep under the same sidewalk that gave me shelter the first night I was in Richmond. . . .

When I had saved what I considered enough money with which to reach Hampton, I thanked the captain of the vessel for his kindness, and started again. Without any unusual occurrence I reached Hampton, with a surplus of exactly fifty cents with which to begin my education. . . .

As soon as possible after reaching the grounds of the Hampton Institute, I presented myself before the head teacher for assignment to a class. Having been so long without proper food, a bath and change of clothing, I did not, of course, make a very favorable impression upon her, and I could see at once that there were doubts in her mind about the wisdom of admitting me as a student. . . . After some hours had passed, the head teacher said to me: "The adjoining recitation-room needs sweeping. Take the broom and sweep it."

It occurred to me at once that here was my chance. . . . I swept the recitation-room three times. Then I got a dusting-cloth and I dusted it four times. . . . I had the feeling that in a large measure my future depended upon the impression I made upon the teacher in the cleaning of that room. When I was through, I reported to the head teacher. . . . When she was unable to find one bit of dirt on the floor, or a particle of dust on any of the furniture, she quietly remarked, "I guess you will do to enter this institution."

I was one of the happiest souls on earth. The sweeping of that room was my college examination, and never did any youth pass an examination for entrance into Harvard or Yale that gave him more genuine satisfaction. I have passed several examinations since then, but I have always felt that this was the best one I ever passed. . . .

1874

Captain Jones Helps Make a Steel King

Andrew Carnegie arrived in America from Scotland in 1848 as a penniless lad of thirteen. After making money in many enterprises, in 1874 he concentrated on the steel industry and by 1900 controlled the bulk of United States steel production. He didn't do all this by himself, of course, and in his autobiography Carnegie acknowledges the help of many men, such as "Captain" Jones.

Source: MILLER, MARGARET CARNEGIE (copyright holder). *The Autobiography of Andrew Carnegie*, pp. 195–197. Houghton Mifflin Company, Boston, 1948.

The (Thomson) mills were at last about ready to begin and an organization the auditor proposed was laid before me for approval. I found he had divided the works into two departments and had given control of one to Mr. Stevenson . . . and control of the other to a Mr. Jones. Nothing, I am certain, ever affected the success of the steel company more than the decision which I gave upon that proposal. Upon no account could two men be in the same works with equal authority. An army with two commanders-in-chief, a ship with two captains, could not fare more disastrously than a manufacturing concern with two men in command upon the same ground, even though in two different departments. I said:

"This will not do. I do not know Mr. Stevenson, nor do I know Mr. Jones, but one or the other must be made captain and he alone must report to you."

The decision fell upon Mr. Jones and in this way we obtained "The Captain," who . . . made his name famous wherever the manufacture of Bessemer steel is known.

The Captain was . . . quite young, spare and active, bearing traces of his Welsh descent even in his stature, for he was quite short. He came to us as a two-dollar-a-day mechanic from the neighboring works at Johnstown. We soon saw that he was a character. Every movement told it. He had volunteered as a private during the Civil War and carried himself so finely that he became captain of a company which was never known to flinch. Much of the success of the Edgar Thomson Works belongs to this man.

In later years he declined an interest in the firm which would have made him a millionaire. I told him one day that some of the young men who had been given an interest in the company were now making more than he was and we had voted to make him a partner. . . .

"No," he said, "I don't want to have my thoughts running on business. I have enough trouble looking after these works. Just give me a h_ _l of a salary if you think I'm worth it."

"All right, Captain, the salary of the President of the United States is yours."

"That's the talk," said the little Welshman.

Our competitors in steel were at first disposed to ignore us . . . and declined to recognize us as competitors. . . . But so perfect was our machinery, so admirable the plans, so skillful were the men selected by Captain Jones, and so great a manager was he himself, that our success was phenomenal. . . .

Young Garland Does a Grown Man's Job

> Even with the help of crude machinery, farming on the western plains in the 1870's and 1880's was hard work. In his autobiography, Hamlin Garland gives this realistic picture of harvest-time activities.
>
> Source: GARLAND, HAMLIN. *A Son of the Middle Border*, pp. 148–151. The Macmillan Company, New York, 1923.

Reaping generally came about the 20th of July, the hottest and dryest part of the summer, and was the most pressing work of the year. It demanded early rising for the men, and it meant an all day broiling over the kitchen stove for the women. Stern, incessant toil went on inside and out from dawn until sunset, no matter how the thermometer sizzled. On many days the mercury mounted to ninety-five in the shade, but with wide fields all yellowing at the same moment, no one thought of laying off. A storm might sweep it flat, or if neglected too long, it might "crinkle."

Our reaper in 1874 was a new model of the McCormick self-rake. . . . True the McCormick required four horses to drag it but it was effective. It was hard to believe that anything more cunning would ever come to claim the farmer's money. Weird tales of a machine on which two men rode and bound twelve acres of wheat in ten hours came to us, but we did not . . . believe these reports. On the contrary we accepted the self-rake as quite the final word in harvesting machinery and cheerily bent to the binding of sheaves with their own straw in the good old time-honored way.

No task save that of "cradling" surpassed in severity "binding on a station." It was a full-grown man's job, but every boy was ambitious to try his hand, and when at fourteen years of age I was promoted from "bundle boy" to be one of the five hands to bind after the reaper, I went to my corner with joy and confidence. . . .

I was short and broad-shouldered with large strong hands admirably adapted for this work, and for the first two hours, easily held my own with the rest of the crew, but as the morning wore on and the sun grew hotter, my enthusiasm waned. . . . My breakfast had been ample, but no mere stomachful of food could carry a growing boy through five hours of desperate toil. Along about a quarter to ten, I began to scan the field with anxious eye, longing to see my sister Harriet and the promised luncheon basket.

Just when it seemed that I could endure the strain no longer she came bearing a jug of cool milk, some cheese and some deliciously fresh fried-cakes. With keen joy I set a couple of tall sheaves together like a tent and flung myself down flat on my back in their shadow to devour my lunch. . . . It took resolution to rise and go back to my work, but I did it, sustained by a kind of soldierly pride.

At noon we hurried to the house, surrounded the kitchen table and fell upon our boiled beef and potatoes with such ferocity that in fifteen minutes our meal was over. . . . Then came a heavenly half-hour of rest on the cool grass in the shade of the trees . . . but alas!—this "nooning," as we called it, was always cut short by father's word of sharp command, "Roll out, boys!" . . . Again the big white jugs were filled at the well, the horses, lazy with food, led the way back to the field, and the stern contest began again.

All nature at this hour seemed to invite to repose rather than to labor. . . . The sunlight was a golden, silent, scorching cataract—yet each of us must strain his tired muscles and bend his aching back to the harvest.

Supper came at five, another delicious interval—and then at six we all went out again for another hour or two in the cool of the sunset. However, the pace was more leisurely now for the end of the day was near. . . . At last, father's long-drawn and musical cry, "Turn OUT! All hands TURN OUT!" rang with restful significance through the dusk. Then, slowly, with low-hung heads the freed horses moved toward the barn, walking with lagging steps like weary warriors going into camp.

A Coed Courts Disaster Wearing Four
Fraternity Pins

In the 1870's, not many colleges or universities in the United States would admit young women as well as young men. Ida Tarbell, who later became one of our greatest women journalists, relates experiences at Allegheny College, Meadville, Pa.

Source: *All in the Day's Work; An Autobiography.* By IDA M. TARBELL. New York: The Macmillan Company, 1939, pp. 40–47. Permission granted by Ella Tarbell Price.

Allegheny did not of course admit women at the start; but the ferment caused by the passing of the Fourteenth Amendment, making it clear that only men were to be regarded as citizens, stirred the Allegheny constituents mightily. Allegheny's chief patron . . . was the Methodist Church. . . . Leaders among Methodist women had been abolitionists, aggressive temperance advocates, and now they became militant suffragists. Their influence began to tell.

In 1870, with misgivings in not a few minds, the admission of women to Allegheny was voted. This was the same year that the University of Michigan opened its doors to women, and two years before Cornell. In the six years before I entered ten women had graduated. When I came there were but two seniors, two juniors, and no sophomores. I was a lone freshman in a class of forty hostile or indifferent boys. The friendly . . . professor charged with the care of the "young ladies" put it that I was "Lost in the Wilderness of Boy."

From the first I was dimly conscious that I was an invader, that there was abroad a spirit of masculinity challenging my right to be there, and there were taboos not to be disregarded. . . .

The sloping green of the campus below Bentley Hall was inviting. Between classes I made my way one day to a seat under a tree only to hear a horrified call from the walk above, "Come back, come back quick!" An imperative summons from an upper class woman. "You mustn't go on that side of the walk, only men go there."

It was not so simple to find a spot where you could go and be comfortable. If Bentley Hall, where all the classes were held, was a beautiful piece of architecture, its interior could hardly have been more severe. The rooms were heated with potbellied cast-iron stoves, seated with the hardest wooden chairs, lighted by kerosene lamps. . . . But of all that I was unheeding. . . . I realized . . . that I had found what I had come to college for, direction in the only field in which I was interested—science. . . . I was given the free run of the laboratory along with a few as crazy as myself. . . .

And such good talks! Much of it was concerned with fresh scientific thought, the inventions and discoveries which were stirring the world. An omnivorous reader of the scientific publications of Europe and America, Professor Tingley, kept us excited, not only by what had been done but what it might mean. There was the telephone. I had been in college but a few weeks when my father asked me to go with him and my brother to the Centennial Exposition of 1876. President of the college Bugbee . . . was heartily in favor of my going. I went, and when I returned, Professor Tingley's first question was, "Did you see the telephone?" I hadn't even heard of it. . . . Professor Tingley was greatly disappointed, and I did not understand why until a few weeks later he called the student body together to explain and illustrate the telephone by a homemade instrument. "You'll talk to your homes from these rooms one day," he told us. "New York will talk to Boston." He didn't suggest Chicago. "Dreamer," the boys said.

. . . Life at college was lightened by my discovery of the Boy. Incredible as it seems . . . I had come to college at eighteen without ever having dared to look fully into the face of any boy of my age. . . . My brother and his friends, my father and his friends, these I had always hobnobbed with; but those who naturally should have been my companions, I shunned. I was unable to take part in those things that brought the young people of the day together. I did not dance. . . . I was incredibly stupid and uninterested in games. . . . I had no easy companionable ways, was too shy to attempt them. . . .

But the daily association in the classroom, . . . the mutual interests, . . . the continual procession of college doings which in the nature of things required that you should have a masculine attendant, soon put me at my ease. . . . I still had a stiff-necked

determination to be free. To avoid entangling alliances of all
kinds had become an obsession with me. I was slow in laying it
aside when I began to take part in the social life of the college,
and because of it I was guilty of one performance which was
properly enough a scandal to the young men.

There were several men's fraternities in the college; most of
the boys belonged to one or another. It was an ambition of the
fraternities to put their pins on acceptable town and college girls.
You were a Delta girl, or a Gamma girl or a Phi Psi girl. I re-
sented this effort to tag me. Why should I not have friends in all
the fraternities? And I had; I accumulated four pins and then,
one disastrous morning, went into chapel with the four pins on
my coat. There were a few months after that when, if it had not
been for two or three non-Frat friends, I should have been a
social outcast. . . .

1880

Chicago Recovers from the Great Fire

All American cities grew rapidly in the 1870's and 1880's, but
Lady Duffus Hardy, a traveling English noblewoman, was particularly impressed by Chicago. Her criticism of the neglect of
the fine arts and science was frequently echoed by foreign visitors to the United States during this period.

Source: HARDY, LADY DUFFUS. *Through Cities and Prairie
Lands: Sketch of An American Tour*, pp. 76–79. R. Worthing-
ton, New York, 1881.

Knowing of the fiery scourge which a few years ago had marred
and scarred the beauty of Chicago we expected to find traces of
ugliness and deformity everywhere, crippled buildings, and lame,
limping streets running along in a forlorn crooked condition,
waiting for time to restore their old vigor and build up their
beauty anew. But . . . the city has risen up out of its own ashes,
grander and statlier than ever. On the outskirts the line of fire
can still be traced; gaunt skeletons of houses still remain to point
the way it took . . . while in the suburbs picturesque shells of
once beautiful homes greet us here and there.

But once within the boundaries of the city we lose all traces of the conflagration. The business streets are lined with handsome massive houses, some six or seven stories high, substantially built, sometimes of red brick with stone copings and elaborate carving, while others are built of that creamy stone which reminds one of the Paris boulevards. No wooden buildings are allowed to be erected within a certain distance of the city.

The fashionable trading localities are State and Clark streets, though there are several others which are well patronized by a less fashionable multitude. . . . The different banks, churches, and municipal buildings which had been destroyed by the great fire . . . are all re-erected in a substantial style. . . .

Chicago is indeed a great city, full of energy and enterprise. Signs of its hidden strength and powers of progress greet us everywhere; but at present it appears to be wholly devoted to money-making. Art, science (except such science as serves its purpose), and literature are in a languishing state. But it is young yet. Perhaps when it is fully developed, and grown strong in muscle, and bone, and brain, the soul may be born to glorify the commonplace, and stir the latent genius of this city into life and beauty.

1887

A Young Apache Learns the White Man's Ways

The famous Indian school at Carlisle, Pennsylvania attempted to teach English, a trade, and basic skills to young Indians of both sexes and all tribes. A young Apache, who had fought with Geronimo against white Americans, tells here of his experiences at the school.

Source: Betzinez, Jason with W. S. Nye. *I Fought with Geronimo*, pp. 152–156. The Stackpole Company, Harrisburg, Pennsylvania, 1959.

. . . Our train stopped on a siding just outside the post of Carlisle Barracks, where we were met by a delegation of faculty and students. . . . After we had been assembled on the steps of the mess hall for a photograph the boys were separated from the girls and each group was led to its respective dormitory. . . . Here we were each given a haircut and a bath but not as yet issued new clothing. . . . As I look today at our first photographs I realize what unkempt and wild-looking creatures we were.

But this was soon to change. The school tailor shop turned out blue Army-type uniforms for the boys while the dress shop made neat dresses for the girls. We wore these uniforms proudly. Never before had I owned such fine-looking clothing.

We soon learned that the school was run on military lines. There were rules to be observed as well as a schedule. I suppose that some of the young Indians, who had had little discipline, fretted under this just as do children of other races who have not had the benefit of firm control. But we conformed. I am happy to say that for my own part I took to this regulated life quite naturally. From the outset I made up my mind to be a true young man, to obey the rules, and try to please the warmhearted man who had brought us there. This was my great good fortune, to have determined to make something of myself, to lift myself to a more useful life than the old pitiful existence to which I had been born.

Our rising bell in the morning was at six o'clock, breakfast at six-thirty, cleaning up our quarters and other work at eight, school at nine, dinner at twelve, supper at six, study period from eight to ten, then lights out. During the evening study period we were not allowed to visit back and forth between rooms, sing Indian songs, or make any noise. For those who could speak English there was a rule against speaking Indian. We were not allowed to use tobacco or profanity. Each Saturday night we were expected to report ourselves for any violation of these rules. . . .

Our first teacher was a nice little lady, Miss Flora F. Low, who gave us names and taught us to write them on the blackboard. My childhood name of Nah-delthy, which means Going-to-Run, had been changed in 1878 to Batsinas. Batsinas was an old Indian at San Carlos, a great friend of my mother who had given me his name. Miss Low now changed the spelling of this to Betzinez. I suppose she thought it was a Spanish or Mexican word though actually I think "Batsinas" was Apache. It was also the custom at the school to give those of us, who had only one name, another name—to be our first name. Miss Low selected for me the name of Jason. She said that Jason was some man who hunted the golden fleece but never found it. I thought this was too bad but it didn't mean anything to me at that time so I accepted the name. . . .

It was extremely difficult for me to learn to speak English. At first I was unable to make many of the sounds. I even had trouble pronouncing the letters of the alphabet. I couldn't tell the difference between the strange sounds as readily as the younger people in the class. As a result I progressed very slowly, so slowly, in fact, that for the first three years it didn't seem that I would ever learn. Luckily I wasn't ashamed of myself or discouraged, saying simply that I would have to work extra hard to catch up with the others. . . .

One day Mr. W. P. Campbell, a Chippewa Indian who was our first disciplinarian, called me out and took me to the old blacksmith shop where he assigned me as an apprentice. [There Jason learned to weld and other techniques of the blacksmith, following that trade for thirty-two years after he left Carlisle.] . . .

During my ten years in Pennsylvania I became well acquainted with the country, and very fond of it, too. In addition to the Saturday night sociables, and other entertainment which was provided for us at the school, I used to go down to Carlisle on Saturday evenings to loaf on the street corners just like the young white farmers. One of my most pleasant memories is that of eating oysters at a little stand back of the market square. I must remind you that this is a bit unusual for a western Indian, whose tribe had a taboo against eating anything that lived under the water. But I made strenuous efforts to shed the Indian superstitions. In so doing I suppose I picked up a few of the white man's like carrying a rabbit foot for good luck. . . .

Some people have asked me if I knew Jim Thorpe, the famous Indian athlete who attended Carlisle. No, he was later than my time and besides was from another tribe in another part of the United States. Nevertheless like most of the boys at the school I played baseball, basketball, football, and many other sports and games. In the early days we used to indulge, too, in an old Indian game of shinny, a very rough sport something like hockey except that it is not played on ice.

The most powerful influence on my life at this or any other

time was my introduction to the teachings of Christianity. . . .
This influence became stronger and stronger as I came to understand English better. It changed my whole life.

1887

||||||||||||||||||||||||||||||||||||||||||||||||||||||||||||||||||||||||||||||||||||||||||||||||||||||||||||||||||||||||||||||||||

Edison Develops a Motion Picture Camera

> Thomas A. Edison invented a long list of devices which
> helped create the type of life we live today. Something of his
> philosophy and methods can be gained by reading his account
> of his experiments with motion pictures.
> Source: RUNES, DAGOBERT D. (editor). *The Diary and Sun-
> dry Observations of Thomas Alva Edison*, pp. 71–78. Philosophi-
> cal Library, New York, 1948.

. . . It was in 1887 that I began my investigations, and photog-
raphy . . . was in a decidedly crude state of development.
Pictures were made by "wet" plates, operated by involved mechanisms. The modern dry films were unheard of. . . .

There were many problems connected with the first motion
picture camera, but before everything else came the question of
making a unit machine—that is, one where all of the exposures
needed could be made with the same apparatus and through the
same lens. And this at once brought up the second difficulty.
Obviously, it was quite impossible to construct any single camera
capable of the proper speed and mechanism required for the purpose, and use glass plates for the exposures. I saw at once that
these would have to be discarded entirely, and any experiments
would have to start from a brand new point of departure.

We tried various kinds of mechanisms and various kinds of
materials and chemicals for our negatives. The experiments of a
laboratory consist mostly in finding that something won't work.
The worst of it is you never know beforehand, and sometimes it
takes months, even years, before you discover you have been on
the wrong line all the time. . . .

It was along about this point that George Eastman came into
our experiments. I heard that he was working on a new kind of

216

dry film, and asked him to come down and talk it over. The result was that his representative went back home to see what he could do in making a narrow strip of sensitized film that would operate on a roll. Without George Eastman I don't know what the result would have been in the history of the motion picture. The months that followed were a series of discouragements for all of us. While he was busy with the problem of chemicals we were busy with the problem of mechanics.

It is almost impossible for the layman to appreciate the extreme niceties of adjustment we had to overcome. . . . If there was the slightest variation in the movement of the film, or if it slipped at any time by so much as a hair's breadth, this fact was certain to show up in the enlargements. Finally we completed a mechanism that allowed the film to be moved in the uniform ratio of one-tenth part of the time needed for a satisfactory exposure, and permitted from twenty to forty such exposures per second.

It looked as though we were finished, and we tried the first roll of film jubilantly. Success was in our hands. But we had counted too soon.

The strips (of film) had been made in a one-half inch width that we thought was ample, but it was not enough. We had to make a larger size, allowing a one-inch surface for the emulsion, with a one-half inch margin for the perforations needed for the locking device that we used for starting and stopping the film.

This meant, of course, adjusting our mechanical apparatus also to carry the new-sized roll; but we did it at last, and soon the first of the new cameras was ready to show what it could do.

I didn't apply for the patent until two years later. I was very much occupied with other matters, and while we all congratulated ourselves on what we had accomplished, and knew we had an interesting and novel apparatus, we generally regarded it more or less as a curiosity with no very large practicable possibilities. It probably seems strange to the world now, but such was the fact, even after we had exhibited our first pictures.

These were shown originally in an apparatus that we christened "The Kinetoscope," consisting of a cabinet equipped with an electrical motor and battery, and carrying a fifty-foot band of film, passed through the field of a magnifying glass. They attracted quite a lot of attention at the World's Fair in Chicago in 1893, but we didn't think much of it until we found that two English-

men, who had been interested in the exhibit, finding that I had
carelessly neglected to patent the apparatus abroad, had started
an independent manufacture on a considerable scale.

Of course, it was too late then to protect myself, and I concentrated my efforts in devising a mechanism that would project
the pictures on a screen before an audience. . . .

1889

A Cowboy Survives a Stampede

One of the great dangers of a cowboy's work was a stampede
of frightened cattle. You can see why from this first-hand ac-
count written by a cowboy who lived through one.
Source: WESTERMEIER, CLIFFORD P. (compiler and editor).
*Trailing the Cowboy: His Life and Lore as Told by Frontier
Journalists*, pp. 95–97. The Caxton Printers, Ltd., Caldwell,
Idaho, 1955.

I was with what is known as the Shoesole outfit on the banks
of the Oyee river in Idaho in July, 1889. There were thirty-eight
cowboys in the camp, and on July 23rd we had just completed a
roundup of beef cattle that we were to drive to Shoshone Falls to
ship east. There were between 1,700 and 2,000 head of big steers
in the band, and we had them all safely bunched for the night.
There was a storm brewing all the afternoon and the boss cowboy, Coon Foster, thought we had best not unsaddle our ponies
at all that night. He laid his uneasiness to the weather, and most
of the boys in the outfit took it for granted that . . . was what
was troubling him, but when we crossed a creek I saw moccasin
tracks . . . and I knew better.

I knew that Foster had seen 'em, too, and it was Indians and
not weather that worried him. About six o'clock in the evening it
commenced to rain, and Foster stationed six of the cowboys,
myself among the number . . . as guards over the camp and
cattle. . . .

Everything was quiet, seemingly, but I heard several suspicious
sounds, coyote barks and other noises. . . . Suddenly a big steer

that stood far out on the mesa beyond the herd twisted his tail and let out a bellow that would raise the dead. In an instant the entire herd was on its feet. They came straight at me and only about fifty yards away. Foster came at me yelling like mad for the boys to saddle up and get the cattle stopped. He had just reached my side when the leaders of the herd surrounded us. Our ponies turned and ran with them. The bellowing and rearing of the cattle was frightful.

We were managing to get the steers nearest us separated a trifle so as to get room to turn, and had a fair chance of getting out of the bunch, when Foster's horse stumbled and fell. My pony fell over him and I landed between his body and that of Foster's horse, and that is the only thing that saved my life. The whole herd tumbled and pitched and tossed over us. Foster was literally mangled to sausage meat. His horse was little better, and mine was crushed into a bloody mass. I found that I could not get up, for my leg was broken just below the thigh. I was soon cared for, however, and in six weeks was all right and on the range again. We found 341 dead cattle, two dead horses, one dead cowboy and two more with broken legs after the herd had passed. Indians had stampeded the herd.

1894

A Gruff Voice Says "You Are Under Arrest"

Mary Anderson came to America from Sweden at the age of sixteen. She devoted her life to improving conditions for women workers and was director of the Women's Bureau of the United States Department of Labor from 1919 to 1944. Here she tells of her first interest in the trade union movement.

Source: *Woman at Work: The Autobiography of Mary Anderson* as told to Mary Winslow. University of Minnesota Press, Minneapolis. Copyright 1951 by the University of Minnesota.

By the time I got the job at Schwab's [shoe factory] in Chicago I was twenty-two years old. I had been in America about six years and had had ten different jobs. During that time I had progressed from housework at a dollar and a half a week to a skilled job in the shoe industry at about fourteen dollars a week. I had learned English, had made a few friends, and had seen something of life in a number of different places. . . .

The seven years I spent at Schwab's marked my entrance into the trade union movement. Although I did not know it at the time, this was to be the real beginning of life for me in America. . . . I did not know anything about the union when I first joined. A business agent for the Boot and Shoe Workers Union came to the factory and asked some of the girls if they would join. The girls asked me. I wanted to go along with them just to be friendly but I said I would like to know something about it first. We all went to a meeting, heard that a union would mean better wages and shorter hours, and then we joined. After a few weeks I became the shop collector for the union and in about a year I was elected president of the Stitchers Local 94 of the International Boot and Shoe Workers Union. . . .

It was late in 1894 when I first went to work at Schwab's. I spent all my spare time on trade union matters and did not have a chance to supplement my education at night school or by studying at home. We worked a ten-hour day, from seven thirty in the morning until six in the afternoon. I would have to start to work very early because it was a long walk from my home on the North Side of the city to the factory on the West Side. After work was over I would go home for supper and then I was usually off to meetings that somethimes lasted very late. Fortunately, I was strong and well and enjoyed the work I was doing, so it was not too hard on me physically.

> [After years of work at the local union level, Miss Anderson became a leading member of the Chicago Women's Trade Union League. She assisted in strikes and took great interest in organizing women into trade unions.
> Once, during the Chicago garment workers' strike of 1910, she was arrested.]

I myself was arrested once during this strike and I will always remember my feeling of defilement, both physical and spiritual, after I got out of that cell. In order to keep in touch with the picketers and find out when they were arrested, I was waiting about two blocks away from the picket line when one of the picketers came rushing up to me with the news that several of them were being arrested . . . suddenly I felt a hand on my shoulder and heard a gruff voice say, "You are under arrest."

It was a policeman who had followed the girl bringing me the message. When I asked why I was arrested and said I had done nothing . . . the answer was just "Shut up! You are under arrest." He refused to let me telephone to the office of the Women's Trade Union League . . . and made us walk with him to the . . . police station. About six of the girls who had been picketing were there too. . . .

I was alone in a filthy cell with nothing in it except a dirty old cot and a wooden chair. The cell had an open sewer running through it and the smell was disgusting. [After a few hours in jail, Miss Anderson and the other women were released through the aid of some influential Chicago lawyers.] I went home and took a bath and changed my clothes, but I did not get rid of the feeling of dirt and defilement for a long time afterward.

. . . .

We did everything we could to interest women in the unions, developing special techniques that were very helpful. . . . The men met in halls that were often in back of a saloon, or in questionable districts, dirty and not well kept. I remember the so-called labor temples that were anything but temples. The girls would not go to meetings in these places and we could not ask them to go under the circumstances. . . .

To eliminate this problem we tried to get nice places for the girls to meet. . . . Girls and women like a homelike atmosphere and a social get-together now and then. They get tired of just talking about conditions of work in the factory. So every other meeting we used to try and arrange for some kind of social gathering. Sometimes we would serve coffee or tea and cakes. It was not easy for use to do this. We had no money, we were tired after the day's work, and it was an added burden . . . but it helped and we were probably more successful in our work with women because of it. . . .

A Republican Is Surveyed with a Fishy Eye

William Allen White was owner and editor of a newspaper in Emporia, Kansas. For fifty years he was widely regarded as the Republican voice of the Midwest. Here he describes his meeting with the Bryans.

Source: *The Autobiography of William Allen White*, pp. 327–329. The Macmillan Company, New York, 1946.

It was in 1900 that I met William Jennings Bryan for the first time. McClure's Magazine asked me to write a character sketch of him, and I journeyed to Lincoln, Nebraska, where he lived, to see him. He was a . . . tallish young man who was . . . beginning to get too opulent a crescent under his vest. He had a mop of black hair and a tawny complexion. His eyes were large, expressive, kindly. In all things he was a gentle person, I felt. He was kind to me, though I could see that he suspected me of no good motives because I was a Republican. . . . Nevertheless, we got along gayly.

Bryan, even in that day, was too much a professional politician to suit my tastes. He was getting what all politicians get, a lively sense of his ability to influence people . . . by charming manners, meaningless courtesies, pleasant words, outworn phrases. . . . This did not offend me, but it did steel me a little against him.

. . . When he left me for an hour in his library and told me to look around . . . I found . . . that most of his books dealing with the currency and with the tariff were . . . published by groups interested in propaganda . . . books written not by scholars but by partisans of the creeds that Mr. Bryan preached. It was a shabby library and, to me, revealed much.

Also, I met Mrs. Bryan, who was a born . . . student, an introvert who surveyed me . . . with a fishy eye of distrust. . . . But she was exactly the kind of woman he needed. . . . Such a woman must always have stayed his hand when he was too magnanimous, checked him when he was too gracious, stopped him when he was too impulsive. The two personalities . . . rolled together made a well-balanced person. . . .

The article which I wrote about him was coldly objective but not deeply critical. How she must have disliked it!

1900

Herbert Hoover Enjoys "A Hot Time"

Herbert Hoover had an adventurous and prosperous career as a mining engineer before devoting his life to public service. He and Mrs. Hoover lived in many parts of the world. In his memoirs, Hoover relates their exciting experiences, including this account of the Boxer uprising in China.

Source: *The Memoirs of Herbert Hoover: Years of Adventure, 1874–1920*, pp. 47–52. Copyright 1951 by Herbert Hoover. Used with permission of The Macmillan Company.

In the winter and spring of 1900 we began to hear of the new secret society directed against foreigners. It was named the I Ho Tuan—the mailed fist. The foreigners called it "The Boxers." Their avowed purpose was to expel all foreigners from China, to root out every foreign thing—houses, railways, telegraphs, mines —and they included all Christian Chinese and all Chinese who had been associated with foreign things. . . .

By May 1st, 1900, the danger had grown so great that I called in our geological expeditions from the interior. These men had, however, outlined a field of anthracite coal greater than all the other anthracite fields in the world put together.

[Mr. and Mrs. Hoover were in Peking, where Mrs. Hoover became ill. They returned to Tientsin, a city close to the coast where they had a home, so that Mrs. Hoover could get medical treatment. Her illness was not serious and she quickly recovered.]

Rumors of Boxer attacks upon missionaries and others rumbled all about us. Foreign-drilled Chinese troops were brought up to protect the foreign settlement in Tientsin. On Sunday morning, June 10th, however, we were rudely awakened by shells bursting over the settlement from modern artillery—the foreign-drilled army . . . [had mutinied]. Tientsin had no . . . defense works, but there were about 1,100 sailors and marines of various nationalities in the settlement. . . . They had no artillery except two small cannon and only a dozen machine guns. It was a small force to oppose some 25,000 foreign-equipped Chinese troops. . . .

Quickly the settlement pulled itself together. [A Russian, Colonel Wogack, who was the highest ranking officer in Tientsin, was put in command of all the troops, except those of the British.] Learning of my engineering staff, Wogack sent word to us to organize the Christian Chinese, who had fled to the settlement for safety, to build barricades. The settlement was about a quarter-mile wide and a mile long, protected by the river on one side. In hunting material for barricades, we lit upon the great warehouses filled with sacked sugar, peanuts, rice and other grain. Soon we and other foreigners whom I enlisted had a thousand terrified Christian Chinese carrying and piling up walls of sacked grain and sugar along the exposed sides of the town. . . . By morning we were in a better state. The big attack came the second day, but the marines and sailors repulsed it from behind our bags. . . .

The acute dangers came from two sources—the first, the possibility of mass attack; the second, the incessant and furious artillery fire. Some 60,000 shells were fired into the settlement from first to last. . . .

An increasing number of foreigners, soldiers and civilians, were wounded. We had only one Army doctor and our settlement physician and there was only one professional nurse. Colonel Wogack turned the . . . club into a hospital and soon all the floors were covered with wounded. Mrs. Hoover volunteered at once and I saw little of her during the . . . siege, except when she came home occasionally to eat or catch a little sleep. She became expert in riding her bicycle close to the walls of buildings to avoid stray bullets and shells although one day she had a tire punctured by a bullet. . . .

Somewhat later in the siege Mrs. Hoover and I and our engineering staff returned to our own house for a base, as it had not been hit. Late one evening . . . a shell banged through a back window and then, exploding, blew out the front door and surroundings. Mrs. Hoover, after a long day at the hospital, was sitting in a side room playing solitaire. She never stopped the game. . . .

The siege lasted about a month. . . . Then came word that relief armies were on their way and would be in the next day. We were warned not to fire on them by mistake. During the morning the Chinese stopped firing on us. Soon someone said he heard cannonading in the distance. How we strained our ears! Then it came plainer and plainer. We climbed on the roof of the highest warehouse to get a glimpse. We saw them coming over the plain. They were American Marines and Welsh Fusiliers. I do not remember a more satisfying musical performance than the bugles of the American Marines entering the settlement playing "There'll Be a Hot Time in the Old Town Tonight."

1901

A Notorious Train Robber Reveals His Methods

Desperate outlaws sometimes staged spectacular train robberies on the western railroads. Al Jennings headed the notorious Jennings' Gang which netted over two hundred thousand dollars during two years of robbery before they were caught. After serving a long term in prison, Jennings "went straight" and wrote an account of Western outlawry in which he described his own experiences.

Source: JENNINGS, AL, with the assistance of Will Irwin. *Beating Back*. Appleton-Century-Crofts, 1904.

One train robbery is much like another. There are two ways of going at it. Under the old method, used always by the Dalton boys, two of the gang mount the forward end of the baggage car a station down the line. When the train starts they crawl over the tender, hold up the engineer and fireman, and force them to make a stop at the point where the rest of the gang is waiting. But if the trainmen have a heavy consignment in the express car, and therefore expect to be robbed, they watch the baggage platform; you risk a complete fizzle.

We used another method. We picked a point where the train had to stop for water, or else we held up a signal man and made him "flag" the train. As soon as the train stopped, part of the gang would begin a fusillade . . . in order to cow the passengers and the crew. If a passenger shoved his head out of the window, we would smash the glass over his head. In the meantime two of the gang would attend to the engine, one keeping the engineer and fireman covered while the other turned water into the fire-box. When that was done one remained with the trainmen, and the other went back to help in the actual robbery.

Though we sometimes went through the passengers, the express safe was always our real object—we never robbed a train unless we had a tip on a large sum of money. There isn't very much in robbing the passengers. You can't watch them all. At the first fire the big wads of money and the valuable jewelry generally go under the seats or behind the steam pipes. Mostly, you get only watches, trinkets, and small change.

Occasionally the express messenger showed fight, but a few bullets just over his head always stopped him. Then, with one of my coolest men, I would attend to the express safe. Sometimes we made the messenger open it; generally we blew it with giant powder. We'd empty the contents into sacks, fan a few shots around the train for a warning, and get to our horses.

. . . The hard and dangerous part comes afterward, when the trainmen start up the marshals and vigilantes, and the whole country seems roused against you. I've seen a district alive with armed men an hour after the robbery. We generally held to-gether for a day or so, then . . . we'd scatter, making an appoint-ment, often for months ahead, to meet for the next robbery. Generally I'd pass the intervening time among the cattle ranches in another part of the Oklahoma Territory. Frank Jennings used to loaf around among the nesters. When we found him again, he'd be comfortably settled down in a farmhouse, smoking a corncob pipe, helping the women wipe the dishes, and singing at the melodeon of evenings. He could eat his way into the bosom of a family quicker than any other man I ever knew.

I understand that people are digging all over Oklahoma for the buried treasure of the Jennings gang. I buried my treasure all right, but not that way. It used to run through our fingers like water. First, a big wad went to the territorial or railroad official who had informed us of the shipment. We had our friends to take care of—they were mostly poor. . . . I don't know just where the rest of it went—mostly, I suppose, I dropped it in New York or Chicago for I used to vary life on the ranches by going

East. When the time came for the next job we were always broke.

Our chief trouble, barring the escape from the marshals, was in reassembling. We didn't dare use the mails. Most of us went under assumed names. I usually traveled as "Mr. Edwards," and Frank as "Mr. Williams." Sometimes, when you heard of a chance for a robbery and wanted to gather the riders, you had to hunt for a fortnight. You knew nothing about them except their regular haunts, and even then you were hardly ever right. . . .

1901-1909

"The Capitol Is Scandalized at the Roosevelt Children"

William Allen White, a leading American journalist, knew and loved Theodore Roosevelt and his family. He visited them many times in the White House and recorded his impressions.
Source: *The Autobiography of William Allen White*, pp. 341–343. Copyright 1946 by The Macmillan Company, and used with their permission.

The Roosevelts lived in middle-class simplicity. At family meals the children came to the table. The President . . . was served first and . . . used to apologize for it, indicating that he did not see any sense in the formality, but . . . that he could not overrule the servants. Roosevelt . . . took two helpings of meat generally, and they always had at least three vegetables. Potatoes in those days were standard dinner equipment, generally mashed. He liked gravy. . . . At dinner he ran the table—not that he talked all the time but he primed others and pumped them to talk about what they knew best. . . .

. . . .

But the Roosevelts' meals and the Roosevelt household were always riotous. And he gave them their rambunctious character and keenly enjoyed it. Mrs. Roosevelt once said . . . "How Theodore loves a party!"

It was beautiful to see him with half a dozen guests at his table, with the children there cutting in, for they were never repressed children. . . . Once . . . someone asked the young-sters: "Who are your father's favorite cabinet members?"

As if they were trained to it . . . they took their knives and forks by the handles and drummed on the table and piped in something like unison, "Mr. Root and Mr. Knox." Which made a great hit in the Capitol after the story got around; indeed the Capitol was scandalized at the Roosevelt children.

But they grew up into decent, useful, self-respecting men and women and the liberties they had as children gave them a sense of duty later in life. The Colonel and Mrs. Roosevelt were good parents. . . . The atmosphere of the White House, which be-wildered diplomatic circles by its general informality and occa-sional disregard of usage, was nevertheless typically middle-class American—sincere, wholesome, a bit boisterous, but always well bred in the deep sense of the word, which makes kindness the soul of manners.

1903

"I Fit It Jest the Best I Knew How"

Telephones, better roads, automobiles, and, later, radio and television eventually broke down the isolation and loneliness of farm life in the United States. But here is testimony to show what rural free delivery of mail meant to American farmers.

Source: THRASHER, MAX BENNET. "Thirty Miles with a Rural Carrier," *Independent*, Vol. LV (January 5, 1903), pp. 311–317.

Rural free delivery is as yet so much of a novelty in this coun-try that when . . . a rural mail carrier in Michigan invited me to spend a day driving with him over his thirty-mile route, I was glad to avail myself of the opportunity. . . .

There are four routes in operation from the Cassopolis post office now. I was to go over Route No. 1, the first to be estab-lished. The carrier on this route, Mr. G. B. Warner, was formerly a farmer living several miles out of town and in the district which he now serves. He therefore had the advantage of being well acquainted beforehand with many of the patrons of the route and much of the country over which he now drives daily. This route covers twenty-nine miles. This, I was told, was a little longer than the average, twenty-five miles being reckoned a practical working distance.

We left the post office at Cassopolis at 8:30 A.M. and were back there at 5 P.M. There were 109 boxes on the route over which we drove, and we stopped at over one hundred of them. Into these boxes we distributed 264 papers, 37 letters, 8 postal cards, 12 circulars, and 2 packages. The day was Friday, and on account of the fact that so many weekly papers are printed in the middle of the week, the number of papers delivered that day was considerably above the average. When the route was established there were only five daily papers taken in the district which it was to serve. When I rode over it there were sixty-five, and about twenty-five monthly magazines are taken on this route.

The average number of pieces of mail delivered monthly by the carrier with whom I rode at that time was 5,200. Since the route was established the carrier had issued 262 money orders. . . . The extension of the money order system is one of the benefits of rural delivery. Few of the small discontinued country offices were authorized to issue money orders. We issued two money orders during the trip I made. One of these happened to be asked for by a man whom I had been told was one of the most violent opponents to the establishment of the route. I asked this man—a farmer—how he liked the system.

"Wal," he said, "I'll be honest with you. I fit it jest the best I knew how. I thought we didn't want it. But if I was to sell my farm tomorrow, and go to look for another to buy, I'd give five dollars an acre more for a place where they had rural delivery than I would for one where they hadn't." One other farmer with whom I talked was even more emphatic. He declared that he would never again own a farm at any price outside the limits of rural free delivery.

We made the trip in a small, light, covered wagon, built expressly for this purpose, so as to secure the comfort and convenience of the carrier with the least possible weight. . . . The exterior of the cart is painted a light blue, and from its size and color the vehicle is conspicuous a long way off on the country roads. The carrier wears the gray uniform of the regular postal service. Each carrier is required to furnish his own wagon and the horses to draw it, and to provide for the keep of the horses. Two horses are necessary, so that they may have alternate days in which to rest. It takes a pretty good horse to draw such a wagon over twenty-five to thirty miles of country roads in all kinds of weather, at all seasons of the year, making a hundred or more stops, and yet the horse must be docile enough so that he will halt at a word from the driver, when the wagon is alongside a box, and stand there until he gets the word to go on, since both the driver's hands must be occupied in opening the box and depositing the mail in it. For all this and his own services the carrier receives $600 a year. . . .

The rural carrier is a daily connecting link between the farmer and the world. . . . Along the whole route I improved every opportunity to talk with men and women about rural delivery. I did not find any who did not approve of it, and most were enthusiastic. One man said: "It's one of the things that seems to bring back to us farmers some of the money we've been paying out for years for taxes. . . . Congress votes money, lots of it," he went on, "for armies, and war ships, and river and harbor improvements, and public buildings in cities and towns, and a good many of us live and die and never see none of 'em. But here is something that comes right to our very doors, and we can't help seeing and feeling the good of our money."

1903

A Muckraker Learns about the Boss and His Gang

Lincoln Steffens, sometimes called "The First of the Muckrakers," wrote a series of articles for *McClure's Magazine* which exposed corruption in several of America's largest cities. Like all the Muckrakers, Steffens carefully gathered the facts before he wrote. Here he describes his method.

Source: *The Autobiography of Lincoln Steffens*, pp. 483–486. Harcourt, Brace and Company, New York, 1931.

When I went to Cincinnati . . . I sought out Boss Cox. His office was over his "Mecca" saloon, in a mean little front hall room one flight up. The door was open. I saw a great hulk of a man, sitting there alone, his back to the door, his feet up on the window sill; he was reading a newspaper. I knocked; no response. I walked in; he did not look up.

"Mr. Cox?" I said.

An affirmative grunt.

"Mr. Cox, I understand that you are the boss of Cincinnati."

Slowly his feet came down, one by one . . . and a stolid face turned to let two dark, sharp eyes study me. . . . I gave my name, and explained that I was "a student of politics, corrupt politics, and bosses." I repeated that I had heard he was the boss of Cincinnati. "Are you?" I asked.

"I am," he grumbled in his hoarse, throaty voice.

"Of course you have a mayor, and a council, and judges?"

"I have," he admitted, "but"—he pointed with his thumb back over his shoulder to the desk—"I have a telephone, too."

. . . He stared a long moment . . . then turned heavily around back to his paper. That short interview was a summary of the truth about Cincinnati. . . .

. . . After the first few days in his town, I went back to him one early morning. He was more polite the second visit than he was the first. He whirled around in his chair to receive me.

"Well, what are you getting?"

I told him some stories, well-known incidents. "Lies," he blurted, "all . . . lies."

"Are they?" I asked. . . . "I'll go over the ground again." The next morning I called again, early, and I said: "Those stories are true, Mr. Cox. There are some inaccuracies," and I named and corrected them. "The rest is true." When he did not deny that, I made my proposition.

"Look here, Mr. Cox, you have detectives watching me. You must be curious about whom I see and what I learn. Keep the dicks on; they will give you a check on me, and I'll come in every day or two and tell you what I get. You can correct my information, but you must be square with me. I'm a stranger, I can be misled, but you mustn't mislead me; not you. You need not tell me anything, of course; it's up to me to find my own facts; but I'll give you a chance to nail the lies people tell me, and you . . . since I am depending on you, you mustn't deceive me."

He blinked; he turned to the window and looked out. He turned back, stared, without a flicker of his eyelids, without a word. I had to close the bargain.

"All right," I said. "That's a go then."

"Make it always early," he answered and turned away.

. . . In the course of the weeks I worked in Cincinnati I learned many facts about the boss and his gang. . . . I told them all to him. I made my calls early and often; I gave him always all I had. He would balk at each new one.

"Say, who filled you up with that?"

"Not true?" I would say.

"Not the way you've got it."

All right. I would check it, "a lie"; he watched me write that, and I would go away to come back the next day to say, usually, "That's true, Mr. Cox," or "I have that judgeship story corrected, Mr. Cox." This I would say and look him in the eye. My theory was . . . that I had made him feel that I was trusting him. And I did, and he rose to it.

1905

Theodore Roosevelt Expresses Keen Pride

Theodore Roosevelt, one of our most popular Presidents, reached the height of his popularity in 1904 and 1905. In a letter to George Otto Trevelyan, he writes honestly and realistically of his feelings at that time.

Source: Reprinted by permission of the publishers from *The Letters of Theodore Roosevelt*, Volume 4, edited by ELTING E. MORISON, Cambridge, Mass.: Harvard University Press. Copyright, 1952, by the President and Fellows of Harvard College.

Washington, March 9, 1905

Well, I have just been inaugurated and have begun my second term. Of course, I greatly enjoyed inauguration day, and indeed I have thoroughly enjoyed being President. But I believe I can also say that I am thoroughly alive to the tremendous responsibilities of my position. Life is a long campaign where every victory merely leaves the ground free for another battle, and sooner or later defeat comes to every man, unless death forestalls it. But the final defeat does not and should not cancel the triumphs, if the latter have been substantial and for a cause worth championing.

It has been peculiarly pleasant to me to find that my supporters are to be found in the overwhelming majority among those whom Abraham Lincoln called the plain people. As I suppose you know, Lincoln is my hero. He was a man of the people who always felt with and for the people, but who had not the slightest touch of the demagogue in him. It is probably difficult for his countrymen to get him exactly in the right perspective as compared with the great men of other lands. But to me he does seem to be one of the great figures who loom ever larger as the centuries go by. His unfaltering resolution, his quiet, unyielding courage, his infinite patience and gentleness, and the heights of disinterestedness which he attained whenever the crisis called for putting aside self, together with his farsighted, hardheaded common sense, point him out as just the kind of chief who can do most good in a democratic republic like ours.

Having such an admiration for the great rail-splitter, it has been a matter of keen pride to me that I have appealed peculiarly to the very men to whom he most appealed and who gave him their heartiest support. I am a college-bred man, belonging to a well-to-do family so that, as I was more than contented to live simply, and was fortunate enough to marry a wife with the same tastes, I have not had to make my own livelihood; though I have always had to add to my private income by work of some kind. But the farmers, lumbermen, mechanics, ranchmen, miners, of the North, East and West, have felt that I was just as much in sympathy with them, just as devoted to their interests, and as proud of them and as representative of them, as if I had sprung from among their own ranks; and I certainly feel that I do understand them and believe in them and feel for them and try to represent them just as much as if I had from earliest childhood made each day's toil pay for that day's existence or achievement. How long this feeling toward me will last I cannot say. It was overwhelming at the time of the election last November, and I

judge by the extraordinary turnout for the inauguration it is overwhelming now. Inasmuch as the crest of the wave is invariably
succeeded by the hollow, this means that there will be a reaction.
But meanwhile I shall have accomplished something worth ac-
complishing, I hope.

1906

Jurgis Learns the Secrets of the Jungle

Upton Sinclair was an angry young man when he wrote *The
Jungle* which revealed the evil conditions existing at that time in
the Chicago stock yards and meat packing plants. This excerpt
from his influential novel shows why it helped support a public
demand for the Pure Food and Drug Act and similar regula-
tory legislation.

Source: SINCLAIR, UPTON. *The Jungle*, pp. 96–97. Doubleday & Company, Inc., New York, 1906.

. . . It seemed as if every time you met a person from a new
department, you heard of new swindles and new crimes. There
was, for instance, a Lithuanian who was a cattle butcher for the
plant where Marija had worked, which killed meat for canning
only; and to hear this man describe the animals which came to
his place . . . it seemed they must have agencies all over the
country, to hunt out old and crippled and diseased cattle to be
canned. There were cattle which had been fed on "whisky-malt,"
the refuse of the breweries, and had become what the men called
"steerly"—which means covered with boils. It was a nasty job
killing these, for when you plunged your knife into them they
would burst and splash foul-smelling stuff into your face; and
when a man's sleeves were smeared with blood, and his hands
steeped in it, how was he ever to wipe his face, or to clear his
eyes so that he could see? It was stuff such as this that made the
"embalmed beef" that had killed several times as many United
States soldiers as all the bullets of the Spaniards; only the army
beef, besides, was not fresh canned, it was old stuff that had been
lying for years in the cellars.

234

Then one Sunday evening, Jurgis sat puffing his pipe by the kitchen stove, and talking with an old fellow whom Jonas had introduced, and who worked in the canning rooms at Durham's; and so Jurgis learned a few things about the great and only Durham canned goods which had become a national institution. They were regular alchemists at Durham's; they advertised a mushroom-catsup, and the men who made it did not know what a mushroom looked like. They advertised "potted chicken,"—and it was like the boardinghouse soup of the comic papers, through which a chicken had walked with rubbers on. Perhaps they had a secret process for making chickens chemically—who knows? said Jurgis' friend; the things that went into the mixture were tripe, and the fat of pork, and beef suet, and hearts of beef, and finally the waste ends of veal, when they had any. They put these up in several grades, and sold them at several prices; but the contents of the cans all came out of the same hopper. And then there was "potted game" and "potted grouse," "potted ham," and "deviled ham"—de-vyled, as the men called it. "De-vyled" ham was made out of the waste ends of smoked beef that were too small to be sliced by the machines; and also tripe, dyed with chemicals so that it would not show white; and trimmings of hams and corned beef; and potatoes, skins and all; and finally the hard cartilaginous gullets of beef, after the tongues had been cut out. All this ingenious mixture was ground up and flavored with spices to make it taste like something. Anybody who could invent a new imitation had been sure of a fortune from old Durham, said Jurgis' informant; but it was hard to think of anything new in a place where so many sharp wits had been at work for so long; where men welcomed tuberculosis in the cattle they were feeding, because it made them fatten more quickly; and where they bought up all the old rancid butter left over in the grocery stores of a continent, and "oxidized" it by a forced-air process, to take away the odor, rechurned it with skim milk, and sold it in bricks in the cities! Up to a year or two ago it had been the custom to kill horses in the yards—ostensibly for fertilizer; but after long agitation the newspapers had been able to make the public realize that the horses were being canned. Now it was against the law to kill horses in Packingtown, and the law was really complied with—for the present, at any rate.

Chrysler Describes How He Learned to Drive

Walter P. Chrysler tells how he bought and learned to drive his first automobile. It was a historic occasion, for it inspired an interest which later led him to found the corporation which became one of the "Big Three" of American automobile manufacturing.

Source: WALTER P. CHRYSLER, in collaboration with BOYDEN SPARKS. *Life of an American Workman*. New York: Dodd, Mead & Company, 1950, pp. 99-109.

. . . In 1908 I went to Chicago to see the automobile show. That is where it happened. I saw this . . . touring car; it was painted ivory white and the cushions and trim were red. The top was khaki, supported on wood bows. . . . On the running board there was a handsome tool box that my fingers itched to open. Beside it was a tank of gas to feed the front head lamps; just behind the hood on either side of the cowling was an oil lamp, shaped quite like those on horse drawn carriages. I spent four days hanging around the show, held by that automobile as by a siren's song. The price tag meant just what it said, as I found out by repeated inquiries: $5000 cash. I had $700. I must confess that I never stopped to ask myself if I should, if I could afford to go in hock to buy that car. All I asked myself was: Where could I raise the money?

> [Chrysler managed to borrow the money from some banker friends although they thought he was crazy to go so greatly in debt for an automobile.]

The automobile arrived in a freight car, anchored to the floor. I did not know how to run it, but I certainly was not going to allow another person to be the first behind its wheel. I arranged with a teamster to haul it to my house and put it in the barn. . . . If it had been a jewel of fantastic size, I could not have been more careful of it.

My wife was wild with enthusiasm then and wanted to take a ride immediately. But I put the car in the barn, and it stayed in there so long that she despaired of ever getting a ride. Sometimes she sat in it when I cranked up and let the engine run.

Night after night, I worked in the barn. . . . Saturday afternoons and all day on Sundays I worked on that car. . . . There was no single function that I did not study over and over. Finally, I proved to myself that I knew and understood it, because I had taken it apart and put it all together. . . .

Finally, my wife asked, "What is the use of having an automobile if we're never going to ride?"

"Now, don't be impatient, Della."

"Impatient! You've had the car three months and it's never been out of the barn!"

It was a Saturday afternoon, and I said "In the barn three months, you say? Well, this afternoon she's coming out. Come look!"

. . . I had a gallery of neighbors, as I cranked up, and got behind the wheel, one hand devoted to steering and one to fiddling with that confounded sliding transmission lever. . . . She had a chain drive, of course, and that was what made her seem to growl and snarl every time I touched the transmission lever. . . . But the engine was purring, and when I looked behind, I could see that she was not smoking, much. Then I clamped my teeth on a fresh cigar and engaged the clutch.

The big touring car bucked like a mustang saddled for the first time. We shot forward; as some of the neighbors whooped and yelled, she bucked again and lurched into a ditch, rolled half a length farther and stalled, axle deep, in my neighbor's garden patch.

I had chewed up about one third of my cigar on that short run. I sent off for a man who had a team of horses. . . . We pulled her out; I settled with the teamster and promised monetary satisfaction to my irate neighbor. I heard a few mocking laughs, and so I cranked her up, jumped in behind the throbbing wheel and started off. This time I got her into high and let her roll. All I was doing was to grip the wheel and steer. . . . We were at the edge of town right in the country.

A few hundred yards ahead, I saw a cow emerging from behind an osage hedge that bordered a lane. She was headed for the road. I bulbed the horn until it had made its goose-like cry four or five times, but the cow . . . kept right on her course and never changed her pace. Nor did I change the pace of the automobile. I could not; all that I could do was to grip the wheel and steer, biting on my cigar until my teeth met inside of it.

Well, I missed the cow, though I was close enough to touch her. I missed few of the ruts and holes along that country road to . . . where there was an intersecting road, and there I turned around. I fed more gas to the four-cylinder engine on the way toward home. On the basis of ratings today, that car would be said to have about eighty horse-power. As I came up the grade, the neighbors saw me riding fast, maybe twenty miles an hour. I stopped at the barn. My neighbors helped me push the car inside. I closed the doors and then discovered I was so tired I trembled. There was not a dry stitch of clothing on me; that perspiration came from nervousness and excitement. It was six o'clock in the evening then. I went into the house, stripped off my clothes, took a bath and got into bed. I was all in from that wild ride. Well, that's the way I learned to drive.

1910

"Yer Never Worked Nights, Did Yer?"

During the Progressive Era, several states enacted laws regulating hours and working conditions for women and children. That such laws were needed is revealed in this selection, written by a woman journalist who worked in the Pennsylvania silk mills to gather authentic material.

Source: SANVILLE, FLORENCE LUCAS. "A Woman in the Pennsylvania Silk-Mills," *Harper's Magazine* (April, 1910), pp. 651–662, *passim*. Copyright, 1910, by Harper & Brothers. Reprinted by permission of *Harper's Magazine*.

The length of a factory girl's work-day varies from a legal limit of eight hours in one or two advanced States to ten, eleven, or twelve in less enlightened communities; and in some States where the law still fails to protect its women from industrial exploitation the hours are regulated only by the needs of the industry.

In Pennsylvania . . . the law prescribes a limit of twelve hours daily and sixty hours weekly for women over eighteen; for girls under that age the law restricts this further to fifty-eight hours a week and an average of ten hours a day. . . . But in the factories scattered through the villages and small mining-towns, in which great numbers of young girls are employed—such as are established by the silk industry—I found in a period of industrial depression that over half of the mills were working ten and a half to eleven hours a day. . . .

Eleven hours of work a day means entering the factory at 6.45 in the morning and leaving it at 6.15 at night, with a half-hour at midday. During a large part of the year it means that for day after day the sun does not shine upon these hosts of working women and children, as they come in the chill of the early morning and return in the dusk of the evening.

The work which fills these crawling minutes is not absorbing—is not even interesting. . . . In fact, I found that the passage of the time becomes the most absorbing question of the day about an hour after work has commenced. In mills where the employer failed to provide a clock I quickly found that, as the discovered possessor of a watch, my life became a burden. . . . I ran the gauntlet of a continuous volley of questions—"What's the time, please?" "Let's see your watch." . . . The second day I found it hard not to be impatient, despite the wistful questions. . . . The third day in self-defence I left my watch at home—although my penalty was to share the prevailing ignorance of how the day was passing.

The evils of prolonged hours of labor for girls are intensified when this labor is performed at night. . . . I saw this most clearly when I first applied for work on the night shift. As we went into the factory our passage was blocked by a return stream of girls, and the announcement that "the boiler has burst and there was no work that night." In the outpouring throng . . . were so many short skirts that it might well have been a group of schoolgirls, dismissed late by the teacher. We naturally fell in with the girls whose way led in the same direction as ours, and we walked down the railroad track together.

"Yer never worked nights, did yer?" was the first question put to us. We confessed not. "Y'll git more fer it—but it's terrible hard." I asked about the hours and found that they were from 6.30 in the evening until 6 in the morning, with a half-hour at midnight. "They keep the doors locked so that no one can't git out—they didn't use ter." . . .

Finally, all our escort had dispersed except Lena R_ _ _, a thin-shouldered anaemic-looking girl, with a sweet, bright face. She looked so young that I asked her age. "I'll be fourteen in the winter," she replied, and added that she had been doing night work since she was eleven. . . .

One of the most striking evils in the physical environment of women in the factories is the lack of seats. . . . Very few mills . . . provide the seats which are required by the Pennsylvania law. . . . The harmful effect of continuous standing upon young and growing girls, is too well established a fact to require any elaboration. In addition to the permanent ill effects, much immediate and unnecessary suffering, especially in hot weather, is inflicted by the prohibition of sitting. I could always detect the existence of this rule by a glance at the stocking-feet of the workers, and at the rows of discarded shoes. . . . For after a few hours the strain upon the swollen feet becomes intolerable, and one girl after another discards her shoes. . . .

Another harsh and very common practice of employers is to cover the lower sashes of the windows with paint, and to fasten them so that they cannot be raised in hot weather. This is done so that the girls "don't waste time looking out." . . .

It would be grossly unfair were I to indicate that every mill in which we worked, or with which we came in contact, was characterized by such brutal indifference on the part of the management. In some factories the girls spoke with enthusiasm of the generosity and consideration of their employers. And one mill which we visited in an effort to obtain work was not only spotlessly clean, but was even brightened by pots of growing plants and great bunches of mountain laurel placed throughout the work rooms. . . .

1913

A Freshman Congressman Describes a Freshman President

> Alben W. Barkley of Kentucky, while serving as Truman's Vice-President (1949–1953), earned the affectionate title of "Veep." His autobiography, *That Reminds Me—*, contains many stories and impressions of the political leaders that he knew during his forty-seven years of public service. This is his impression of President Wilson.
>
> Source: BARKLEY, ALBEN W. *That Reminds Me—*, pp. 91–93. Doubleday & Company, Inc., New York, 1954.

Woodrow Wilson was inaugurated on March 4, 1913, the same day on which I was sworn in as a freshman congressman. I came to revere him as the greatest statesman and greatest President under whom I ever served. It was said of President Wilson that he loved humanity en masse but not individually. This was not true. . . . Though Wilson . . . was no extrovert, he had a deep and abiding love for people as individuals, and he displayed his warm humanity in many homey little ways.

President Wilson revealed his own true nature in a remark I once heard him make in talking about men who enter public life. "Some men grow; others swell," he said. Wilson grew but did not swell. With the weight of the country—and later of the world —on his shoulders, he never became too big to listen sympathetically to the problems of those in lesser positions. . . .

. . . I recall vividly how Wilson, in commenting to me on the large number of new congressmen who were carried into office with him in the Democratic landslide, said to me, "I look upon you younger members of Congress much as I looked upon my students at Princeton. You have had no experience yet in legislative matters, but you will learn." He went on to say that he too had lacked experience when he became president of Princeton and later Governor of New Jersey, and that he now looked forward to learning, along with the newcomers in the House and Senate, more about the machinery of government. The sincerity and humility of his manner won me completely. . . .

Though an intellectual, Wilson was no ethereal cloud dweller.

241

He loved vaudeville, and . . . I often saw the President and Mrs. Wilson at the theater enjoying a Saturday matinee. He particularly relished the slapstick comedy acts, and his deep-throated laughter could be heard halfway across the theater. He had a deft turn of his own with the humorous phrase. His Vice President, Thomas R. Marshall, once came to him with one of Wilson's scholarly volumes on American history, and Wilson unhesitatingly inscribed it: "To My Favorite Vice."

He also poked fun at what he insisted was his personal lack of beauty. I have heard him recite a Limerick which . . . went . . . like this:

> As a beauty I'm not a great star.
> Others are handsomer far
> > But my face—I don't mind it
> > Because I'm behind it
> It's the folks out in front that I jar.

1913

Only One Step, No Stooping, and No Hurry

> Although the idea of the moving assembly line had many ancestors, Henry Ford first applied it successfully to the manufacture of automobiles. Here he describes the principles involved.
> Source: FORD, HENRY, in collaboration with SAMUEL CROWTHER. *My Life and Work*, pp. 76–84, *passim*. Doubleday, Page and Company, 1922.

The more economical methods of production . . . began gradually. . . . In our first assembling we simply started to put a car together at a spot on the floor and workmen brought to it the parts as they were needed in exactly the same way that one builds a house. . . . The first step forward in assembly came when we began taking the work to the men instead of the men to the work. We now have two general principles in all operations—that a man shall never have to take more than one step, if possibly it can be avoided, and that no man need ever stoop over.

The principles of assembly are these:

(1) Place the tools and the men in the sequence of the operation so that each component part shall travel the least possible distance while in the process of finishing.

(2) Use work slides or some other form of carrier so that when a workman completes his operation, he drops the part always in the same place—which place must always be the most convenient place to his hand—and if possible have gravity carry the part to the next workman for his operation.

(3) Use sliding assembly lines by which the parts to be assembled are delivered at convenient distances.

The net result of the application of these principles is the reduction of the necessity for thought on the part of the worker and the reduction of his movements to a minimum. . . .

Along about April 1, 1913, we first tried the experiment of an assembly line. We tried it on assembling the fly-wheel magneto. . . . I believe that this was the first moving line ever installed. The idea came in a general way from the overhead trolley that the Chicago packers use in dressing beef. We had previously assembled the fly-wheel magneto in the usual method. With one workman doing a complete job he could turn out from thirty-five to forty pieces in a nine-hour day, or about twenty minutes to an assembly. What he did alone was then spread into twenty-nine operations; that cut down the assembly time to thirteen minutes, ten seconds. Then we raised the height of the line eight inches—this was in 1914—and cut the time to seven minutes. Further experimenting with the speed that the work should move at cut the time down to five minutes. . . . That line established the efficiency of the method and we now use it everywhere. . . .

About the best we had done in stationary chassis assembling was an average of twelve hours and twenty-eight minutes per chassis. We tried the experiment of drawing the chassis with a rope and windlass down a line two hundred fifty feet long. Six assemblers traveled with the chassis and picked up the parts from piles placed along the line. This rough experiment reduced the time to five hours fifty minutes per chassis. In the early part of 1914 we elevated the assembly line. We had adopted the policy of "man-high" work; we had one line twenty-six and three quarter inches and another twenty-four and one half inches from the floor —to suit squads of different heights. The waist-high arrangement and a further subdivision of work so that each man had fewer movements cut down the labour time per chassis to one hour thirty-three minutes. . . .

It must not be imagined, however, that all this worked out as quickly as it sounds. The speed of the moving work had to be carefully tried out; in the fly-wheel magneto we first had a speed of sixty inches per minute. That was too fast. Then we tried eighteen inches per minute. That was too slow. Finally we settled on forty-four inches per minute. The idea is that a man must not be hurried in his work—he must have every second necessary but not a single unnecessary second. We have worked out speeds for each assembly. . . . The chassis assembling line, for instance, goes at a pace of six feet per minute. . . . In the chassis assembling are forty-five separate operations or stations. . . . The motor arrives on the tenth operation. . . . Some men do only one or two small operations, others do more. The man who places a part does not fasten it—the part may not be fully in place until after several operations later. The man who puts in a bolt does not put on the nut; the man who puts on the nut does not tighten it. On operation number thirty-four the . . . motor gets its gasoline; it has previously received lubrication; on operation forty-four the radiator is filled with water, and on operation number forty-five the car drives out on to the street.

1917

"We'll Get a Second Lieutenant to Run It"

World War I brought governmental regulation and control of the economy through the War Industries Board and similar governmental agencies. Bernard Baruch, who headed WIB, gives an example of some of the difficulties encountered.

Source: BARUCH, BERNARD M. *Baruch: The 'Public Years*, pp. 65–69. Holt, Rinehart and Winston, New York, 1960.

[WIB had drawn up a price control schedule for coke, iron, and steel. Baruch presented this plan at a meeting with sixty-five of the nation's leading steel executives.]

The meeting was a stormy one with much heated argument and impassioned oratory. In fairness to the steel industry, it should be said that its leaders were perfectly willing to fix prices on purchases by our government. They insisted, however, that the price to the public and to the Allies should continue to be determined by a free market. This was in direct conflict with the rule laid down by President Wilson that the price for the government must also be the price for the public and the Allies.

The climax occurred when I asked Judge Gary [head of U.S. Steel] if he would be interested in a letter I possessed, and handed it to him. . . . It was a letter from the President, stating that he would take over the United States Steel Corporation or any other business on WIB's recommendation. Gary read the letter with an expressionless face and handed it back.

"You haven't got anybody to run the Steel Company," he said.

"Oh yes I have, Judge," I told him.

"Who?"

"Oh, we'll get a second lieutenant or somebody to run it."

That must have stung Gary to the quick.

"But that won't trouble you very much," I added. "If those mill towns find out why we've taken over, they'll present you with your mills brick by brick."

Gary rose from his seat and walked away. I could see the fingers of each hand rubbing one against the other. You could almost hear his mind turning over.

Suddenly he turned around, came back, and said, "Can't we fix this up?"

"Sure we can," I said.

The steel people went into a private conference. When they returned, one of them, long my friend, stormed over to see me. Belligerently thrusting his face near mine, he shook his finger and shouted: "Bernie, the steel people thought you were friendly to them but they've found out you're their archenemy. They'll never forgive you as long as you live."

"Is that the steel people's message to me?" I asked him.

"It is," he shouted, apparently in a rage.

"All right," I said, "if that's the message to me, let me give you my answer." Assuming a stance as belligerent as his, I told him in unadorned language what I thought of the steel leaders, and assured him that they were not going to get away with any bluff.

That was the last shaft in the steel men's quiver. When we resumed negotiations they were more amenable. . . . On September 24th the President proclaimed the new prices which the WIB and the steel industry had agreed upon. . . . The steel industry accepted these new prices in good faith and they remained almost unchanged till the end of the war. It has been estimated that this regulation of steel prices saved the government more than a billion dollars. The steel industry also did a superb job of production; but there is no question that profits . . . were still excessive.

The government's interference with the affairs of the United States Steel Company always rankled Judge Gary, and he never forgave the threat I made. After the war, he publicly charged that . . . the government . . ., meaning WIB, had sought to nationalize the steel industry as the first step in undoing America's free enterprise system. I had to set the record straight and publicly reveal the uncooperative attitude of the steel industry in the midst of war that had compelled the government to resort to a show of force.

. . . Gary . . . typified the problem which WIB faced in educating American businessmen to the new facts of life. They had not made the transition in their thinking from Main Street to Washington, and their values were still the values of the market place. Their pride in the achievements of industry and their mistrust of government made it difficult for them to put national interest above unenlightened self-interest.

1918

"All We Can Do Is Wait for Fortune's Decision"

The author of this diary was a corporal in the famous Rainbow Division which fought gallantly in France.

Source: BERGER, JOSEPH, and BERGER, DOROTHY (editors). *Diary of America*, pp. 541–543. Simon and Schuster, New York, 1957.

October 17, 1918. I talked to a sergeant whom I had known back in Lorraine. He told me that replacements had filled the great gaps in . . . the old regiments until only non-coms and a few officers remained of those who had come across with the Division. He said the new men were filling the places well and got right into the spirit of the Division. Of course some of them can't stand the strain. The history books won't tell, for example, of the green private who blew off his trigger finger with his rifle yesterday because he couldn't stand the gaff up here. . . .

October 30. Last night the Germans put on a whale of a bombardment, and I don't see how any of us escaped to tell the story. In the thick of it our communications were knocked out and I was detailed to repair the telephone line. . . . I . . . breathed a little prayer, climbed out of my foxhole, and darted out into the inferno.

Flashes of exploding artillery at intervals lighted up the blackness of the night. Explosions of enemy shells on every hand and the scream of big ones going overhead to back areas added to the thunderous uproar. . . . Boy! I was glad when I came to that break in the line. I was splicing the wire when—Shriek! Bang! A ton of steel came over me. Just as I finished the job . . . another hit knocked the line out in another place.

For once I lost my . . . self-assurance, and I wasn't so certain that I would ever see home and Mother again. But finally . . . I came upon the next break and spliced it in a hurry. Then I raced back to my hole after reporting communications in order. . . .

November 4. German bombers visited us again last night. They must have dropped a hundred bombs or more on this town during the raid. It is difficult to describe our feelings during an air raid. We hear the hum of motors over our heads. Our anti-aircraft guns and machine guns fire into the darkness hoping . . . they may be lucky enough to hit an enemy plane. Then a series of explosions shake the earth and throw up debris like a volcano in eruption. All we can do is to lie still while the cold sweat pops out on our foreheads, and wait for fortune's decision—life or death.

November 8. [Advancing toward Sedan, France.] The battle has changed from a slow, bloody, inch-by-inch fight to a mad chase. The enemy is in full retreat.

November 11. [At Harricourt, France.] Just before eleven,

Lieutenant Bennett, looking at his watch, said to me, "In four minutes the war will be over." At eleven the great rumble of artillery and small arms was stilled. Eleven o'clock! How strangely solemn, almost painful to ears long accustomed to the din and tumult of the front!

> [November 11 was the day on which all fighting stopped in World War I at eleven o'clock. Until after World War II this date was a holiday known as Armistice Day. Now it is called Veterans Day, in honor of veterans of all our wars.]

1919

Abraham Flexner Gets Excited— and Almost Fifty Million

> After accumulating a great fortune from the activities of the Standard Oil Company, John D. Rockefeller donated vast sums to worthy purposes throughout the world. Here Abraham Flexner, who spearheaded the reform of medical education in the United States, tells how Rockefeller money helped in this cause.
> Source: *Abraham Flexner: An Autobiography*, pp. 176–178. Simon and Schuster, New York, 1960.

In the spring of 1919 I raised . . . the question of possibly obtaining from Mr. Rockefeller a fund earmarked for medical education, which would be spent . . . within a relatively brief period for the purpose of building up in various sections institutions which would point the way to other medical schools and at the same time induce the hopeless ones to discontinue altogether. . . .

I shall never forget the important interview with Mr. Gates. [A Rockefeller assistant who screened the many requests for money which Rockefeller received.] I went to his office at 26 Broadway after making an appointment and described the plan. . . . Mr. Gates listened without comment until I had finished. Then he said, "What will it take? What will it cost?"

"To complete the job with a limited number of schools will . . .

require several hundred millions. Part of it will have to be in cash, part of it can be supplied by making the right kind of connections between existing and well-supported hospitals and medical schools. In any event, Mr. Rockefeller will not and should not contribute the entire amount of cash required. . . . The schools should become matters of local . . . pride, so that they and the general public should shoulder a large part of the burden."

"That is sound," commented Mr. Gates. "How much do you want from Mr. Rockefeller?"

I had in my own thinking not reached this point, though I knew well that we could use as much as we could obtain. I had therefore very quickly to make a guess as to how much Mr. Rockefeller might . . . give. I replied, "Oh, if Mr. Rockefeller would give us fifty million dollars earmarked for medical education, I believe that we could add several hundreds of millions directly and indirectly to the resources of the schools selected for development."

"Will you write me a memorandum on the subject," asked Mr. Gates, "which I can present to Mr. Rockefeller?"

"Yes," I answered. "How much will be read?"

"Oh, five pages," replied Mr. Gates.

"Very well," I answered, "I shall try to get it into four."

I returned to the office . . . and set about the preparation of the memorandum, which . . . was revised over and over in order that it might be clear, persuasive, and devoid of everything that was not to the point. In its final form I handed it to Mr. Gates, who read it approvingly and said that he would hand it to Mr. Rockefeller. For a few months nothing happened. In the autumn . . . I met Mr. Rockefeller, Jr. . . . and ventured to ask him whether his father had spoken to him on the subject of medical education.

"Yes," he replied, "I think he is interested and will do something. I don't know what, perhaps a million, perhaps several. We shall have to wait."

A short time later, Starr J. Murphy, Mr. Rockefeller's counsel, asked me over the telephone to come to see him at once. As I entered his office he said, "I have something for you," and handed me a brief letter . . . in which Mr. Rockefeller pledged himself to give upward of $20,000,000 to . . . medical education. . . .

I was, of course, excited and grateful, but when Mr. Murphy asked what we intended to do, I said:

"Not much until we get the other thirty million."

"Can't you do anything with twenty million?"

"Oh, yes," I said, "we can do a good deal, but if we begin on a scale of twenty million, the program will be radically different from that which we would adopt if we had fifty million."

. . . Soon Mr. Rockefeller increased his gift until it reached the huge total of almost fifty million. . . .

1923

Father Coolidge Calls Calvin and Grace

Calvin Coolidge, Republican President during most of the prosperous 1920's, was a prudent man. Also, he had the distinction of being the only President whose father administered his oath of office. A newspaper reporter who was there describes the unusual and dramatic circumstances.

Source: LANG, LOUIS J. "How Coolidge Got the News," *Outlook* (Sept. 5, 1923), pp. 22-24.

[Vice President Coolidge and his wife were vacationing at his father's farmhouse in the Green Mountains, near Plymouth, Vermont, in August, 1923, when newspaper reporters brought him news of President Harding's death. The reporters arrived at 1 A.M. in an ancient automobile driven by an old neighbor of Coolidge's father.]

. . . Painfully laboring up the last series of precipitous hills, we suddenly shot into an open space. . . . We caught a glimmer of light. ". . . Father Coolidge always keeps an old kerosene lamp burning, because he gets up before daylight to milk the cows," said our ancient pilot.

We drew up at the porch of the Coolidge farmhouse. All jumped out. Except for the dim flame just described, the house was an inky blot. Atkinson and I crept up on to the porch. . . . Atkinson fumbled for the bell. It could not be found.

"There ain't no bell. We are all honest here. . . . Walk right into the house," said our driver in a loud whisper.

Atkinson pushed open the door into the mite of a room where the . . . lamp sputtered. The Coolidge collie pup barked. "Who is there?" was the husky inquiry from the adjoining room.

Atkinson, who recognized the voice of Father Coolidge, answered: "The newspaper men. President Harding is dead. We must see your son at once."

There was a swish of clothing inside the father's bedroom. Then appeared the aged father of the President. He wore a nightgown tucked into a pair of overalls. His feet were bare. Rubbing his blinking eyes, Father Coolidge said: ". . . I'll call Calvin and Grace." . . .

Lights began to gleam through the narrow staircase, at the top of which the President and the future mistress of the White House were presumably dressing. . . . Hours seemed to elapse. We correspondents were wondering if the President ever would come downstairs. . . .

. . . There was a step on the stair. There came from the bottom of the flight an apparition in black. A white face was silhouetted in the flutter of flame from the single lamp. It was the face of the new President. It was ashen in hue. This was intensified by a suit of black, a black tie, and black shoes.

The new President strode silently, almost majestically, into the room. He greeted each of us with a hand-shake. We each addressed him as "Mr. President." . . . With dignity and precision, he said: "Mr. Geisser, [his acting secretary] will you please come with me into the other room?"

The President and Mr. Geisser started for the room on the left. Father Coolidge had dug up another greasy, flickering lamp. He preceded the President with it. The three disappeared. The door was closed.

Nearly 2 A. M.! Not a line from the President for the many millions who awaited it.

Two-fifteen A. M.! The door opened. The President reappeared with a few sheets of paper. . . . The President, still silent to the correspondents, handed them individually . . ,. his first message to the American people. . . .

The correspondents glanced hastily through the document. The unprecedented feature was the announcement that the President was to take the oath of office from his father, a mere notary public. I asked the President: "Has it not been invariably the custom that a President should be sworn in by a Justice of the United States Supreme Court?"

The President replied: "Maybe. But it is good law, in my judgment, that a President can be sworn in by anybody who has authority to administer an oath, even if that body happens to be his father." . . .

Clustered about the President were . . . witnesses. . . . These grouped themselves about the old table, on which still burned the smoky kerosene lamp. The old family Bible was alongside it. Father Coolidge took up his station on one side of the table. The President with Mrs. Coolidge faced him.

Elder Coolidge asked his son to raise his right hand. The President obeyed. Elder Coolidge then read the . . . oath. . . . The President, with deep emotion, repeated each word of the oath after his father. . . . Then he tenderly embraced and kissed his wife. The proud father walked over and seized his son's hand with a crushing grip. The witnesses shook the President's hand. Then neighbors trooped in, and there was quite an affectionate exchange of mingled grief and congratulations.

It was near daylight. The President said to his wife: "We are due at Rutland at 9 A. M. Better hurry with your grip." Mrs. Coolidge disappeared, first to prepare a breakfast of corn-cakes and coffee, and then to get ready for her first journey to Washington as the First Lady in the Land.

1924

Will Rogers Comments on Sinking Ships and Cheating Children

Americans in the 1920's and 1930's called Will Rogers our "Cowboy Philosopher." From the stage, in a daily newspaper column, in books, and in magazine articles he commented sharply and humorously on domestic politics and world affairs. Here are his remarks on two vital issues of the 1920's.

Source: DAY, DONALD (editor). *The Autobiography of Will Rogers*, pp. 103–104; 104–105. Houghton Mifflin Company, Boston.

Well, we were all last week trying to sink our greatest Battleship, the Washington. . . . A great many people don't understand just how this sinking came about. You see we had a conference over here a few years ago. It was called by America. We were building a lot of Battleships and we had plenty of money to do it on, and it looked like in a couple of years we might have the largest Navy in the World. Well, the League of Nations gathering in Paris had attracted a lot of attention and got quite a lot of publicity, none of which had been shared in this country by the Democrats. So, when the Republicans got in, they conceived the idea of a publicity stunt for the Republicans. Why not then have a conference? But what would they confer about? . . .

So Secretary of State Hughes happened to think of an idea: "Let us confer on sinking battleships." Well, the idea was so original that they immediately made him the Toastmaster. You see, up to then, Battleships had always been sunk by the enemy, and when he proposed to sink them yourself it was the most original thought that had ever percolated the mind of a Statesman. So, when he communicated the idea to England and Japan that we had an idea whereby we would sink some of our own Battleships, why they come over so fast, even the butler wasn't dressed to receive them when they arrived.

England was willing to tear her blueprints on planned building into half, Japan was willing to give up her dreams of having more ships on the seas than any nation and stop building up to 3/5 of the size of England and America, and Secretary Hughes met that with "Now, Gentlemen, I will show you what America is prepared to do. FOR EVERY BATTLESHIP YOU FELLOWS DON'T BUILD AMERICA WILL SINK ONE."

Now they are talking of having another Naval Disarmament Conference. We can only stand one more. If they ever have a second one we will have to borrow a Boat to go to it.

You see, we don't like to ever have the start on any Nation in case of war. We figure it looks better to start late and come from behind. . . . Sinking your own Boats is a military strategy that will always remain in the sole possession of America.

. . . .

As I am writing this 2 blocks away the body of Samuel Gompers, the Great Labor Leader, is being viewed and wept over by hundreds of big strong men, who are appreciative of what he had spent his life in doing for them. . . . He has done more for the working man than any man living. . . .

. . . I see a lot in the Papers about . . . Child Labor . . . and I have been asked how I stand on that. If Congress would just pass one law, as follows . . . "EVERY CHILD, REGARDLESS OF AGE, SHALL RECEIVE THE SAME WAGE AS A GROWN PERSON." That will stop your child labor. They only hire them because they pay them less for the same work than they would have to pay a man. If Children don't do more for less money, why is it that they want to use them? No Factory or Farmer or anybody else hires a Child because he is so big hearted he wants to do something for the Child. He hires him because he wants to save a man's salary. It's becoming a habit and a custom that if a Child does something for us, no matter how good and prompt they do it, to not give them as much as we would a grown person, because, I suppose, people think they would just spend it foolishly if they had too much.

1924

Red Grange Gives Thousands the Thrill of Their Lives

> The 1920's have been called the "Golden Age of Sports," and it was during that time that college football became the popular spectator sport that it is today. Red Grange of the University of Illinois was one of the great stars of the period.
> Source: *Associated Press*, New York, October 18, 1924.

Urbana, Ill., Oct. 18, 1924 (Associated Press)

A flashing, red-haired youngster, running and dodging with the speed of a deer, gave 67,000 spectators jammed into the new $1,700,000 Illinois Memorial Stadium the thrill of their lives to-

day when Illinois vanquished Michigan, 39 to 14, in what probably will be the outstanding game of the 1924 gridiron season. . . .

Harold (Red) Grange, Illinois phenomenon, All-America half-
back . . . was the dynamo that furnished the thrills. Grange
doubled and redoubled his football glory in the most remarkable
exhibition of running, dodging and passing seen on any gridiron
in years—an exhibition that set the dumb-founded spectators
screaming with excitement.

Individually, Grange scored five of Illinois' six touchdowns in
a manner that left no doubt as to his ability to break through the
most perfect defense. He furnished one thrill after another. On
the very first kickoff Grange scooped up the ball on the Illinois
five-yard line and raced 95 yards through the Michigan eleven
for a touchdown in less than ten seconds after the starting
whistle blew.

Before the Michigan team could recover from its shock, Grange
had scored three more touchdowns in rapid succession, running
sixty-five, fifty-five and forty-five yards, respectively, for his next
three scores. Coach Bob Zuppke took him out of the line-up
before the first quarter ended. He returned later to heave several
successful passes and score a fifth touchdown in the last half. . . .

Grange surpassed all of his former exploits in every department. He handled the ball 21 times, gained 402 yards and scored
5 touchdowns. Unbiased experts agree that his performance was
among the greatest ever seen on an American gridiron. . . .

1926

A Champion Battles Cross Tides
and Rough Seas

A British expert on channel swimming tells how Gertrude
Ederle became the first woman to swim the English Channel.
Miss Ederle's feat was an example of women's continuing quest
for equality with men, which was so marked during the 1920's.
Source: RUTHERFORD, ALEX. "Plucky Gertrude Ederle Swims
the English Channel," New York Times, Aug. 6, 1926.

Dover (England), Aug. 6.

Gertrude Ederle, the nineteen-year-old New York champion girl swimmer, is one of the pluckiest persons that ever attempted the huge task of swimming the English Channel. I watched this pretty, tiny atom of humanity in her red bathing suit and . . . cap, with goggles like a motorist's, battle for fourteen hours today against the merciless elements. . . .

Miss Ederle entered the Channel at Cape Gris-Nez (France) at 7:09 this morning amid the wild cheers of the Channel swimmers assembled at the training camp there. She was accompanied by the tug *Alsace*, carrying the Stars and Stripes and a wireless apparatus for flashing to America messages during each mile of progress. . . . Chalked on the . . . side of the tug in front of Miss Ederle's eyes were the words, "This Way, Ole Kid!" with an arrow pointing forward.

The wind at the start was southwest, the temperature was 61 and there was a rough sea. Miss Ederle set off with strong strokes and covered the first four miles in three hours. She was swimming with a strong crawl and she refused to go slow when ordered to by her trainer.

Her party hung over the side of the boat singing American songs, including frequently "The Star-Spangled Banner." Miss Ederle responded from the water. . . . At 10:30 this morning she had her first meal—beef extract drunk while floating on her back and also chicken eaten during ten minutes of rest. . . .

Wild enthusiasm, to which Gertrude responded, greeted her arrival in mid-channel just about midday. "The Star-Spangled Banner" was again sung. The demonstration lasted several minutes.

At 1:30, nine miles from the English coast, rain started, with a strong, fierce wind causing a heavy swell difficult to battle against.

At 3:00 the swimmer was drifting toward Dover with the incoming tide and the rain was stronger than ever.

At 5:00 the wind was increasing in power and velocity and the sea was choppy and angry. The tug party was singing "Yes, We Have No Bananas." A second meal of chocolate was now served to the swimmer. . . . The weather was becoming worse every moment and the sea rougher.

At 6:00 there was talk of giving up, since the weather and the sea appeared too bad for victory. Miss Ederle seemed to swim more strongly against the terrible conditions and pluckily shouted, "No! No!" On she struggled a few yards, only to fall back twice as many.

At 6:30 o'clock she was still going strong, holding her own against the cross tides. It was a great swim.

It was when Miss Ederle had passed south of Goodwin Lightship that the party for the first time decided that victory seemed possible. The crowds on shore began to gather in thousands all along the beach, and automobiles by the hundreds all sounded their horns. Tugs in the Channel hooted their sirens and scores of flares were lit on the beach to guide her in.

As she approached the shallow water, hundreds of people, regardless of their clothes, waded in the water and surrounded her. Miss Ederle walked ashore unaided, quickly followed by her father, who clasped her in his arms and wrapped her in a dressing gown. . . .

1927

The Babe Slams Number Sixty

> During the 1920's, the names of George Herman "Babe" Ruth and "baseball" became synonymous. James S. Carolan tells this tale of Ruth's sixtieth home run which set a major-league record (almost tied by Roger Maris in 1961).
> Source: CAROLAN, JAMES S. "The Babe Slams No. 60," *New York Times*, Oct. 1, 1927.

New York, Oct. 1, 1927.

Babe Ruth scaled the hitherto unattained heights yesterday. Home run 60, a terrific smash off the southpaw pitching of Tom Zachary, nestled in the Babe's favorite spot in the right-field bleachers, and before the roar had ceased it was found that this drive not only had made home-run record history but also was the winning margin in a 4–2 victory over the Senators. The Yanks' last league game of the year will be played today. . . .

The first Zachary offering was a fast one for a called strike. The next was high. The Babe took a vicious swing at the third pitched ball and the bat connected with a crash that was audible in all parts of the stand. It was not necessary to follow the course of the ball. The boys in the bleachers indicated the route of the record homer. It dropped about half way to the top. Boys, No. 60 was some homer, a fitting wallop to top the Babe's record of 59 in 1921.

While the crowd cheered and the Yankee players roared their greetings the Babe made his triumphant, almost regal tour of the paths. He jogged around slowly, touched each bag firmly and carefully and when he imbedded his spikes in the rubber disk to record officially Homer 60, hats were tossed into the air, papers were torn up and thrown liberally and the spirit of celebration permeated the place. . . .

The only unhappy individual within the stadium was Zachary. He realized he was going down in the records as the historical home-run victim, in other words the goat. Zachary was one of the most interested spectators of the home-run flight. He tossed his glove to the ground, muttered to himself, turned to his mates for consolation and got everything but that. There is no denying that Zachary was putting everything he had on the ball.

The ball that the Babe drove was a pitch that was fast, low and on the inside. The Babe pulled away from the plate, then stepped into the ball, and wham! According to Umpire Bill Dinneen at the plate and Catcher Muddy Ruel the ball traveled on a line and landed a foot inside fair territory about half way to the top of the bleachers. . . .

The ball which became Homer 60 was caught by Joe Forner of 1937 First Avenue, Manhattan. He is about 40 years old and has been following baseball for thirty-five, according to his own admission. He was far from modest and as soon as the game was over rushed to the dressing room to let the Babe know who had the ball. . . .

The Lone Eagle Almost Drowns in a Human Sea

> Charles A. Lindbergh made the first successful solo flight
> from New York to Paris in thirty-four hours. The greatness of
> his feat can be judged from his description of the tumultuous
> reception he received at Le Bourget airfield in Paris.
> Reprinted with the permission of Charles Scribner's Sons from
> *The Spirit of St. Louis*, pp. 495–497, by CHARLES A. LINDBERGH.
> Copyright 1953 Charles Scribner's Sons.

. . . I was completely unprepared for the welcome which
awaited me on Le Bourget. I had no idea that my plane had been
so accurately reported along its route between Ireland and the
capital of France. . . . When I circled the aerodrome it did not
occur to me that any connection existed between my arrival and
the cars stalled in traffic on the roads. When my wheels touched
earth, I had no way of knowing that tens of thousands of men
and women were breaking down fences and flooding past guards.

I had barely cut the engine switch when the first people
reached my cockpit. Within seconds my open windows were
blocked with faces. My name was called out over and over again,
in accents strange to my ears—on this side of my plane—on that
side—in front—in the distance. I could feel the *Spirit of St. Louis*
tremble with the pressure of the crowd. I heard the crack of
wood behind me when someone leaned too heavily against a
fairing strip. Then a second strip snapped, and a third, and
there was the sound of tearing fabric. That meant souvenir
hunters were going wild. It was essential to get a guard stationed around my plane before more damage was done.

"Are there any mechanics here?" I asked.

I couldn't understand a single word that came back in answer—
from a half-dozen different mouths.

"Does anyone here speak English?" I shouted.

The noise and excitement made a reply impossible. There were
rips of fabric every few seconds. . . . I was afraid the *Spirit of
St. Louis* might be seriously injured. . . . I decided to get out of
the cockpit and try to find some English-speaking person who
would help me organize a guard to hold back the crowd.

I opened the door, and started to put my foot down onto ground. But dozens of hands took hold of me—my legs, my arms, my body. No one heard the sentences I spoke. I found myself lying in a prostrate position, up on top of the crowd, in the center of an ocean of heads that extended as far out into the darkness as I could see. Then I started to sink down into that ocean, and was buoyed up again. Thousands of voices mingled in a roar. Men were shouting, stumbling. My head and shoulders went down, and up, and down again, and up once more. It was like drowning in a human sea. I lost sight of the *Spirit of St. Louis*. I heard several screams. I was afraid that I would be dropped under the feet of those milling, cheering people; and that after sitting in a cockpit-fixed position for close to thirty-four hours, my muscles would be too stiff to struggle up again.

I tried to sit up—to slip down into the crowd—to roll over onto my hands and knees. It was useless. I was simply wasting strength that I might need for a final effort to save myself, if my head angled beneath my feet too far. It seemed wisest to relax as much as I could, and let time pass. I realized that the men under me were determined that no matter what happened to them, I would not fall.

After the lapse of minutes whose number I cannot judge, I felt my helmet jerked from my head. Firmer hands gripped on my body. I heard my name more clearly spoken. And suddenly I was standing on my feet—on European ground at last. With arms linked solidly in mine, I began moving slowly . . . through the crowd.

In the week I spent at Paris, between ceremonies and engagements which crammed almost every hour of each day, I pieced together the story of what happened that Saturday night at Le Bourget. . . . The French authorities had prepared for my reception. Extra guards were detailed to the aerodrome; and when reports of my plane being sighted over Ireland, England, and Normandy, brought automobiles pouring out from Paris by the thousands, two companies of soldiers were sent to reinforce the civil police. . . .

When the crowd broke down steel fences and rushed out onto the field, all these arrangements collapsed. Police and soldiers were swept away in the rush which followed. Two French aviators—the military pilot Detroyat and the civil pilot Delage—

found themselves close to me in the jam of people. Delage grabbed Detroyat's arm and cried, "Come, they will smother him!" Detroyat, being in uniform, and tall, was able to exercise some authority over the men who had me on their shoulders. Once my feet were on the ground, it was too dark for my flying suit to be very noticeable. I soon became an inconspicuous member of the crowd. Meanwhile my helmet had somehow gotten onto the head of an American reporter. Someone had pointed to him and called out, *"There is Lindbergh! There is Lindbergh!"* The crowd had taken over the reporter and left me free.

1927

A Director Struggles with Two Stars

By the late 1920's, making motion pictures was the nation's fourth largest industry and an estimated 50,000,000 Americans attended the movies each week. Here two English visitors describe the shooting of a movie scene in Hollywood, California, the world's film capital.

Source: JAN and CORA GORDON. *Star-Dust in Hollywood.* George G. Harrap and Co. Ltd., London: 1930, pp. 75–79.

Round a long curtain of backcloth we came on to the set. . . . Suspended from the invisible roof overhead were grids of mercury lights floating like immense square moons of powerful green cheese. . . . The cameras, like small machine guns, were perched high on massive legs, and the cameramen . . . stood on piles of boxes to reach the level of their instruments. . . .

Among the camera-legs . . . crouched a line of square canvas chairs. Each had a name painted on the back. . . . Would you learn the importance of any person on the set? See if he has a chair. If not, you may almost with safety disdain him. . . .

The scene that we perceived between the silhouettes of lights, cameras, operators, and workmen was that of a low-class, dockside drinking den, the sublimation of a hundred romantic bars. . . . For a movie set it was very complete, since almost every corner was to be used as the background of some scene or other.

The chairs marked "Betty Compton" and "Geo. Bancroft" were empty since the two . . . were taking their positions under the distilled glare of a few thousand candle-power. Green and purple illumination from the mercury moons above, and yellow from the sun-arcs, mottled their faces with contrasting and death-like tints, while the director issued his instructions. . . .

To the left an additional battery of lights played on a group of toughs beyond the camera's range. The director, a thick-set young man with wild hair and a rough tweed coat, addressed them:

"Now then, you boys, when I say go, put some pep into it. Don't just punch one another about as if you were a bunch of babies."

He sat back in the chair marked "Mr. Von Sternberg" and placed a small megaphone to his lips.

"Now try it over. Ready? Music!"

From the darkness behind the big sun-arcs a violin wailed and a harmonium grunted like a passionate duet between a musical hyena and a melodious wart-hog. The director allowed a few moments for this stimulus to work on the feelings of his actors, then through the megaphone bellowed: "Go!"

The actors sprang into motion. But Von Sternberg was not satisfied. He bellowed "Stop!" through the megaphone, and turning it toward the musicians, shouted: "That tune's no good. Stir us up a bit. Put more spirit into it. Gee, nobody feels like fighting to a . . . waltz."

He jumped from his seat and, pushing Bancroft aside, gesticulated in his place. "Like this, George, see!"

"Well, now, I thought that it would be more natural if I . . ." the burly sailor began.

"That is all right perhaps, George, but I can see how the whole thing works together, see? I'm looking at this thing not as one piece of individual action, but as a whole. You try it as I say. And, Betty dear, what I want you to do is more like this. I mean keep it quieter. Eh?"

A little grudgingly the highly salaried stars submitted. . . . We were witnessing a mute struggle between Von Sternberg and his stars. The former, in order to bring out the full intensity of this dockside drama, wished to hold his characters down to harsh realism. He wanted them to seem really degraded. But the stars could not afford to think exclusively of the artistic merits of the final picture. They dared not risk their whole careers in order to make one masterpiece for Director Von Sternberg. The actress had to preserve her famous charm under all circumstances: the public expected it from her. If she deliberately lowered herself too far for the sake of the picture, heaven only knew what might happen to her in the future. The actor had his well-known rough and careless good-fellowship to maintain: his public demanded that from him. So, no matter what the character in the actual cast might be, he had to hold on to this rough good-fellowship to the last. They could not afford to forget that public approval is the last appeal controlling every star's occupation. . . .

1929

Watching a Motion Picture of Waning Wealth

The stock market crash of late October, 1929, did not cause the depression of the 1930's, but it was a dramatic sign of the weakening American economy. These newspaper accounts show the effect and the extent of the crash.

Source: *The New York Times*, October 25, 1929, and October 30, 1929.

The most disastrous decline in the biggest and broadest stock market of history rocked the financial district yesterday. In the very midst of the collapse five of the country's most influential bankers hurried to the office of J. P. Morgan & Co., and after a brief conference gave out word that they believe the foundations of the market to be sound. . . .

The break was one of the widest in the market's history. . . . It carried down with it speculators, big and little, in every part of the country, wiping out thousands of accounts. It is probable that if the stockholders of the country's foremost corporations had not been calmed by the attitude of leading bankers . . . the business of the country would have been seriously affected. Doubtless business will feel the effects of the drastic stock shake-out. . . .

The total losses cannot be accurately calculated, because of the large number of markets and the thousands of securities not listed on any exchange. However, they were staggering, running into billions of dollars. Fear struck the big speculators and little ones, big investors and little ones. . . . Losses were tremendous and thousands of prosperous brokerage and bank accounts, sound and healthy a week ago, were completely wrecked in the strange debacle, due to a combination of circumstances, but accelerated into a crash by fear. . . .

Under these circumstances . . . the entire financial district was thrown into hopeless confusion and excitement. Wild-eyed speculators crowded the brokerage offices, awed by the disaster which had overtaken many of them. . . . Rumors, most of them wild and false, spread throughout the Wall Street district and thence throughout the country. One of the reports was that eleven speculators had committed suicide. A peaceful workman atop a Wall Street building looked down and saw a big crowd watching him, for the rumor had spread that he was going to jump off. Reports that the Chicago and Buffalo Exchanges had closed spread throughout the district, as did rumors that the New York Stock Exchange and the New York Curb Exchange were going to suspend trading. These rumors and reports were all found, on investigation, to be untrue. . . .

. . . .

Stock prices virtually collapsed yesterday, swept downward with gigantic losses in the most disastrous trading day in the stock market's history. Billions of dollars in open market values were wiped out as prices crumbled. . . .

Efforts to estimate yesterday's market losses in dollars are futile because of the vast number of securities quoted over the counter and on out-of-town exchanges on which no calculations are possible. However, it was estimated that 880 stocks, on the New York Stock Exchange, lost between $8,000,000,000 and $9,000,000,000 yesterday. Added to that loss is to be reckoned the depreciation on issues on the Curb Market [American Exchange], in the over the counter market and on other exchanges. . . .

Groups of men, with here and there a woman, stood . . . watching spools of ticker tape unwind and as the tenuous paper with its cryptic numerals grew longer at their feet their fortunes shrunk. Others sat stolidly on tilted chairs in the customers' rooms of brokerage houses and watched a motion picture of waning wealth as the day's quotations moved silently across a screen.

It was among such groups as these, feeling the pulse of a feverish financial world whose heart is the Stock Exchange, that drama and perhaps tragedy were to be found. . . . The crowds about the ticker tape, like friends around the bedside of a stricken friend, reflected in their faces the story the tape was telling. There were no smiles. There were no tears either. Just the camaraderie of fellow-sufferers. Everybody wanted to tell his neighbor how much he had lost. Nobody wanted to listen. It was too repetitious a tale. . . .

1930

Bobby Jones Makes Golf History

> Bobby Jones, an amateur from Atlanta, Georgia, has become a legendary figure as a golfer. This newspaper account tells how Bobby won the last of four major tournaments during 1930, a time when golf was beginning its climb to mass popularity as a sport.
> Source: RICHARDSON, WILLIAM D. *New York Times*, September 27, 1930.

Ardmore, Pa.,
Sept. 27, 1930.

When Gene Homans' ball grazed the side of the cup on the twenty-ninth hole at the Merion Cricket Club today, Bobby Jones not only became the national amateur champion for 1930 but the holder of a record that probably will survive through the ages. . . .

At twenty-eight, this rare-gifted golfer from Atlanta, . . . has performed a feat that no one hitherto had considered possible.

Within the short span of five months, Bobby has played in the four major golf events—the British amateur and open championships and the American open and amateur—and won them all, outscoring the professionals at their own game in the two open tournaments and outstripping all his fellow amateurs in the others. . . .

It was no more than appropriate that all these honors should be spread at Bobby's feet on the same golf course where, as a boy of fourteen, he made his debut in championship golf. . . .

No one in the vast throng of fully 18,000 spectators, who made a great human fringe around the green and a solid mass packed in the fairway that Jones had just played from, could help but feel that here was golf history being made. . . .

Both sides of the fairway were lined with persons . . . as he and Homans drove off. Homans . . . drove to the left.

Having nothing to lose, Bobby lit into . . . a long drive, almost reaching the edge of the little stream that runs across the fairway near the 300-yard mark. Homans had to play first and sent a beautiful . . . shot onto the green, a trifle beyond the hole. A moment later Bobby's ball came sailing on, stopping short of the pin.

Despite the fact that all those thousands were standing as close as they could get, the dropping of a pin in the grass would have been heard as Bobby, looking a little haggard and drawn, walked over to his ball after his caddie had handed him his pet putter, known the world over as Calamity Jane. Then followed one of those quizzical glances that he gives the hole, the familiar cocking of the Jones' head, a slight movement of the wrists as they brought the club back and then forward.

The ball started on its journey up to the hole over the closely cropped grass. He didn't quite have the line, but it stopped so close to the side of the hole that Homans would have had to sink his in order to prevent the match from ending there and then. Knowing full well that it was all over Gene took comparatively little time over his own putt, hit the ball and, almost before it passed by the side of the hole he was wringing Bobby's hand.

Immediately a great shout went up, and the tumult . . . lasted for several minutes. There was a wild rush toward Jones who, had it not been for the presence of a squad of marines, would have been crushed.

It was some moments before order was restored and an opening made through which Jones and Homans could walk over to the No. 12 fairway and begin their journey back to the clubhouse.

And over the entire distance Jones was cheered on as triumphant a journey as any man ever traveled in sport. . . .

1933

When the Big Trouble Came . . . There We Were

One of depression's tragedies was the large number of young people who left home to keep from being an expense to their families. A sociologist from the University of Minnesota who traveled and lived with these boy and girl tramps, recorded these facts about their nomadic life.

Source: From *Boy and Girl Tramps of America*, pp. 21–23, 53–54, 62–64, by Thomas Minehan. Copyright 1934 by Thomas Minehan. Reprinted by permission of Holt, Rinehart and Winston, Inc.

"It wasn't so bad at home," says Texas to me in the early weeks of our wandering, "before the big trouble came. . . . We got along pretty good. Dad, of course, never was very well. He was in the war and he got some kind of sickness . . . but he couldn't get a pension. He was always sick for about a month every year, and that meant he had to look for a new job each time he got well. If he had been husky it might have been easy to get a good job, but he was kinda small and then sick you know.

"But we got along swell before the big trouble came even if there were seven of us kids. I shined shoes in a barber shop. Jim carried papers. And Marie took care of Mrs. Rolph's kids. Mother always did some sewing for the neighbors. We had a Chevvie and a radio and a piano. I even started to high school mornings, the year the big trouble came.

"Dad got sick as usual but we never thought anything of it. When he comes to go back to work he can't get a job, and everybody all of a sudden-like seems to be hard up. I cut the price of shines to a nickel, but it didn't help much. I even used to go around and collect shoes and shine them at the houses or take them away, shine and return them, but even then some weeks

267

I couldn't make a dime. Mrs. Rolph's husband got a cut and she cans Marie. Jim had to quit the paper route because he lost all his cash customers, and the others never paid. Nobody wanted Mother to sew anything. And there we were, seven of us kids and Dad and Mother, and we couldn't make a cent like we could before the big trouble came. . . .

"But the big trouble came . . . and there we were. Oh, we tried hard enough, and everybody did their best. Marie made the swellest wax flowers. The kids peddled ironing cloths. Mother tried to sell some home made baked goods. And Dad did everything. We did our best, I guess, but it wasn't good enough, for the big trouble had come and nobody had any money.

"Dad gave up pipe smoking in the fall. All last winter we never had a fire except about once a day when Mother used to cook some mush or something. When the kids were cold they went to bed. I quit high school of course, but the kids kept going to school because it didn't cost anything and it was warm there.

"In February I went to Fort Worth. Mother used to know a man there, and she thought maybe he could help me get a job. But he was as hard up as anybody else. I didn't want to return home and pick bread off the kids' plate so I tried to get work for a farmer for my board. Instead, I got a ride to California. Near Salinas I worked in the lettuce fields, cutting and washing lettuce. I made $32 and I sent $10 home. But that was my first and last pay check. I got chased out of California in June. . . . Since then . . . I just been traveling."

. . . .

"Where have I traveled?" Tow-headed, freckled-faced Bob, a lad of sixteen, was talking as we crouched in the front corner of a gondola for protection against a cold wind. "Fellow, I've traveled to every city in this country big enough to have a flop house. Last winter I spent in New Orleans. Two years ago it was California. This winter it's going to be Alabama and Georgia. You can't name a main street I haven't hit or a road I didn't ride. Right now I'm on my way to Seattle, but I'm not staying there over two or three days."

. . . .

. . . The young tramps must utilize the railroads to travel in gangs. At home, in high school, in colleges, boys tend to associate

268

in gangs, clubs, and fraternities. Girls have sororities and clubs. On the road there is not only this natural gregariousness of youth, but the need for mutual protection. A hitch-hiker on the highway is alone amongst enemies—the men who work and have money and who are suspicious of travelers who have no money, do not work, and yet live. On the railroad he is with friends. Hitch-hikers, too, must be clean and neat. No motorist stops to pick up a dirty beggar, but the police do. Box cars carry all classes. Boys who have only a ragged pair of overalls, a dirty shirt, and decrepit tennis shoes can still travel and live in the jungles. On the highways somebody will sic the dog on them.

In traveling in box cars the child tramps ordinarily require no techniques. They merely climb into a box car and wait until the train pulls out. . . . In . . . places the railroad police are inflexible about enforcing the rule that the hoboes must not board a train until it is in motion. After it is in motion, it is the task of the train crew to keep the transients off—a task obviously impossible. It is not at all unusual to see several hundred transients lined up beyond the railroad property fence. A train is being made up a track or two away. The intervening space is patrolled by railroad police.

"Get back there, I tell you, get back," shouts an officer to a pair of boys crossing the tracks.

"Don't let me catch a one of you," warns another as he swings a club in our faces, "putting a foot upon railroad property until that train gets in motion."

The transients are silent. . . . Imperceptibly the train moves as the fireman rings the bell. Like a group of race horses . . . or football players surging forward when the ball is snapped, the boys and girls surge en masse across the tracks. They . . . swarm all over the train as a cloud of locusts . . . swarm over an orchard. Some climb ladders to the roofs. Others pile into gondolas. The majority chooses box-car doors.

And here is one fertile source of the accidents which daily cripple boy and girl tramps for life. The train is in motion. Scores of boys and girls crowd, boost, and shove one another. Youths in the car reach down and lift others. Boys on the ground boost friends or try to leap up themselves, and all the time the speed of the train is accelerating. . . . And in the jumble and confusion, the stumbling over cinders and tripping over ties, someone may fall. If the train is moving . . . slowly . . . the youth has time to recover and slide out of the way. But not always—and another homeless girl is crippled for life, another boy killed.

1933

Frances Perkins Primes a Pump

Frances Perkins, who served as Franklin D. Roosevelt's Secretary of Labor from 1933 until his death, was the first woman Cabinet member in history. In her book *The Roosevelt I Knew* she related many inside stories of the New Deal, including this description of the unemployment relief measures Roosevelt started.

Source: FRANCES PERKINS. *The Roosevelt I Knew*, pp. 182–186. Copyright 1946 by Frances Perkins. Reprinted by permission of The Viking Press, Inc.

It is hard today to reconstruct the atmosphere of 1933 and to evoke the terror caused by unrelieved poverty and prolonged unemployment. The funds of many states and localities were exhausted. . . . The situation was grim in city, county, and state. Public welfare officers had reached the end of their rope, and special committees, appointed by governors, mayors, and county officials had exhausted their imagination as well as their funds. The Federal Government and its taxing power were all they could think of.

Whatever plans the Roosevelt government might make to revive the normal economic life of the country, the urgent need was for direct relief to the unemployed. . . . Unemployment had been increasing steadily since the autumn of 1929. When Roosevelt took office in March, 1933, it had reached its peak. No one has ever known the exact number out of work and in need. The kind of statistical information now capable of giving us a fairly good answer to that question was not available, but the estimates of persons out of work ranged from 13,300,000 to 17,900,000. The true figure is probably somewhere between, and the number in actual distress approached seventy-five per cent of the unemployed.

. . . As the Roosevelt administration took up its task, the un-employed had just struggled through the third severe winter since President Hoover had proclaimed, in the summer of 1930, that "the depression is over." . . . Banks were collapsing through-out the nation. Relief stations were closing down for lack of funds. Hunger marchers were on parade. Food riots were be-coming more common. Crime, born of the need for food, cloth-ing, and other necessities of life, was on the upsurge.

There were insecurity and terror in the agricultural regions, where sober farm people forcibly prevented sheriffs' sales on fore-closed mortgages. The increase in petty larceny was alarming. An honorable man like Dan Willard, president of the Baltimore & Ohio Railroad, when asked at a public meeting what he thought about the situation, said, "If a man whose family is hungry steals, I cannot blame him. I think I would do the same."

Shortly after Inauguration Day, Harry Hopkins and William Hodson came down from New York to see me. Hopkins was chairman of the New York State Temporary Emergency Relief Administration, which had been established by Roosevelt when he had been Governor. . . . Hopkins, Hodson, and I met at the Women's University Club, which was jammed. We found a hole under the stairs, and there, in cramped, unlovely quarters, they laid out their plan. It was a plan for the immediate appropriation by the Federal Government of grants-in-aid to the states for un-employment relief. I was impressed by the exactness of their knowledge and the practicability of their plan.

They told me they had not been able to get to the President to present their program. . . . Feeling certain of my ground, I cut across the usual formalities and made an appointment for Hopkins and Hodson with the President.

> [President Roosevelt approved the Hopkins-Hodson plan. A bill to enact it was drawn up and rushed through Con-gress, establishing the Federal Emergency Relief Admin-istration, with Harry Hopkins as its head.]

The fortunes of the unemployed took a turn for the better the day FERA began to operate. . . . In its brief span of life FERA received and spent $4,000,000,000 on all projects. It was the first step in the economic pump priming that was to break the back of the depression. FERA spent money for many things, all necessi-ties of life—food, clothing, fuel, shelter, medicine. In an analysis of how the money was spent, Harry Hopkins said, "We can only say that out of every dollar entrusted to us for lessening of distress, the maximum amount humanly possible was put into the people's hands. The money, spent honestly and with constant remembrance of its purpose, bought more of courage than it ever bought of goods."

Thus the relief program was launched. While even its most enthusiastic sponsors never thought it was the complete answer, it kept people alive and instilled courage. In looking back, moreover, one sees that it provided a substantial stimulus to the revival of industry by creating purchasing power in a class previously destitute, and that it had a tremendous effect on raising the standards of living of the poorest and lowest paid people. . . .

1938

The Brown Bomber Squares an Account

By 1938, President Roosevelt had branded Germany as an aggressor in world affairs, so to many observers the boxing match between the American Joe Louis and the German Max Schmeling seemed like a contest for prestige between the two nations. One of the shortest heavyweight championship bouts in history is related in this account.

Source: Dawson, James P. "Louis Evens Score with Schmeling." *New York Times*, June 23, 1938.

New York, June 23, 1938.

The exploding fists of Joe Louis crushed Max Schmeling last night in the ring at the Yankee Stadium and kept sacred the time-worn legend of boxing that no former heavyweight champion has ever regained the title.

The Brown Bomber from Detroit with the most furious early assault he has ever exhibited here, knocked out Schmeling in the first round of what was to have been a 15-round battle, to retain the title he won last year from James J. Braddock. He has now defended it successfully four times.

In exactly 2 minutes and 4 seconds of fighting Louis polished off the Black Uhlan from the Rhine. The battle was short, but it was furious and savage while it lasted, packed with drama that included three knockdowns of the ambitious ex-champion, every moment tense for a crowd of about 80,000.

This gathering . . . paid receipts estimated at between $900,000 and $1,000,000 to see whether Schmeling could repeat the knock-out he administered to Louis just two years ago here and be the first ex-heavyweight champion to come back into the title, or whether the Bomber could avenge this defeat as he promised. . . .

With the right hand that Schmeling held in contempt Louis knocked out his foe. Three times under its impact the German fighter hit the ring floor. The first time Schmeling regained his feet laboriously at the count of three. From the second knock-down Schmeling, dazed but game, bounced up instinctively before the count had gone beyond one.

On the third knockdown Schmeling's trainer and close friend, Max Machon, hurled a towel into the ring, European fashion, admitting defeat for his man. . . . The signal is ignored in American boxing, has been for years. Referee Arthur Donovan . . . gathered the white emblem in a ball and hurled it through the ropes.

Returning to Schmeling's crumpled figure, Donovan took one look and signaled an end to the battle. The count at that time was five on the third knockdown. Further counting was useless. Donovan could have counted off a century and Max could not have regained his feet. The German was thoroughly "out." . . .

Louis wanted to erase the memory of that 1936 knockout he suffered in twelve rounds. It was the one blot on his brilliant record. He aimed to square the account, and he did. . . .

In addition to those looking on at the spectacle, there were millions listening in virtually all over the world. This battle was broadcast in four languages, English, German, Spanish, and Portuguese, so intense was the interest in its outcome. . . .

1940

The Boss Falls for Fala

> Grace Tully, who called President Roosevelt "The Boss," wrote a book about her experiences as his private secretary from 1932 until his death in April, 1945. The book contains many informal glimpses into the public and private life of President Roosevelt, including this one about his favorite Scotch terrier.
>
> Reprinted with the permission of Charles Scribner's Sons from *F. D. R. My Boss*, pp. 128–130, by GRACE TULLY. Copyright 1949 by Grace Tully.

Fala was a present to F. D. R. in 1940 . . . and had been carefully "White House broken" before moving to Washington. . . .

The Boss, who loved animals to begin with, was particularly a captive of Fala's personality. The little Scotsman's sleeping quarters were established in the President's bedroom, his breakfast came in on the President's tray, his outdoor pen was located where the Boss could watch him racing himself dizzy during the day, and he had a regular afternoon appointment to frolic around F. D. R.'s office. . . .

In a rather condescending fashion, Fala learned such conventional tricks as standing on his hind legs, rolling over on orders, hurdling outstretched feet and so forth. . . . He was not above gnawing at Presidential trouser cuffs when he wanted attention, sniffing noisily at shoes, or tossing a rubber ball or bone around with all the vigorous frenzy of a Scottish soccer player.

Fala not only made many of the Presidential trips out of Washington, he also made a few excursions on his own around town. On one occasion he was picked up while jogging casually down "F" Street and on another while sniffing around the Treasury Department. The Boss explained the latter jaunt by pointing out that it occurred on the 15th of a month, pay day.

"He had probably run out of spending money," the Boss laughed, "almost everybody else does on that day."

Fala's dinner, his real meal of the day, was usually served in the President's Study in the White House with the bowl of food ordinarily given to the Boss for transmission to his young friend. Usually he demanded that Fala ask for it in politely doggy manner and if the performance was a bit too eager the bowl was kept

274

on the desk briefly. In such case, Fala would play his part by repeating his request in more piteous accent or perhaps by nuzzling his wet nose against the Boss' ankles.

Fala considered himself thoroughly eligible for all Presidential trips and he sulked quite obviously if he found himself left behind. He went to sea several times and became a regular commuter to Hyde Park . . . and to Warm Springs. He disrupted the timing of the 1941 inaugural procession slightly by taking up occupancy of the back seat of the car lined up for the President. . . . The Secret Service had to deal with that situation.

The Secret Service also had Fala trouble on other occasions, particularly during the war when the Roosevelt travels were presumably highly secret affairs. Since Fala was almost as well known as the President himself, the secrecy would break down whenever a train stop enabled Fala to persuade someone to take him out for a track-side walk. As a consequence, Mike Reilly [a Secret Service man] gave him a code name of "The Informer."

The American public fell for Fala just about as completely as the President did. Hundreds of letters came to the White House addressed to him, some signed by paw prints and many from the very old or very young lovers of dogs. . . . We had a constant stream of visitors or inquiries from people who wanted opportunity to see not the President but Fala. . . .

1941

F. D. R. Looks Forward to Four Freedoms

In his Annual Message to Congress, January 6, 1941, President Roosevelt explained the hopes of American democracy. Within a year we would be fighting to defend the "Four Freedoms" he describes at the end of his message.

Source: "President Roosevelt, Annual Message to Congress, January 6, 1941." *Congressional Record*, 77th Congress, First Session, Part I, Vol. LXXXVII, pp. 46–47.

. . . There is nothing mysterious about the foundations of a healthy and strong democracy. The basic things expected by our people of their political and economic systems are simple. They are:

Equality of opportunity for youth and for others.

Jobs for those who can work.

Security for those who need it.

The ending of special privilege for the few.

The preservation of civil liberties for all.

The enjoyment of the fruits of scientific progress in a wider and constantly rising standard of living.

These are the simple and basic things that must never be lost sight of in the turmoil and unbelievable complexity of our modern world. The inner and abiding strength of our economic and political systems is dependent upon the degree to which they fulfill these expectations. . . .

In the future . . . we look forward to a world founded upon four essential human freedoms.

The first is freedom of speech and expression everywhere in the world.

The second is freedom of every person to worship God in his own way everywhere in the world.

The third is freedom from want, which . . . means economic understandings which will secure to every nation a healthy peacetime life for its inhabitants everywhere in the world.

The fourth is freedom from fear—which . . . means a worldwide reduction of armaments to such a point and in such a thorough fashion that no nation will be in a position to commit an act of physical aggression against any neighbor—anywhere in the world.

This . . . is a definite basis for a kind of world attainable in our own time. . . . A good society is able to face schemes of world domination and foreign revolution alike without fear.

Since the beginning of our American history we have been engaged in change—in a perpetual peaceful revolution—a revolution which goes on steadily, quietly adjusting itself to changing conditions. . . . The world order which we seek is the cooperation of free countries, working together in a friendly, civilized society.

A Huge White Hog Brings Covetous Comment

> Ernie Pyle, World War II's best known war correspondent, lived with our troops in England and went with them on the North African invasion. He interpreted for the folks back home the normal life of the front-line soldier, such as this description of how soldiers fed themselves in North Africa.
>
> Source: From *Here Is Your War* by ERNIE PYLE. Copyright 1943 by Lester Cowan. Reprinted by permission of Holt, Rinehart and Winston, Inc.

Our soldiers at the front learned quickly how to keep their stomachs filled during emergencies. Ordinarily, the soldier's food was prepared for him in army mess kitchens, but at the front many things could happen. Small parties went out for days at a time and had to carry their own rations. On the battle front, kitchen trucks came up only at night and sometimes not even then. With our mobile armies on the move it wasn't always possible for kitchen trucks to be in the right place at the right moment, and as a consequence every soldier learned how to feed himself. Every vehicle from jeep to tank had a few spare cans of rations hidden away somewhere.

Soldiers cooked their own meals when on the move. They made a fire in one of two ways, each involving the use of gasoline: For a short fire they dug a hole about the size of a man's hand, poured gasoline into it, sprinkled sand over the gasoline, and then threw in a match. The sand kept the gas from burning too quickly. On a small fire like that they could heat a canteen or cup of coffee. For a bigger fire, they filled a small can with gasoline and buried it even with the surface of the ground. They piled rocks around to set their cooking utensils on, and then tossed a match at the gas.

I never saw a real skillet, pan or stewpot. The soldiers made their own utensils out of those famous five-gallon gasoline tins. I don't believe there's anything in the world that can't be made out of a five-gallon gasoline tin. . . .

Despite their primitive forms of cooking, the soldiers did eat well. They got either British or American rations, or a mixture

of the two. Soldiers . . . actually preferred the British "compo"
to our own famous C ration. The reason being that the C ration
had so little variety that after three meals a man could hardly
look a C can in the face.

The British compo was more diverse. It had such things as sausage, puddings, chocolate bars, salt, jam, butter, and cheese. . . .

Although a general order was issued against buying food from
the Arabs, in order to avoid using up their supply, we bought it
anyhow. Mess sergeants scoured the country and came back with
eggs, sheep, and chickens. You might say we lived partly off
the country.

Of course ridiculous prices were paid to the Arabs, which in-
furiated the Europeans in North Africa because it ran up the prices
for them too. But the American's attitude was usually expressed
something like this: "Well, money means nothing to us here, and
from the looks of most of the Arabs a few extra francs won't
hurt them."

We had more eggs right at the front than anywhere else in the
whole European and African theaters of war. The love of Americans for eggs has become almost a legend. Along the roads over
which our motor convoys were passing constantly, Arabs stood by
the score, even out on the limitless desert, holding up eggs for
sale. The natives paid one franc for an egg. Mess sergeants paid
three francs when buying in bulk, and individual soldiers paid
five francs [about seven cents] for an egg.

One day I was at a command post in a farmyard in a prosperous
irrigated valley. The grounds were full of officers and soldiers
who has just arrived. All of a sudden across the barnlot there
came plodding a huge white hog.

It was touching and funny to see the wave of desire that swept
over the soldiers. Everybody looked longingly at that hog. Everybody had some crack to make.

"Oh, you big juicy blankety-blank! How I'd like to eat you!"

Another soldier said, "I never stuck a hog in my life, but I'll
bet I could find his jugular vein with my bayonet."

Another, obviously a city man, said, "But how could we skin
him?"

A truck driver answered scornfully, "You don't skin hogs. We'd
boil him in scalding water and scrape him."

A year before none of us would have looked twice at a hog.

But then the grunting passage of a swine across a barnlot brought a flood of covetous comment.

1943

||||||||||||||||||||||||||||||||||||||||||||||||||||||||||||||||||||||||||||||||||||||||||||||||||||||||||||||||||||||||||||||||||||||||||||||||

Four Chaplains Give Their Lives

> In one of the heroic incidents of World War II, four chaplains gave up their life jackets to men without them on the sinking transport *Dorchester*. Daniel A. Poling, father of one of the four brave chaplains, tells the story.
>
> Source: With permission of McGraw-Hill Book Co., Inc. From *Mine Eyes Have Seen* by DANIEL A. POLING. Copyright © 1959 by Daniel A. Poling.

On February 11, 1943, Betty [Mrs. Clark V. Poling] received a telegram from the Adjutant General's office in Washington informing her that Clark was missing in action in the North African area. She telephoned us this news. . . . I was disturbed, but I was able to reassure Betty and myself to a degree, for there was obviously an error in the message: Clark's ship could not have reached North African waters. There had not been time, and I knew where he was headed. . . . Eight weeks were to pass, as it turned out, before we knew for sure that Clark was gone. . . .

On April 10, 1943, the original "missing in action" became "lost in action," and we finally learned something of what had happened in the early-morning darkness of February 3. Ninety miles from its destination in Greenland, the transport ship *Dorchester* had been torpedoed. She had gone down within twenty-seven minutes. Of the 904 men aboard, only 226 survived. The press and radio of the Allied world picked up the story of the four chaplains who had stood praying on the deck while the *Dorchester* disappeared. They represented three faiths. Alexander D. Goode was the Jew. Father John W. Washington was the Roman Catholic. George L. Fox and Clark V. Poling were the Protestants. The fact that these men had linked arms, braced themselves against the rail now awash, and shared the last holy mission of their lives captured the imagination of millions across the world.

The survivors of the *Dorchester* were profoundly moved by their part in the experience. "With utter disregard of self," one of them said later, "having given away their life jackets to four men without them, the chaplains stood together praying . . . for the safety of those men who were now leaving the stricken ship on all sides of them."

. . . I talked with one of the survivors, Engineer Grady Clark, in the Valley Forge Hospital at Phoenixville, Pennsylvania, where he was recovering from shock and exposure. Observing his shipboard orders, Grady had been fully dressed and wearing his life jacket when the torpedo struck. He had been picked up after floating nearly seven hours in the iceberg-chilled waters, and was perhaps the last survivor to be rescued. He confirmed that there had indeed been panic—a fact that the original story had reported. The chaplains had quieted the men milling around on the deck, Grady said, and they had forced a number of the frightened ones over the rails or toward the lifeboats. Only two lifeboats got away. Others were smashed against the side of the *Dorchester.* He had seen the chaplains helping men to adjust their life jackets, and finally he had seen them give away their own jackets. . . . "As I swam away from the ship," Grady said, "I looked back. The flames had lighted everything. The bow came up high and she slid under. The last I saw, the four chaplains were up there praying for the safety of the men. They had done everything they could. I did not see them again." And the engineer concluded: "They themselves had no chance without their life jackets."

1944

D. D. E. Decides on D-Day

From 1942 to June, 1944 in World War II, Allied commanders planned the invasion of Europe that would bring the war against Germany to an end. General Dwight David Eisenhower had to name the day the invasion would actually begin and his decision depended on a factor no man could control.

Source: From *Crusade in Europe,* pp. 239 and 249-50, by DWIGHT D. EISENHOWER. Copyright 1948 by Doubleday & Company, Inc. Reprinted by permission of the publisher.

. . . The combination of moon, tide, and time of sunrise that we considered practicable for the attack occurred on June 5, 6, and 7. We wanted to cross the Channel with our convoys at night so that darkness would conceal the strength and direction of our several attacks. We wanted a moon for our airborne assaults. We needed approximately forty minutes of daylight preceding the ground assault to complete our bombing and preparatory bombardment. We had to attack on a relatively low tide because of beach obstacles which had to be removed while uncovered. These principal factors dictated the general period; but the selection of the actual day would depend upon weather forecasts.

If none of the three days should prove satisfactory from the standpoint of weather, consequences would ensue that were almost terrifying to contemplate. Secrecy would be lost. . . . Complicated movement tables would be scrapped. Morale would drop. A wait of at least fourteen days, possibly twenty-eight, would be necessary—a sort of suspended animation involving more than 2,000,000 men! . . .

. . . .

We met with the Meteorologic Committee twice daily, once at nine-thirty in the evening and once at four in the morning. . . . At these meetings every bit of evidence was carefully presented, carefully analyzed by the experts, and carefully studied by the assembled commanders. With the approach of the critical period the tension continued to mount as prospects for decent weather became worse and worse.

The final conference for determining the feasibility of attacking on the tentatively selected day, June 5, was scheduled for 4:00 a. m. on June 4. . . . When the commanders assembled on the morning of June 4 the report we received was discouraging. Low clouds, high winds, and formidable wave action were predicted to make landing a most hazardous affair. The weatherman said that air support would be impossible, naval gunfire would be inefficient, and even the handling of small boats would be rendered difficult. . . . Weighing all factors, I decided that the attack would have to be postponed. . . .

The conference on the evening of June 4 presented little, if any, added brightness to the picture of the morning, and tension mounted even higher because the inescapable consequences of postponement were almost too bitter to contemplate.

At three-thirty the next morning our little camp was shaking and shuddering under a wind of almost hurricane proportions and the accompanying rain seemed to be traveling in horizontal streaks. . . . It seemed impossible that in such conditions there was any reason for even discussing the situation.

When the conference started the first report given us was that the bad conditions predicted the day before for the coast of France were actually prevailing there and that if we had persisted in the attempt to land on June 5 a major disaster would almost surely have resulted. This they probably told us to inspire more confidence in their next . . . declaration, which was that by the following morning a period of relatively good weather . . . would ensue, lasting probably thirty-six hours. The long-term prediction was not good but they did give us assurance that this short period of calm weather would intervene between the end of the storm we were then experiencing and the beginning of the next spell of really bad weather.

The prospect was not bright because of the possibility that we might land the first several waves successfully and then find later build-up impracticable, and so leave the isolated original attacking forces easy prey to German counteraction. However, the consequences of the delay justified great risk and I quickly announced the decision to go ahead with the attack on June 6. The time was then 4:15 a. m., June 5. No one present disagreed and there was a definite brightening of faces as, without a further word, each went off to his . . . post of duty to flash out . . . the messages that would set the whole host in motion.

1944

A Crucial Switch Determines Which

Grace Tully, private secretary to President Franklin D. Roosevelt from 1932 until his death in April, 1945, tells why Senator Harry S. Truman received the Democratic nomination for Vice-President when Roosevelt ran for a fourth term.

Reprinted with the permission of Charles Scribner's Sons from *F. D. R. My Boss* by GRACE TULLY. Copyright 1949 by Grace Tully.

Bob Hannegan, Chairman of the Democratic National Committee, was one of those who were strongly advising the Boss that Wallace [Henry A. Wallace, who had been Roosevelt's Vice-President during his third term] was not acceptable to the Convention delegates. As an alternative, Mr. Roosevelt suggested Supreme Court Justice William O. Douglas but Hannegan again expressed doubt that he could command sufficient strength among the delegates. Hannegan, a Missourian himself, proposed Harry S. Truman, then a Senator, who had been acquitting himself exceedingly well as chairman of the special committee investigating war expenditures and contracts.

The President finally agreed to accept either of the . . . two and, at Hannegan's request, wrote a letter to that effect. The letter, naming Douglas and Truman in that order, was addressed to Hannegan just before the Convention met in Chicago and we left Washington for the West Coast and [President Roosevelt's] trip to Hawaii and Alaska. En route we stopped, by request, in Chicago for Hannegan to board the Presidential train for a further discussion of political strategy.

The train stood in the Chicago yards during this conference and none of us showed ourselves outside. Hannegan had a lengthy talk with the Boss and when he came out of the President's sitting room he was carrying in his hand the letter naming Douglas or Truman as an acceptable running mate. He came directly to me.

"Grace, the President wants you to retype this letter and to switch these names so it will read 'Harry Truman or Bill Douglas'!"

The reason for the switch was obvious. By naming Truman first it was plainly implied by the letter that he was the preferred choice of the President. The Convention took it that way and Truman was nominated. By that narrow margin and perhaps casual action did one man rather than another, perhaps one policy rather than another, eventually arrive at the head of the American government in April of 1945.

The historic significance of the incident sprang to my mind when the President died in 1945. I searched our files for the carbon copy of the original version of the letter. It was never found. Dorothy Brady, my assistant, had done the actual retyping and apparently had destroyed the first version when she had completed the final letter. It was a routine . . . action on her part—first drafts of letters which are amended before sending are never retained—but it is one case in which an original would have had great historical interest.

1945

Stalin Smiles Blandly

The development of the A-Bomb, which was to be used against Japan on August 6, 1945, was a top-secret project. James Byrnes, Secretary of State, reports Stalin's reactions when told the secret a month earlier at Potsdam.

Source: BYRNES, JAMES F. *All in One Lifetime*, pp. 300–301. Reprinted by permission of Harper & Brothers.

. . . President Truman and I discussed whether or not we were obligated to inform Stalin that we had succeeded in developing a powerful weapon and shortly would drop a bomb in Japan. Though there was an understanding that the Soviets would enter the war with Japan three months after Germany surrendered, which would make their entrance about the middle of August . . . the President and I hoped that Japan would surrender before then. However, . . . we agreed that because this was uncertain, and because the Soviets might soon be our allies in that war, the President should inform Stalin of our intention, but do so in a casual way.

. . . Upon the adjournment of the afternoon session, when we arose from the table, the President, accompanied by our interpreter, Bohlen, walked around to Stalin's chair and said . . . "You may be interested to know that we have developed a new and powerful weapon and within a few days intend to use it against Japan." I watched Stalin's expression as this was being interpreted, and was surprised that he smiled blandly and said only a few words. When the President and I reached our car, he said that Stalin had replied only, "That's fine. I hope you make good use of it against the Japanese."

I did not believe Stalin grasped the full importance of the

President's statement, and thought that on the next day there would be some inquiry about this "new and powerful weapon," but I was mistaken. I thought then and even now believe that Stalin did not appreciate the importance of the information that had been given him; but there are others who believe that, in the light of later information about the Soviets' intelligence service in this country, he was already aware of the atom bomb, and that this accounted for his apparent indifference. . . .

1945

Makoto Would Rather Blind Himself

The second atom bomb used in warfare was dropped on Urakami, a highly industrialized suburb of Nagasaki, Japan, three days after Hiroshima. A young Japanese boy, Makoto Nagai, describes the result.

Source: TAKASHI NAGAI (translated by Ichiro Shirato and Herbert B. L. Silverman). *We of Nagasaki: The Story of Survivors in an Atomic Wasteland*, pp. 22–28. Duell, Sloan and Pearce, New York, 1951.

I was ten. We were staying at the cottage in Koba [a village about three miles northeast of Urakami and separated from it by Mount Kawabira] and I was down at the river swimming.

All of a sudden there was an airplane. It came from down the river. I looked up at the sky. I was at the bottom of the valley so I could see only a narrow strip of sky between the hillsides. . . . Suddenly there was an awful light in the sky, toward Urakami. I just dived head-first into the water. . . . From down the river came a noise like thunder. It was a terrific rush of wind. The leaves were torn off all the trees and came racing along. My pants that I had left on a rock were blown along with the leaves.

It was getting dark and cold very fast. I thought an airplane must have crashed into the sun. Without anything on I started running up the hill toward the cottage. Somebody I couldn't see shouted at me from behind some bushes:

"What the devil are you doing? Hide! Quick! They'll spot you!"

I ran and got under a taro. [A plant with large, broad leaves, sometimes called the "elephant's ear."] The big leaves hid me completely. But I was worried about my little sister Kayano. I picked a taro leaf and held it over my head and ran to the house that way.

Everything was smashed. The pots had been blown off the stove. Kayano was all right but she was very excited. She was watching something over Mount Kawabira.

"Brother!" she yelled, "Look! Look! Over there!" I looked toward the mountain, where she was pointing.

What a sight! The biggest thing I ever saw, the biggest that ever was, was sticking way up into the sky from the other side of the mountain. It was like a cloud but it was like a pillar of fire too. It looked hard and soft and alive and dead all at the same time, and beautiful and ugly, too, all at once. The light it sent out was all the colors of the rainbow. It almost blinded me with the glare. It kept getting taller and taller all the time, and wider and wider, twisting and rolling around just like smoke from a chimney. It was growing from the top, I mean, the top was getting pushed up from inside. Then the top began to spread out, so that it looked like an umbrella opening up. . . .

Kayano said it was all red when she first saw it and she said it had a shape like a tree, but by the time I saw it, it was very swollen and beginning to get whitish.

Where we were, we were about three miles away from it. . . . I began to be worried about my mother because the thing was in the direction of Urakami. [His mother was killed by the bomb.] I was just burning up inside, I was so worried. I couldn't stand it. I ran back down to the river and jumped right into the water to cool off. . . .

After a few minutes I saw something coming up the road along the river that looked like a parade of roast chickens. Some of them kept asking for "Water! Water!"

I wasn't burning up any more. I shivered. I ran back to the cottage.

I would rather blind myself than ever have to see such a sight again!

. . . .

When the war stopped my father and little sister and I went back to Urakami—although there wasn't much left of it. One day in October an order from the school was posted: "All pupils of Yamazato Grade School will assemble immediately in the school yard!" I went right to school. There were three teachers and thirty pupils in the yard. Twenty-five teachers and about twelve hundred pupils had died. Another teacher and about three hundred pupils didn't turn up; they were out sick on account of wounds or atomic sickness. There had been about sixty of us in my class, but only four turned up. My own teacher was too overcome to speak. He just looked at us and dismissed us. The school looked like an old baker's oven. There was still lots of charred wood left on the playground from the cremations almost two months ago.

1945

Jackie Robinson Gets His Chance

After starring in athletics at college, serving with the Army in World War II, and playing with a Negro baseball team, Jackie Robinson was given the chance to crack the color bar in organized baseball by Branch Rickey, President of the Brooklyn (now the Los Angeles) Dodgers. While Jackie was playing with the Kansas City Monarchs, Clyde Sukeforth, a Dodger scout, called on him and said Mr. Rickey wanted to see him in New York. Jackie tells the story of his meeting with Mr. Rickey.

Source: ROBINSON, JACKIE, as told to WENDELL SMITH. *My Own Story*, pp. 21–23. Greenberg, New York, 1948.

When I walked into his office that bright August morning, Mr. Rickey was sitting behind his big desk. He smiled broadly and his deep-set eyes sparkled under his bushy eyebrows. "Come in, come in," he said hospitably. "I'm very glad to see you. Clyde Sukeforth tells me you're quite a ball player, Jackie."

I guess I was a little awkward. I didn't want to appear too modest, and yet I didn't want to convey the impression that I had a big head. Sukeforth, standing beside me, rose to the occasion.

"He's the Brooklyn type of player," Sukey said. . . . "The boy can run like blazes and looks like he might be a pretty fair country hitter."

Mr. Rickey nodded approvingly. . . . He looked at me like a pawn broker examining some trinket brought in by an unfamiliar customer. His piercing eyes roamed over me with such meticulous care, I felt almost naked.

It was a little embarrassing. I shifted uneasily and for want of something to do jammed my hand down in my coat pocket. I don't know what I expected to find there, but I guess I was searching for something to hold on to. . . .

"Do you drink?" Mr. Rickey suddenly asked.

"No, sir," I said rather proudly.

"That's fine," he said, relaxing in his chair. . . . "I am interested in bringing you into the Brooklyn organization. I have never seen you play, but my scouts have. If Sukeforth says you're a good ball player, I'll take his word for it. . . . He thinks, as do some of my other men, you could make good on one of our top farm clubs."

Needless to say, I was excited. The thought of playing on a farm club of a Major League team sent little electric shocks up and down my spine. Here was my chance—the chance to be affiliated with a Big League team. Even if I weren't good enough, I could someday tell my grandchildren that I had at least had the opportunity.

Then Mr. Rickey told me I would have to stand a lot of gaff without losing my temper or making a scene. He even acted out several situations I'd be likely to face, and then asked how I would meet each one of them. I wasn't too happy over the prospect he foresaw, but I knew too, that I was pretty sure to run into some name-calling, some insults, some Jim Crow.

I told him I felt pretty sure I would stay out of rhubarbs on the field and trouble of any sort away from it, but that I couldn't become an obsequious, cringing fellow. Among other things, I couldn't play hard, aggressive ball if I were that sort of man.

Mr. Rickey seemed satisfied because he changed the subject:

"I haven't made up my mind which farm club we'll put you on," Mr. Rickey continued, "but wherever it is, I want you to understand one thing: there'll be no limitations as to how far you can go. We will not consider you in any way different from the rest of the players we have in this organization. You are simply another ball player trying to make the grade. If you are good enough, you'll wind up on top. If you aren't, you'll be sent down to another league or released outright."

You could have knocked me over with a feather! Had my ears betrayed me? Could I be wide awake and of sound mind? Yes, as he continued to talk, I realized that he was serious and that I was not dreaming. . . .

[Jackie Robinson was assigned to the Montreal Royals, a Dodger farm team in the International League for the 1946 season. He starred for that team and the next year came up to the Big Leagues with the Brooklyn Dodgers. His first year he helped the Dodgers win the pennant and won for himself the Rookie of the Year Award in the National League. Now all Major League teams and most Minor League teams have Negro ballplayers, but Jackie Robinson was the first.]

1946

Mrs. Roosevelt Wins a Victory

Mrs. Eleanor Roosevelt served for several years as an American delegate to the United Nations, concerning herself chiefly with humanitarian, educational, and cultural questions. At the organizational meeting in London, she helped win a significant victory, as she describes here.

Source: ROOSEVELT, ELEANOR. *On My Own*, pp. 49-52. Copyright © 1958 by Anna Eleanor Roosevelt. Copyright © 1958 by the Curtis Publishing Company. Reprinted by permission of Harper & Brothers.

. . . It was while working on Committee 3 that I really began to understand the inner workings of the United Nations. It was ironical perhaps that one of the subjects that created the greatest . . . heat of the London sessions came up in this "unimportant" committee to which I had been assigned.

The issue . . . arose from the fact that there were many displaced war refugees in Germany when the armistice was signed—Ukrainians, Byelorussians, Poles, Czechoslovaks, Latvians, Lithuanians, and others . . . who were still living there in temporary camps because they did not want to return to live under the Communist rule of their own countries. There also were the pitiful Jewish survivors of the German death camps. . . .

The Yugoslav—and, of course, the Soviet Union position . . . was that any war refugee who did not wish to return to his country of origin was either a quisling or a traitor to his country. Their representatives argued that the refugees in Germany should be forced to return home and to accept whatever punishment might be meted out to them. . . .

The position of the Western countries, including the United States, was that large numbers of the refugees were neither quislings nor traitors and that they must be guaranteed the right to choose whether or not they would return to their homes. Since . . . Committee 3 was the scene of one of the early clashes between the Soviet Union and the West, the newspapers found it convenient to make much of the refugee controversy. I felt very strongly on the subject, as did others, and we spent countless hours trying to frame some kind of resolution on which all could agree. We never did, and our chairman . . . had to present a majority report to the General Assembly which was immediately challenged by the USSR.

In the Assembly the minority position was handled, not by the Soviet representative on Committee 3, but by the head of the Soviet Union's delegation, Andrei Vishinsky. . . . Vishinsky was one of the Russians' great legal minds, a skilled debater, a man with ability to use the weapons of wit and ridicule. And Moscow apparently considered the refugee question of such vital importance that he spoke twice before the Assembly in a determined effort to win over the delegates to the Communist point of view. . . . It was apparent that in view of the importance of the issue someone would have to speak for the United States. The question of who this was to be threw our delegation into a . . . dither. There was a hurried and rather uncomfortable consultation among the male members and when the huddle broke up John Foster Dulles [later Secretary of State but at the time an American delegate to the UN] approached me rather uncertainly.

"Mrs. Roosevelt," he began . . . rather lamely, "the United States must speak in the debate. Since you are the one who has carried on for us in this controversy in the committee, do you think you could say a few words to the Assembly? I'm afraid nobody else is really familiar with the subject."

"Why, Mr. Dulles," I replied as meekly as I could manage, "in that case I will do my best."

Actually, I was badly frightened. I trembled at the thought of speaking against the famous Mr. Vishinsky. But when the time came, I walked, tense and excited, to the rostrum and did my best. There was a little more than met the eye in this situation. The hour was late and we knew the Russians would delay a vote as long as possible on the theory that some of our allies would get tired and leave. I knew we must, if possible, hold our South American colleagues until the vote was taken because their votes might be decisive. So I talked about Simon Bolivar and his stand for the freedom of the people of Latin America. I talked and I watched the delegates and to my joy the South American representatives stayed with us to the end and, when the vote came, we won.

This vote meant that the Western nations would have to worry about the ultimate fate of the refugees for a long, long time, but the principle of the right of an individual to make his own decisions was a victory well worth while. . . .

1950

The UN Resists Aggression

On June 25, 1950, Communist-trained forces from North Korea crossed the 38th Parallel and attacked the Republic of South Korea. These resolutions show how the Security Council of the United Nations acted with promptness and determination against this aggression.

Source: "Review of United Nations Charter; A Collection of Documents," pp. 593–594. *Senate Document*, No. 87, 83d Congress, Second Session (1954).

June 25, 1950

The Security Council. . . . Noting with grave concern the armed attack upon the Republic of Korea by forces from North Korea,

Determines that this action constitutes a breach of the peace,

I. Calls for the immediate cessation of hostilities; and

Calls upon the authorities of North Korea to withdraw forthwith their armed forces to the thirty-eighth parallel;

II. Requests the United Nations Commission on Korea

(a) To communicate its fully considered recommendations on the situation with the least possible delay;

(b) To observe the withdrawal of the North Korean forces to the thirty-eighth parallel; and

(c) To keep the Security Council informed on the execution of this resolution;

III. Calls upon all Members to render every assistance to the United Nations in the execution of this resolution and to refrain from giving assistance to the North Korean authorities.

June 27, 1950

The Security Council . . . having noted from the report of the United Nations Commission for Korea that the authorities of North Korea have neither ceased hostilities nor withdrawn their armed forces to the 38th parallel and that urgent military measures are required to restore international peace and security, and

Having noted the appeal of the Republic of Korea to the United Nations for immediate and effective steps to secure peace and security,

Recommends that the Members of the United Nations furnish such assistance to the Republic of Korea as may be necessary to repel the armed attack and to restore international peace and security in the area.

July 7, 1950

The Security Council . . . welcomes the prompt and vigorous support which governments and peoples of the United Nations have given to its resolutions of 25 and 27 June 1950 to assist the Republic of Korea in defending itself against armed attack and thus to restore international peace and security in the area;

Notes that Members of the United Nations have transmitted to the United Nations offers of assistance for the Republic of Korea;

Recommends that all members providing military forces and other assistance . . . make such forces and other assistance available to a unified command under the United States;

Requests the United States to designate the commander of such forces;

Authorizes the unified command at its discretion to use the United Nations flag in the course of operations against North Korean forces concurrently with the flags of the various nations participating.

1954

An Englishman Sees a Nation on Wheels

Visitors from abroad, such as the Englishman James Morris, can give us the power "to see ourselves as others see us." He writes here of the important role automobiles play in mid-twentieth century American civilization—an importance we sometimes do not realize.

Source: MORRIS, JAMES. *As I Saw the U. S. A.*, pp. 163–170. Pantheon Books Inc., New York, 1956.

The American civilization is inextricably enmeshed with the internal combustion engine. . . .

It is an old joke that the Americans are soon going to lose the use of their legs . . . but it is true that few Americans will walk anywhere if they can help it, either for practical purpose or for pleasure. You can do your banking from your car, without leaving the driving seat, by choosing a bank with a "curbside teller." You can post your letters in mailboxes that protrude to the level of your car window. You can watch a film from your car in a "drive-in" cinema. At many stores you can be served in your car. At innumerable restaurants waitresses will hitch trays to the car door, so that you can eat without moving. In Florida there is even a "drive-in" church. . . . There is no more characteristic gesture of American life than the casual rolling-down of a car window and the emergence of a hand, to grasp a hot dog or a theater ticket, a pound of apples or an evening paper, a check book or a soft drink from a roadside stall. . . .

Imagine yourself, for a moment, as a travelling motorist in America. . . . The road is likely to be smooth and wide, and you are tempted to speed, not least because almost everyone else on the road is speeding already. The limit varies, according to the state you are in. . . . If you go too fast, you may be stopped by the traditional "speed cop," with his howling sirens. . . . It is more likely nowadays that you will be intercepted by radar. Notices will warn you beforehand—"Watch Your Speed! Checked by radar!"—and your progress will be picked up by instruments mounted beside the road or in other cars, infallibly recording your speed and probably photographing your license plate.

Take no risks on the roads. . . . The American is a dashing driver, and often a reckless one; and statistics have shown that it is thirty-two times safer to fly in an American aircraft than it is to drive on an American road. Whatever you do, avoid the low-priced car driven by the single young man; he is probably a sales-man . . . and he likes to devise . . . dangers on the road, as a relief to the monotony. If you see a woman driving, with small children in the back of the car, keep with her. She is probably just as skillful as the men, and, with all her responsibilities con-centrated on four wheels, she is prudent too.

. . . Every state has different license plates, often prettily colored, and with fancy slogans like "Minnesota: Land of 10,000 Lakes"; "Illinois: Land o' Lincoln"; "New Mexico: Land of En-chantment"; "New York: The Empire State." . . . There are many other odd things to see on the passing cars. Some people invent slogans of their own. "Official Car," says a pompous plate . . . and adds in smaller print: "Tax payer." Another popular one, during my stay in America [1954], was: "Don't Blame Me! I voted Democratic!" Often motorists buy stickers to record the states and "scenic wonders" they have visited, and their rear windows are a gaudy mess of colored posters, with reproductions of decorative hanging bridges, Puritans, geysers, bears, country houses, the Capitol, Indians, and caves. . . . The whole makes a pattern of souvenirs that is . . . dangerous, in that it blocks the view through the car windows. . . .

In any small town en route you may buy an excellent cup of coffee; but be careful how you park the car. . . . Once you have found a place you must have a nickel or a dime for the parking meter. Put the coin in the slot, and the machine records how long you have been standing there. If you overstay the limit a red flag will show, and the chances are that a slowly wandering policeman will happen by . . . pause to examine the evidence, and then . . . will . . . affix a notice to your windshield instructing you to pay a small fine by such-and-such a time. It is a painless process, for you need not appear in court. Indeed, in some places you can pay the fine there and then, by wrapping your dollar in your police ticket, and depositing it in a box conveniently affixed to a neighboring lamppost. . . . It is an admirable device, the parking meter, relieving policemen of unnecessary duties, involving the minimum of paper work and administration, and making it easy for the motorist to comply with the law and have his coffee too.

Finally, at the end of your day, you decide to put up for the night, and you will find the motels. There are rows of them, each with its neon sign . . . announcing a vacancy. . . . Your room is clean and comfortable . . . and your car is parked freely and conveniently directly outside your window. . . . So you sink into your soft, squashy bed, while the night traffic roars by. . . . In the morning, so gentle is the civilization of the automobile, you need only walk a pace or two across the carpeted floor before you can sink refreshed into the welcoming driving seat. . . .

1954

The Supreme Court Issues an Historic Decision

In the case of *Brown v. Board of Education of Topeka*, the Supreme Court ruled that racial segregation in the public schools of the nation was unconstitutional. Here is the unanimous decision of the Court, as read by Chief Justice Earl Warren.
Source: 347 U. S. 483 (1954).

. . . These cases come to us from the States of Kansas, South Carolina, Virginia, and Delaware. They are premised on different facts and different local conditions, but a common legal question justifies their consideration together in this consolidated opinion.

In each of the cases, minors of the Negro race, through their legal representatives, seek the aid of the courts in obtaining admission to the public schools of their community on a nonsegregated basis. In each instance, they had been denied admission to schools attended by white children under laws requiring or permitting segregation according to race. This segregation was alleged to deprive the [Negro children] of the equal protection of the laws under the Fourteenth Amendment. In each of the cases other than the Delaware case, a three-judge federal district court denied relief to the plaintiffs on the so-called "separate but equal" doctrine announced by this Court in *Plessy v. Ferguson* (1896). . . . Under that doctrine, equality of treatment is accorded when the races are provided substantially equal facilities, even though these facilities be separate. . . .

The plaintiffs contend that segregated public schools are not "equal" and cannot be made "equal," and that hence they are deprived of the equal protection of the laws. . . .

In approaching this problem, we cannot turn the clock back to 1868 when the [Fourteenth] Amendment was adopted, or even to 1896 when *Plessy v. Ferguson* was written. We must consider public education in the light of its full development and its present place in American life throughout the Nation. Only in this way can it be determined if segregation in public schools deprives these plaintiffs of the equal protection of the laws.

Today, education is perhaps the most important function of state and local governments. Compulsory school attendance laws and the great expenditures for education both demonstrate our recognition of the importance of education to our democratic society. It is required in the performance of our most basic public responsibilities, even service in the armed forces. It is the very foundation of good citizenship. Today it is a principal instrument in awakening the child to cultural values, in preparing him for later professional training, and in helping him to adjust normally to his environment. In these days, it is doubtful that any child may reasonably be expected to succeed in life if he is denied the opportunity of an education. Such an opportunity, where the state has taken to provide it, is a right which must be made available to all on equal terms.

We come then to the question presented: Does segregation of children in public schools solely on the basis of race, even though the physical facilities and other "tangible" factors may be equal, deprive the children of the minority group of equal educational opportunities? We believe that it does. . . .

296

The effect of this separation on . . . educational opportunities was well stated by a . . . Kansas . . . court. . . .

"Segregation of white and colored children in public schools has a detrimental effect upon the colored children. The impact is greater when it has the sanction of the law; for the policy of separating the races is usually interpreted as denoting the inferiority of the negro group. A sense of inferiority affects the motivation of a child to learn. Segregation with the sanction of law, therefore, has a tendency to [retard] the educational and mental development of Negro children and to deprive them of some of the benefits they would receive in a racially integrated school system." . . .

We conclude that in the field of public education the doctrine of "separate but equal" has no place. Separate educational facilities are inherently unequal. Therefore, we hold that the plaintiffs and others similarly situated . . . are, by reason of the segregation complained of, deprived of the equal protection of the laws guaranteed by the Fourteenth Amendment. . . .

1956

Ninety Degrees Below Freezing

Rear Admiral George J. Dufek commanded Task Force 43 in "Operation Deepfreeze," our Navy's expedition to Antarctica in support of the International Geophysical Year. He tells the exciting story of an American plane's landing at the South Pole as part of the scientific expedition.
From *Operation Deepfreeze*, © 1957, by GEORGE J. DUFEK. Reprinted by permission of Harcourt, Brace & World, Inc.

Over the intercom Hawkes asked, "Admiral, should we land now . . .?"

"Use your own judgment," I replied.

"We have a fair surface here," said Shinn.

"Set her down when you are ready," I said. . . .

The plane came in smoothly, touched the surface, bumped a little—but I knew she was under control. She slowed to a stop, but Shinn kept his engines turning over. It was 8:34 P. M., October 31 [1956].

Strider opened the door and I stepped out onto the South Polar Plateau. It was like stepping out into a new world. We stood in the center of a sea of snow and ice that extended beyond our vision. How deep the ice that lay beneath our feet was, no one has as yet determined. . . . The bitter cold struck me in the face and chest as if I had walked into a heavy swinging door. The temperature was − 58° Fahrenheit; 90° below freezing. . . .

Doug Cordiner handed me the pointed staff with the American flag attached to it. We . . . attempted to force it into the snow. It could not be done—too hard. . . . With an alpine ax I dug a hole eighteen inches deep. We put the flagstaff into it, and I said: "Let's fill it in and stamp it down before I fall in myself." The altitude, the cold, and my exertions had nearly exhausted me. . . .

I looked at Doug Cordiner, and though we had only been there a few moments, noticed that more than half of his . . . nose and cheekbones had turned white.

"You have frostbite on your face, Doug," I said. "Cover your face."

"You have it too, Admiral," he said.

We watched each other as we went about our work. When white spots appeared the other would point and with a circular motion of his hand indicate "frostbite—take care of it." Of course, we should have had face masks but at this time of year we had not anticipated these low temperatures.

The rest of the plane's crew piled out onto the polar plateau with one exception—there was always a pilot in the cockpit to keep the engines running.

Strider worried about his engines leaking oil and was concerned about the skis freezing to the snow-ice surface. Hawkes and Cordiner busied themselves with erecting the radar reflectors to guide other aircraft to this best-choice landing. . . . We tried to take some movies and still pictures. My own efforts were a complete failure; my cameras were frozen. But the others were more successful.

Time passed more rapidly than I thought. Trigger came up to me and said, "Boss, I can't move the fingers of this hand. I think they're frozen. We've done everything here we can. I suggest we leave."

"Good," I said. "Let's get . . . out of here."

We embarked—exactly forty-nine minutes after we had landed. Strider slammed the door. We strapped ourselves into our seats. Shinn revved up the engines for the take-off. Nothing happened. The plane did not move. Her skis were frozen to the ice of the plateau. With engines turning over full power . . . the plane rocked—and moved forward—slowly. The plane bounced along the rough surface—and then staggered into the air. . . .

The windshield of the cockpit was completely frosted inside and out, and the pilots could not see through it. Shinn was taking off on instruments. . . .

"Port engine losing oil pressure rapidly—we may have a forced landing," came the message from the cockpit.

"Oh, no," I thought. We waited in silence—then came the reassuring voice from up forward. "Oil pressure building up—we're all right."

We settled back for the three-hour flight to our Beardmore Base. . . . I leaned back and closed my eyes.

Only seventeen men in the history of mankind had set foot on the South Pole—Amundsen and his four men; Scott and his four; and the seven of us. We were the first Americans ever to set foot on the Pole. The Russians had been the first to land by plane at the North Geographic Pole—May 21, 1937. Now, on October 31, 1956, Americans had been the first to land by plane at the South Geographic Pole. The flags of three nations had been placed there—the Norwegian in December 1911, the British in January 1912, and now, forty-four years later, the Stars and Stripes of the United States. It was a good feeling. . . .

"Oh God, Thy Sea Is So Great, and My Boat Is So Small"

> Nuclear submarines are able to cruise under the Arctic ice and can surface by crashing through thin spots. Commander Calvert here describes a history-making experience.
> Source: *Skate's Breakthrough at the Pole*, by COMMANDER JAMES CALVERT, USN. LIFE, May 4, 1959, pp. 131–145. The main story of the *Skate* is told in the book *Surface at the Pole*, by Commander James Calvert, USN. McGraw-Hill Book Company, New York, 1960.

. . . Now in March the Arctic was at its worst. There would be only partial daylight, the temperature would average 30° below zero, and the welcoming leads [elongated cracks in the ice] and *polynyas* [larger, lakelike bodies of water] would in all probability be sealed. But we hoped to prove conclusively that arctic submarine operations are possible at all times of the year. We were going back, and what was more, we intended to surface.

. . . .

People often ask me how it feels to journey into the dark seas under the ice aboard a steel cylinder packed with more than 100 men and some of the 20th Century's most complex mechanism. . . . All *Skate's* officers and half her men are trained in nuclear propulsion, and everyone in the ship's company is an experienced submarine sailor. . . . They trust God and they also trust the machine. . . . We trust it will not fail. On our polar voyage this trust, coupled with the crew's calm skill, paid off.

The report I received from the officer of the deck that first morning under the pack was not encouraging. Solid ice stretched away over our heads in all directions. No sign of an opening appeared either on the television or on the upward beam Fathometer, whose sonic waves probed the underside of the ice. . . . There was no open water in the winter ice pack. We would have to hunt for thin spots where we could try with *Skate* a whale's trick Stefansson [author of *The Friendly Arctic*, a classic account of the great explorer's polar adventure] had seen 45 years ago.

At that time, Stefansson had been astonished to see great schools of beluga whales rising through the thinnest portions of the newly frozen leads. They would strike the bottom of the ice with their huge backs and break through a six- or eight-inch thickness of frozen polar sea. Anything the whales could do, *Skate*, which weighs 3,000 tons and is almost the length of a football field, could also do.

Later that first day we got lucky. Prowling along our course at 16 knots, we spotted what looked very much like a newly frozen *polynya*. . . . We slowed *Skate* and began to investigate what we called Skylight Number One. . . . I talked the situation over with my officers. . . . They agreed that this might be our best opportunity, so I decided to attempt a surfacing.

Following procedures we learned in the arctic last summer, we placed the ship precisely underneath the skylight and stopped her forward motion. Then we began to pump water out of her variable ballast tanks, thus slowly removing the ballast which held us beneath the surface. . . .

Like a great balloon we floated upward in silence. . . .

The sail hit the ice with a gentle thump and we stopped dead. Nothing happened. It was like being in an elevator that stalls between floors. After a long moment of surprise, the reason became obvious: either we had risen too slowly or the ice was too thick.

The initial tension gone, we took *Skate* down a few feet and then started up again, this time lightening our tanks at a greater speed. The absorbing drama on television was repeated, but this time when the sail hit, the screen was suddenly filled with great broken chunks of ice and sloshing sea water. The periscopes picked up clear daylight. We had broken through!

With this opening into the outer world, we brought the sub up the rest of the way. . . .

. . . .

On March 17 we arrived in the vicinity of the geographic North Pole. . . . No frozen leads or *polynyas*. . . . Then suddenly we spotted the faint light of a small lead and we started up. This was our toughest surfacing so far. . . . It took us two hours of careful maneuvering before at last our sail buckled the ice at the precise top of the world. [Here Commander Calvert scattered the ashes of Sir Hubert Wilkins to the arctic winds—thus carrying out the last wishes of that great man who had pioneered the attempt to take the sub under the ice in 1931. A simple burial service was also performed at that "precise top of the world." Another task which they carried out was to leave a token behind commemorating the 50th anniversary of Peary's arrival at the pole in 1909. They made a small cairn of ice blocks and put inside it a waterproof cylinder containing a record of their visit and of the burial ceremony for Sir Hubert Wilkins. An American flag on a steel shaft was placed on top of the cairn. *Skate* also contributed greatly to the U. S. store of arctic information. Happy family news awaited many members of the crew when the voyage was completed a few days later.]

. . . But a more personal message awaited me in the mail when *Skate* reached New London [Connecticut]. It was a small package from the office of Vice Admiral Hyman Rickover, the man responsible for the development of the Navy's nuclear submarines. Admiral Rickover is a relentlessly dedicated and driving man. Having worked directly under him, I know that he is not a sentimentalist, either about himself, his mission or his men.

The package contained no accompanying card, only a small bronze paperweight carrying in raised letters the quotation: "Oh God, thy sea is so great and my boat is so small."

1961

Three Astronauts Take the Dare

Early in 1961, after nearly two years of intensive training, three American astronauts were chosen as candidates to become America's first man in space. Here, in their own words, they express their feelings about participation in the Project Mercury space program.

Source: WAINWRIGHT, LOUDON S. "The Chosen Three for First Space Ride," *Life*, Vol. 50, No. 9, March 3, 1961, pp. 26, 28, 30. Copyright 1961 *Time* Inc.

John H. Glenn, Jr., Lieutenant Colonel,
United States Marine Corps:
"A lot of people ask . . . why a man is willing to risk . . . something like this. Well, we've got to do it. We're going into an age

of exploration that will be bigger than anything the world has ever seen. I guess I'm putting my family up against some risks. I could do other jobs which might increase my life expectancy. But this could help my kids, too. I want them to be better off than I was as a young man. With risks you gain.

"I've got a theory about this. . . . People are afraid of the future, of the unknown. If a man faces up to it and takes the dare of the future, he can have some control over his destiny. That's an exciting idea to me, better than waiting with everybody else to see what's going to happen."

Virgil Grissom, Captain,
United States Air Force:

"There's a big difference between us and Columbus and Lindbergh and the Wright brothers and all these people we're compared to. They did it themselves. We didn't think up this thing. We're just going to ride the capsule.

"This is the best thing that's ever happened to me. . . . Here's a big new project with nothing but future. It's the first step in a great program that will go on as long as there are people. . . . But the notoriety the first man gets will only last for a little while and in a year or two the excitement of this will be forgotten in bigger things."

Alan B. Shepard, Jr., Commander,
United States Navy:

"Once in a while I begin to wonder how . . . I'm going to feel, but I don't dwell on it. It's fine to think it's going to be a thrill, but it's more important to know what to do with all the knobs and levers. Fear or distress comes from the unknown. The training in this program has helped us to know. It's a matter of confidence. I don't know just where the confidence begins, but it's there."

All America Rode with Him

> On May 5, 1961, Commander Alan B. Shepard became the
> first American to penetrate outer space. Lucian C. Warren, one
> of five reporters chosen for a close-up view of this historic
> launching, wrote this eye-witness account.
>
> Source: WARREN, LUCIAN C. "Space Feat Gives All America
> a Lift," *Courier Express* (Buffalo), Saturday, May 6, 1961,
> pp. 1–2.

CAPE CANAVERAL, FLA., May 5. It was a small capsule that
carried Navy Cmdr. Alan B. Shepard, Jr. in and out of space
today, but all America rode with him.

As the capsule lifted its way into weightlessness 115 miles up,
America's respect got a lift, too. As the Navy—302 miles out in
the Atlantic—made a perfect recovery and found the 37-year-old
astronaut in soaring spirits, America's spirits also soared. . . .

At 3 this morning, I was whisked to Hangar "S," NASA's
[National Aeronautics & Space Administration] headquarters for
the final preparations made by astronaut Shepard. . . .

At 3:59 word was flashed to the waiting group—"Here he
comes." . . .

Looking neither right nor left, the silver-suited spaceman
strode the 11 steps to a waiting van, which rolled off shortly to
the launch pad while the medical attendants continued to make
their checks. . . .

I shall never forget the eerie sight in the pre-dawn hours, as
searchlights concentrated on the 83-foot rocket, its capsule, its
escape tower, the temporary scaffolding or "gantry" surrounding
it and gaseous oxygen fumes spewing forth with the same
ghoulish effect as the witches' caldron in Macbeth.

The vapors, coming from exhaust pipes and the bird itself,
were produced by the loading of liquid oxygen, at 193 degrees
below zero Fahrenheit, into a rocket fuel system containing as a
prime ingredient denatured alcohol.

It was a warm morning, but you wouldn't have known it from
the ice which coated the lower part of the rocket and which
occasionally chipped off into snowflakes.

Shepard was supposed to leave the van at 5 a. m., and the rocket and capsule were ready then. But last minute instructions inside held him up.

Then at 5:15 he emerged. It was a dramatic moment to see him stop, shade his eyes from the glaring searchlights, and eye the Mercury-Redstone bird from bottom to top.

He took a couple of sideward steps, then repeated the operation. Finally, he walked about 20 feet to a gantry elevator and was slowly lifted to "level 3" [capsule level] while scanning a checkboard, presumably of things he must keep in mind. . . .

. . . I saw him pause briefly at level 3, then enter the capsule for his long vigil on his back before being lifted into space about four hours later. . . .

There was deafening handclapping and cheering . . . as the bird gracefully lifted itself into the sky, its rocket belching from the lower end, soared through a few thin clouds, began a vapor trail, then disappeared into space history. . . .

1963

"An Assassin's Bullet Has Thrust Upon Me the Awesome Burden of the Presidency"

President John F. Kennedy was killed in Dallas, Texas, on Friday, November 22, 1963—the fourth American President to die at the hands of an assassin. The entire nation shared a profound feeling of shock and grief. Probably no one better expressed the sense of bereavement and "the tragedy and torment of these terrible days" than the new President, Lyndon B. Johnson. His Address to the Joint Session of Congress was at once a beautiful eulogy, a firm rededication to principles, and a clear call to action.

Source: PRESIDENT LYNDON B. JOHNSON, *Address to the Joint Session of Congress*, November 27, 1963.

Mr. Speaker, Mr. President, members of the House, members of the Senate, my fellow Americans:

All I have I would have given gladly not to be standing here today. The greatest leader of our time has been struck down by the foulest deed of our time. . . .

No words are sad enough to express our sense of loss. No words are strong enough to express our determination to continue the forward thrust of America that he began. . . .

This nation will keep its commitments from South Vietnam to West Berlin. We will be unceasing in the search for peace; resourceful in our pursuit of areas of agreement even with those with whom we differ; and generous and loyal to those who join with us in common cause. . . .

Those who test our courage will find it honorable. We will demonstrate anew that the strong can be just in the use of strength, and the just can be strong in the defense of justice. . . .

We will carry on the fight against poverty and misery and disease and ignorance in other lands and in our own.

We will serve all the nation, not one section or one sector or one group—but all Americans. . . .

An assassin's bullet has thrust upon me the awesome burden of the Presidency. I am here today to say I need your help. I cannot bear this burden alone. I need the help of all Americans in all America.

This nation has experienced a profound shock, and in this critical moment it is our duty, yours and mine, as the Government of the United States, to do away with uncertainty and doubt and delays and to show that we are capable of decisive action. . . .

From this chamber of representative government let all the world know, and none misunderstand, that I rededicate this Government to the unswerving support of the United Nations—to the honorable and determined execution of our commitments to our allies—to the maintenance of military strength second to none—to the defense of the strength and stability of the dollar—to the expansion of our foreign trade—to the reinforcement of our programs of mutual assistance and cooperation in Asia and Africa —and to our Alliance for Progress in this hemisphere. . . .

On the 20th day of January in 1961, John F. Kennedy . . . said, "Let us begin."

Today, in this moment of new resolve, I would say to all my fellow Americans, let us continue.

This is our challenge: Not to hesitate, not to pause, not to turn about and linger over this evil moment, but to continue on our course so that we may fulfill the destiny that history has set for us.

Our most immediate tasks are here on this Hill: [Here the President called for tax reduction, aid to education, and "the earliest possible passage of the civil rights bill."]

. . . We have talked long enough in this country about equal rights. We have talked for a hundred years or more. It is time now to write the next chapter, and to write it in the books of law. . . . This is no time for delay. It is a time for action—strong forward-looking action. . . . I believe in the ability of the Congress . . . to act wisely, to act vigorously, to act speedily when the need arises.

The need is here. The need is now. I ask your help. We meet in grief, but let us also meet in renewed dedication and renewed vigor. Let us meet in action, in tolerance and in mutual understanding. . . .

The time has come for Americans of all races and creeds and political beliefs to understand and respect one another. So, let us put an end to the teaching and preaching of hate and evil and violence. Let us turn away from the fanatics, from the far left and the far right, from the apostles of bitterness and bigotry, from those defiant of law, and those who pour venom into our nation's bloodstream.

I profoundly hope that the tragedy and the torment of these terrible days will bind us together in new fellowship, making us one people in our hour of sorrow.

So let us here highly resolve that John Fitzgerald Kennedy did not live—or die—in vain. And on this Thanksgiving Eve, as we gather together to ask the Lord's blessing and give him our thanks, let us unite in those familiar and cherished words:

America, America, God shed His Grace on thee,
And crown thy good with brotherhood
From sea to shining sea.

"We Shall Never Let You Down"

> The most dramatic incident in President Johnson's 27,000-mile mission to the Manila Conference and Pacific area in November, 1966, was his surprise visit to the American troops at Cam Ranh Bay, South Vietnam. The following excerpts are from news reports of his impromptu remarks to some seven thousand men assembled there.

You know what you are fighting against: a vicious and illegal aggression across this little nation's frontier. . . . Make no mistake about it: the American people whom you serve are proud of you. . . .

We depend upon you. We know that a nation that stops producing brave men soon ceases to be a nation. I give you my pledge that we shall never let you down. . . .

You stand today in a long line of brave men—the kind of men that our nation has produced when they were needed—the kind of men who fought at Valley Forge and Gettysburg, in the Argonne and Iwo Jima, on the Pusan perimeter and at the 38th parallel. . . .

One day when they know peace, the whole world will acknowledge that what you have done here was worth the price. . . .

American fighting men, I salute you! You have the respect, you have the support, you have the prayers of a grateful President and of a grateful nation. . . .

Index

309

311

Additional Acknowledgments

The selections on pages 168, 186, 191, are reprinted by permission of the publishers, The Arthur H. Clark Company, from [Ulrich B. Phillips' *Documentary History of American Industrial Society*, Vols. IX and X].

The selections on pages 198 and 208 are reprinted from *A Son of the Middle Border* by Hamlin Garland. Copyright 1914, 1917 by P. F. Collier and Son, 1917, 1923 by Hamlin Garland, renewed 1945 by Mary L. Lord and Constance G. Williams. Used with permission of The Macmillan Company.

The cover reproduction is "Old Reminiscences" by John F. Peto, Phillips Collection, Washington.

FGHIJK 0698
PRINTED IN THE UNITED STATES OF AMERICA